D1527815

COMPENDIUM OF THE CONFEDERATE ARMIES

KENTUCKY, MARYLAND, MISSOURI, THE CONFEDERATE UNITS AND THE INDIAN UNITS

Stewart Sifakis

Facts On File®

AN INFOBASE HOLDINGS COMPANY

To
the Memory of James Sifakis
1893–1961

COMPENDIUM OF THE CONFEDERATE ARMIES: KENTUCKY, MARYLAND, MISSOURI, THE CONFEDERATE UNITS AND THE INDIAN UNITS

Facts On File, Inc.
460 Park Avenue South
New York NY 10016

Library of Congress Cataloging-in-Publication Data
Sifakis, Stewart.
Compendium of the Confederate armies.

Includes bibliographical references and indexes.
Contents: Alabama — Florida and Arkansas — Kentucky, Maryland, Missouri, the Confederate units and the Indian units — [etc.]
ISBN 0-8160-2294-1
1. Confederate States of America, Army—History.
2. United States—History—Civil War, 1861–1865—Regimental histories. I. Title.
E546.S58 1992 973.7'42 90-23631

Facts On File books are available at special discounts when purchased in bulk quantities for businesses, associations, institutions or sales promotions. Please call our Special Sales Department in New York at 212/683-2244 or 800/322-8755.

Text design by Ron Monteleone
Printed in the United States of America

MP FOF 10 9 8 7 6 5 4 3 2 1

This book is printed on acid-free paper.

CONTENTS

ACKNOWLEDGMENTS

I am deeply indebted for this work to the personnel, past and present, of Facts On File, especially to Edward Knappman, Gerry Helferich and my editors: Kate Kelly, Helen Flynn, Eleanora von Dehsen, Traci Cothran, Nicholas Bakalar, Susan Schwartz and Michelle Fellner. Thanks also go to Joe Reilly, Michael Laraque, Jackie Massa and Kevin Rawlings. Also I would like to thank the staffs of the National Archives, Library of Congress, the various state archives and the New York Public Library for their patience and assistance. Over the past decades the staff of the National Park Service, Edwin C. Bearss, chief historian, have proven very informative on my frequent visits to the various battlefields. To Shaun and Christina Potter and Sally Gadsby I am indebted for keeping me at my work. For the logistical support of the management of the Hotel Post, Zermatt (Karl Ivarsson, Ursula Waeny and Lesley Dawkins), I am very grateful. And last, but certainly not least, I owe thanks to John Warren for his knowledge of computers, without which this project would have ground to a halt, and to his computer widow, Evelyne.

INTRODUCTION

This work is intended to be the companion set to Frederick H. Dyer's *Compendium of the War of the Rebellion* for the Confederacy. The compendium was first published as a three-volume work in 1909. A study of all the Union regiments, battalions, batteries and independent companies, it has since been reprinted in two- and one-volume editions.

It has been estimated that for every day since the end of the American Civil War, one book, magazine or newspaper article has appeared dealing with some aspect of that fratricidal struggle. Many ask: If so much has been written on the Civil War, is there really a need for more? The answer is an emphatic yes. Many aspects of the conflict have been covered only superficially and require much more in-depth research. But for such research a bedrock of reference works is essential.

There are many such works available, including the U.S. War Department's 128-volume *The War of the Rebellion: A Compilation of the Official Records of the Union and Confederate Armies* and the U.S. Navy Department's 31-volume *Official Records of the Union and Confederate Navies in the War of the Rebellion*. Registers of military personnel include: George W. Cullum's two-volume *Biographical Register of the Officers and Graduates of the United States Military Academy*, Francis B. Heitman's two-volume *Historical Register and Dictionary of the United States Army From Its Organization, September 29, 1789, to March 2, 1903*, Guy V. Henry's two-volume *Military Record of Civilian Appointments in the United States Army*, Robert K. Krick's *Lee's Colonels: A Biographical Register of the Field Officers of the Army of Northern Virginia* and Ezra J. Warner's *Generals in Gray: Lives of the Confederate Commanders* and *Generals in Blue: Lives of the Union Commanders*. Politics are covered in Jon L. Wakelyn's *Biographical Dictionary of the Confederacy* and Ezra J. Warner's and W. Buck Yearns' *Biographical Register of the Confederate Congress*. E. B. Long's *The Civil War Day by Day: An Almanac 1861-1865* provides an excellent chronology. Collective biographies include Mark M. Boatner's *The Civil War Dictionary*, Patricia L. Faust's *Historical Times Illustrated Encyclopedia of the Civil War* and Stewart Sifakis' *Who Was Who in the Civil War*. Then, of course there is Dyer's compendium.

To date there has not been a comprehensive equivalent to Dyer's work for the South as a whole. Basically work has been done by individual states. North Carolina has an excellent work currently nearing completion. Other commendable works have been done for Tennessee, Virginia and Texas. Works were begun for Georgia and South Carolina but did not proceed far. State government agencies in Florida and Kentucky made some efforts in the early years after the war. However, none of these draws a consolidated picture of the Confederate States Army. That is where the *Compendium of the Confederate Armies* comes in.

This work is organized into volumes by state. One volume includes the border state units—Kentucky, Maryland and Missouri; units organized directly by the Confederate authorities from various state companies; and those units from the Indian nations allied with the Confederacy. The final volume consists of the tables of organization of the various armies and departments throughout the war.

There are chapters in each volume on the artillery, cavalry and infantry. Those units having a numerical designation are listed first, followed by those units using the name of their commander, home region or some other name. Units are then broken down alphabetically by size—for example, battalions, batteries, companies and regiments. If two or more units still have the same sorting features, they are then further broken down alphabetically by any special designation—1st or 2nd Organization, Local Defense Troops, Militia, Provisional Army, Regulars, Reserves, Sharpshooters, State Guard, State Line, State Troops or Volunteers and so on. The company designation for artillery batteries that served within an artillery battalion or regiment is listed at the end of the battalion or regiment designation. If heavy artillery battalions or regiments served together as a unit through most of the war, they are treated as a whole with no breakdown of the companies.

Each entry starts with the unit's name. Any nicknames or other mistaken designations follow. Then comes a summary of its organizational details: its date and location of organization, mustering into service, the number of companies for battalion organizations, armament for artillery batteries, surrenders, paroles, exchanges and disbandment or mustering out. The next paragraph starts with the first commanding officer and continues with an alphabetical listing of the other field-grade officers. (Captains are listed chronologically for artillery batteries.) The next paragraph is the brigade and higher-level command assignments of the unit. This is followed by a listing of the battles and campaigns the unit was engaged in. Note that the unit was not necessarily present on each date that is indicated for multiday actions. The final paragraph is the suggested further reading, if any.

Because records are incomplete, I have dropped the list of casualties of each unit that Dyer includes for the Northern units. But I have added to Dyer's format by including the first commanding officer and the field-grade officers of each unit. Selected bibliographies are included for each volume. Also, as available, unit histories and personal memoirs are listed with some units as suggested further reading.

KENTUCKY

KENTUCKY UNITS

Although Kentucky never seceded from the Union, it was admitted to the Confederacy on December 10, 1862.

Throughout the war there were Confederate incursions into the state. At these times the recruits were often placed in new units, for which the records are often incomplete as the units never made it back to the Confederate lines.

Note: The index for the Kentucky units begins on page 211.

ARTILLERY

1. Kentucky 1st Artillery Battery

Also Known As: Lyon's Artillery Battery

Cobb's Artillery Battery

Organization: Organized by the conversion of 1st Company F, 3rd Infantry Regiment to artillery service at Bowling Green on September 20, 1861. It was armed with four 6-lb. Smoothbores and two 12-lb. Howitzers on April 6- 7, 1862. Byrne's Mississippi and Kentucky Artillery Battery was merged into this battery at Corinth, Mississippi in May 1862. Graves' Mississippi and Kentucky Artillery Battery was merged into this battery at Murfreesboro, Tennessee in November 1862. It was armed with four 12-lb. Napoleons from July 1863 to April 1, 1864. Green's Kentucky Artillery Battery, Humphreys' Arkansas Artillery Battery, and Company B, 2nd Alabama Light Artillery Battalion were merged into this battery in January 1864. Surrendered by Lieutenant General Richard Taylor, commanding the Department of Alabama, Mississippi, and East Louisiana, at Citronelle, Alabama on May 4, 1865.

First Commander: Hylan B. Lyon (Captain)

Captain: Robert Cobb

Assignments: Central Geographical Division of Kentucky, Department #2 (September-October 1861)

Artillery, Buckner's Division, Central Army of Kentucky, Department #2 (October 1861-January 1862)

Bowen's Brigade, Central Army of Kentucky, Department #2 (January-February 1862)

Breckinridge's Brigade, Reserve, Central Army of Kentucky, Department #2 (February-March 1862)

Kentucky Brigade, Reserve Corps, Army of the Mississippi, Department #2 (March-April 1862)

Preston's Brigade, Reserve Corps, Army of the Mississippi, Department #2 (June-July 1862)

T. B. Smith's Brigade, Clark's Division, Breckinridge's Command, District of the Mississippi, Department #2 (July-August 1862)

Kentucky Brigade, Army of Middle Tennessee, Department of Tennessee (October-November 1862)

Kentucky Brigade, Breckinridge's Division, 1st Corps, Army of Tennessee (November-December 1862)

Kentucky Brigade, Breckinridge's Division, 2nd Corps, Army of Tennessee (December 1862-May 1863)

Kentucky Brigade, Breckinridge's Division, Department of the West (May-July 1863)

Artillery Battalion, Breckinridge's Division, Department of the West (July 1863)

Artillery Battalion, Breckinridge's Division, Department of Mississippi and East Louisiana (July-August 1863)

Artillery Battalion, Breckinridge's Division, 2nd Corps, Army of Tennessee (August 1863-February 1864)

Cobb's Battalion, Artillery, 2nd Corps, Army of Tennessee (February-April 1864)

Cobb's Battalion, Artillery, 1st Corps, Army of Tennessee (April-September 1864)

Burnet's Command, Artillery Reserves, etc., District of the Gulf, Department of Alabama, Mississippi, and East Louisiana (March-April 1865)

Burnet's Command, Department of Alabama, Mississippi, and East Louisiana (April-May 1865)

Battles: Shiloh (April 6-7, 1862)

Vicksburg Bombardments (May 18-July 27, 1862)

Baton Rouge (August 5, 1862)

Hartsville (December 7, 1862)

Murfreesboro (December 31, 1862-January 3, 1863)

Jackson Siege (July 1863)

Chickamauga (September 19-20, 1863)

Chattanooga Siege (September-November 1863)

Chattanooga (November 23-25, 1863)

Atlanta Campaign (May-September 1864)

Atlanta Siege (July-September 1864)

Mobile (March 17-April 12, 1865)

Further Reading: Davis, William C., *The Orphan Brigade: The Kentucky Confederates Who Couldn't Go Home*. Thompson, Edward Porter, *History of the Orphan Brigade*.

2. KENTUCKY BELL'S ARTILLERY BATTERY

Organization: Organized on August 10, 1861. It was armed with mountain howitzers. This unit does not appear in the *Official Records*.

First Commander: J. N. Bell (Captain)

3. KENTUCKY BYRNE'S ARTILLERY BATTERY

Organization: Organized as a Mississippi and Kentucky unit on August 21, 1861. It was initially armed with four 6-lb. Smoothbores and two 12-lb. Howitzers. It was armed with five 6-lb. Smoothbores and two 12-lb. Howitzers from October 1861 to May 1862. Merged into 1st Artillery Battery at Corinth, Mississippi in May 1862.

First Commander: Edward P. Byrne (Captain)

Assignments: Artillery, Hardee's Division, Central Army of Kentucky, Department #2 (October 1861-March 1862)

Kentucky Brigade, Reserve Corps, Army of the Mississippi, Department #2 (March-May 1862)

Battle: Shiloh (April 6-7, 1862)

Further Reading: Davis, William C., *The Orphan Brigade: The Kentucky Confederates Who Couldn't Go Home*.

4. KENTUCKY COBB'S ARTILLERY BATTERY

See: KENTUCKY 1ST ARTILLERY BATTERY

5. KENTUCKY CUMBERLAND ARTILLERY BATTERY

Organization: Organized the fall of 1861. It was armed with seven pieces on February 14-16, 1862. The battery was captured at Fort Donelson on February 16, 1862. It was exchanged and reorganized in the fall of 1862. Apparently attached to a Mississippi battery in the spring of 1863. Regiment surrendered at Vicksburg, Warren County, Mississippi on July 4, 1863. Paroled at Vicksburg, Warren County, Mississippi in July 1863. Declared exchanged on September 12, 1863. Merged into the 1st Artillery Battery in January 1864.

First Commander: H. D. Green (Captain)

Captain: W. H. Hedden

Assignments: Clark's Brigade, Central Army of Kentucky, Department #2 (November 1861-February 1862)

Artillery, Floyd's Division, Fort Donelson, Department #2 (February 1862)

Artillery, Tilghman's Division, 1st Corps, Army of West Tennessee, Department of Mississippi and East Louisiana (December 1862-January 1863)

Tilghman's Brigade, Loring's Division, Army of North Mississippi, Department of Mississippi and East Louisiana (January-February 1863)

Tilghman's Brigade, Loring's Division, 2nd Military District, Department of Mississippi and East Louisiana (February-April 1863)

Tilghman's Brigade, Loring's Division, Department of Mississippi and East Louisiana (April 1863)

Battles: Fort Donelson (February 12-16, 1862)

Coffeeville (December 5, 1862)

Fort Pemberton (March 11, 1863)

Fort Pemberton (March 13, 1863)

Fort Pemberton (March 16, 1863)

Fort Pemberton (April 2, 1863)

Fort Pemberton (April 4, 1863)

Vicksburg Campaign (April-July 1863)

Vicksburg Siege (May-July 1863)

6. KENTUCKY GRAVES' ARTILLERY BATTERY

See: KENTUCKY ISSAQUENA ARTILLERY BATTERY

7. KENTUCKY GREEN'S ARTILLERY BATTERY

See: KENTUCKY CUMBERLAND ARTILLERY BATTERY

8. KENTUCKY HARRIS'-ARNETT'S-CORBETT'S ARTILLERY BATTERY

Organization: Organized in mid-1862. Apparently disbanded in the fall of 1862.

First Commander: Joseph E. Harris (Captain)

Captains: R. M. J. Arnett

C. C. Corbett

Assignment: Morgan's Brigade, Department of East Tennessee (July-November 1862)

Battles: Morgan's 1st Kentucky Raid (July 4-28, 1862)

Cynthiana (July 17, 1862)

9. KENTUCKY HEDDEN'S ARTILLERY BATTERY

See: KENTUCKY CUMBERLAND ARTILLERY BATTERY

10. KENTUCKY INGRAM'S ARTILLERY BATTERY

See: KENTUCKY ISSAQUENA ARTILLERY BATTERY

11. KENTUCKY ISSAQUENA ARTILLERY BATTERY

Organization: Organized as a Mississippi and Kentucky unit on November 8, 1861. Company B, 4th Kentucky Infantry Regiment attached to this battery in early 1862. It was armed with two 6-lb. Smoothbores and two 12-lb. Howitzers on November 11, 1862. Merged into the 1st Artillery Battery at Murfreesboro, Tennessee in November 1862.

First Commander: Selden Spencer (Captain)

Captains: Rice E. Graves

J. Ingram

Assignments: Reserve, 1st Geographical Division, Department #2 (October 1861)

Kentucky Brigade, Army of Middle Tennessee, Department #2 (October-November 1862)

Kentucky Brigade, Breckinridge's Division, 1st Corps, Army of Tennessee (November 1862)

Further Reading: Davis, William C., *The Orphan Brigade: The Kentucky Confederates Who Couldn't Go Home*. Thompson, Edward Porter, *History of the Orphan Brigade*.

12. KENTUCKY LYON'S ARTILLERY BATTERY

See: KENTUCKY 1ST ARTILLERY BATTERY

13. KENTUCKY SPENCER'S ARTILLERY BATTERY

See: KENTUCKY ISSAQUENA ARTILLERY

14. KENTUCKY WILLIAMS' ARTILLERY BATTERY

Organization: Organized in 1862. It was armed with six Williams breech-loading guns. Disbanded in 1864.

First Commander: R. S. Williams (Captain)

Assignment: Williams' Cavalry Brigade, Department of East Tennessee (October 1863)

Battle: Blue Springs (October 10, 1863)

CAVALRY

15. KENTUCKY 1ST CAVALRY BATTALION

Organization: Organized in late 1861. Mustered out on November 20, 1862.
First Commander: W. E. Simms (Lieutenant Colonel)
Field Officer: Johnathan Shawhan (Major)
Assignments: Army of Eastern Kentucky, Department #2 (December 1861-May 1862)
District of Abingdon (May 1862)
District of Abingdon, Department of Southwestern Virginia (May-November 1862)
Battle: Middle Creek (January 10, 1862)

16. KENTUCKY 1ST (KING'S) CAVALRY BATTALION

Organization: Organized with six companies in the fall of 1861. Increased to a regiment and designated as the 1st Confederate Cavalry Regiment on April 1, 1862.
First Commander: Henry C. King (Major)
Assignments: 6th (Bowen's) Brigade, 1st Division, 1st Geographical Division, Department #2 (October-November 1861)
2nd Brigade, 4th Division, 1st Geographical Division, Department #2 (November 1861-December 1862)
Unattached, 1st Geographical Division, Department #2 (January-March 1862)
Unattached, 1st Grand Division, Army of the Mississippi, Department #2 (March 1862)
Unattached, 1st Corps, Army of the Mississippi, Department #2 (March-April 1862)
Battle: Paris [skirmish] (March 11, 1862)

17. KENTUCKY 1ST CAVALRY BATTALION, MOUNTED RIFLES

Organization: Organized with five companies in in Southwestern Virginia in early March 1862. Apparently disbanded for marauding in late 1862.

First Commander: Benjamin F. Bradley (Major)
Field Officer: Orville C. Cameron (Major)
Assignments: 1st Brigade, Army of Eastern Kentucky, Department #2 (March-May 1862)
District of Abingdon (May 1862)
District of Abingdon, Department of Southwestern Virginia (May-November 1862)
Battles: Wolf Creek (May 15, 1862)
Princeton (May 15-17, 1862)

18. KENTUCKY 1ST (CLAY'S) CAVALRY BATTALION, MOUNTED RIFLES

See: KENTUCKY 3RD CAVALRY BATTALION MOUNTED RIFLES

19. KENTUCKY 1ST SPECIAL CAVALRY BATTALION

Organization: Organized from the remnants of John Hunt Morgan's old command in early 1864. Disbanded by Brigadier General John Echols, commanding Department of Southwestern Virginia and East Tennessee, at Christianburg, Virginia on April 12, 1865. [NOTE: Part of this command joined President Jefferson Davis' escort on his flight from Richmond.]
First Commander: William W. Ward (Colonel)
Field Officer: Robert A. Alston (Lieutenant Colonel)
Assignment: Martin's-Duke's Cavalry Brigade, Department of Western Virginia and East Tennessee (June 1864-April 1865)
Battle: Morgan's Kentucky Raid (May 30-June 20, 1864)
Further Reading: Duke, Basil, *A History of Morgan's Cavalry.*

20. KENTUCKY 1ST CAVALRY REGIMENT

Organization: Organized on October 19, 1861. The 3rd Cavalry Regiment was merged into this regiment on March 2, 1863. This regiment was captured during Morgan's Ohio Raid in July 1863.
First Commander: Benjamin H. Helm (Colonel)
Field Officers: J. Russell Butler (Colonel)
John W. Caldwell (Major)
Nathaniel R. Chambliss (Major)
Jacob W. Griffith (Lieutenant Colonel)
H. C. Leavell (Lieutenant Colonel)
Thomas G. Woodward (Lieutenant Colonel)
Assignments: Cavalry, Buckner's Division, Central Army of Kentucky, Department #2 (October 1861-February 1862)

Breckinridge's Brigade, Reserve, Central Army of Kentucky, Department #2 (February-March 1862)

Forrest's Cavalry Brigade, Department of East Tennessee (July 1862)

Wheeler's Cavalry Brigade, Left Wing, Army of the Mississippi, Department #2 (September-November 1862)

Morgan's Cavalry Brigade, Army of Tennessee (November-December 1862)

Buford's Brigade, Morgan's Cavalry Division, Army of Tennessee (December 1862-March 1863)

2nd Brigade, Wharton's Division, Wheeler's Cavalry Corps, Army of Tennessee (March-July 1863)

Battles: Elk River, near Bethel [skirmish] (March 9, 1862)

Tullahoma Campaign (June-July 1863)

Hoover's Gap (June 24, 1863)

Morgan's Ohio Raid (July 2-26, 1863)

Further Reading: Dyer, John Will, *Reminiscences; Or Four Years in the Confederate Army, A History of the Experiences of the Private Soldier in Camp, Hospital, Prison, and on the Battlefield, 1861-1865*. Davis, William C., *The Orphan Brigade: The Kentucky Confederates Who Couldn't Go Home.*

21. KENTUCKY [AND TENNESSEE] 1ST CAVALRY REGIMENT, MOUNTED RIFLES

See: KENTUCKY 12TH CAVALRY REGIMENT

22. KENTUCKY 2ND CAVALRY BATTALION

Organization: Organized with four companies in late 1863. No further record after September 20, 1864 other than that Company B was transferred to the Army of Tennessee per S.O. #286, Adjutant and Inspector General's Office, dated December 2, 1864. The battalion was apparantly broken up at about this time.

First Commander: Clarence J. Prentice (Major)

Field Officer: John B. Dortch (Major [acting])

Assignments: Grigsby's Brigade, Kelly's Division, Wheeler's Cavalry Corps, Army of Tennessee (January-February 1864)

Grigsby's-Williams' Brigade, Humes' Division, Wheeler's Cavalry Corps, Army of Tennessee (April-September 1864)

Battles: Atlanta Campaign (May-September 1864)

Sugar Valley (May 9, 1864)

Atlanta Siege (July-September 1864)

23. KENTUCKY 2ND CAVALRY BATTALION, MOUNTED RIFLES

Organization: Organized with four companies ca. March 12, 1862. It was later increased to six companies. Disbanded by Brigadier General John Echols, commanding Department of Southwestern Virginia and East Tennessee, at Christianburg, Virginia on April 12, 1865.

First Commander: Thomas Johnson (Major, Lieutenant Colonel)

Field Officer: Otis S. Tenney (Major)

Assignments: District of Abingdon, Department of Southwestern Virginia (November 1862-January 1863)

District of Abingdon, Department of East Tennessee (January-July 1863)

Preston's Brigade, Army of East Tennessee, Department of Tennessee (July-August 1863)

Tyler's Brigade, Armstrong's Division, Wheeler's Cavalry Corps, Army of Tennessee (October-November 1863)

Tyler's-Hodge's Brigade, Armstrong's Division, Wheeler's-Martin's Cavalry Corps, Department of East Tennessee (November 1863-January 1864)

Hodge's Brigade, Jones' Division, Cavalry Corps, Department of East Tennessee (March-April 1864)

Giltner's Cavalry Brigade, Department of Western Virginia and East Tennessee (April-September 1864)

Cosby's Cavalry Brigade, Department of Western Virginia and East Tennessee (September 1864-April 1865)

Battles: *vs.* Carter's East Tennessee and Southwest Virginia Raid (December 20, 1862-January 5, 1863)

Piketon [skirmish] [Company E] (April 15, 1863)

24. KENTUCKY 2ND SPECIAL CAVALRY BATTALION

Organization: Organized from the remnants of John Hunt Morgan's old command in the spring of 1864. Disbanded by Brigadier General John Echols, commanding Department of Southwestern Virginia and East Tennessee, at Christianburg, Virginia on April 12, 1865. [NOTE: Part of this command joined President Jefferson Davis' escort on his flight from Richmond.]

First Commander: J. T. Cassell (Major)

Field Officer: Richard C. Morgan (Colonel)

Assignment: Martin's Cavalry Brigade-Duke's, Department of Western Virginia and East Tennessee (June 1864-April 1865)

Battle: Morgan's Kentucky Raid (May 30-June 20, 1864)

Further Reading: Duke, Basil, *A History of Morgan's Cavalry.*

25. Kentucky 2nd Cavalry Regiment

Organization: Organized by the increase of Morgan's Cavalry Squadron (four companies) to a regiment with the addition of three companies at Chattanooga, Tennessee in June 1862. Companies K, L, and M were organized in July and August 1862. Company H was assigned on September 1, 1862. 1st Company I was transferred to the 9th Cavalry Regiment and 2nd Company I was assigned on September 10, 1862. The regiment was eventually reduced to 10 companies. Captured during Morgan's Ohio Raid in July 1863.

First Commander: John Hunt Morgan (Colonel)

Field Officers: James W. Bowles (Major, Lieutenant Colonel, Colonel)
John B. Castleman (Major)
Basil W. Duke (Lieutenant Colonel, Colonel)
John B. Hutcheson (Lieutenant Colonel)
Thomas B. Webber (Major)

Assignments: Morgan's Cavalry Brigade, Department of East Tennessee (July-November 1862)
Morgan's Cavalry Brigade, Army of Tennessee (November-December 1862)
Duke's Brigade, Morgan's Cavalry Division, Army of Tennessee (December 1862-March 1863)
Duke's Brigade, Morgan's Division, Wheeler's Cavalry Corps, Army of Tennessee (March-July 1863)

Battles: near Pulaski [skirmish] (May 1, 1862)
Morgan's 1st Kentucky Raid (July 4-28, 1862)
Tompkinsville (July 9, 1862)
Lebanon (July 12, 1862)
Cynthiana (July 17, 1862)
Morgan's Raid on the Louisville & Nashville Railroad (August 1862)
Kentucky Campaign (August-October 1862)
Gallatin (August 12, 1862)
Morgan's 2nd Kentucky Raid (October-November 1862)
Lexington (October 18, 1862)
Morgan's Christmas Raid (December 21, 1862-January 1, 1863)
Muldraugh's Hill Trestle (December 28, 1862)
Milton (March 20, 1863)
Snow's Hill (April 3, 1863)
Horse Shoe Bottom (May 10, 1863)
Morgan's Ohio Raid (July 2-26, 1863)
Lebanon (July 5, 1863)

Further Reading: Brown, Dee Alexander, *The Bold Cavaliers, Morgan's 2nd Kentucky Cavalry Raiders*. Duke, Basil, *A History of Morgan's Cavalry*.

26. KENTUCKY 2ND (WOODWARD'S) CAVALRY REGIMENT

See: KENTUCKY 15TH CAVALRY REGIMENT

27. KENTUCKY 3RD CAVALRY BATTALION

Organization: Failed to complete its organization. This unit does not appear in the *Official Records.* However, Major Owsley was the subject of some communication between the Federal and Confederate authorities the record of which is incomplete. He was apparently captured while recruiting his unit in Kentucky, under orders from Major General Joseph Wheeler, and was tried as a spy. There is no further record of him. However, there is a Federal report that one company of the battalion, under a Captain Estes, was negotiating to surrender on April 26, 1865.

First Commander: C. B. Owsley (Major)

28. KENTUCKY 3RD CAVALRY BATTALION, MOUNTED RIFLES

Also Known As: 1st Kentucky Mounted Rifles

Organization: Organized with six companies on November 29, 1862. Disbanded by Brigadier General John Echols, commanding Department of Southwestern Virginia and East Tennessee, at Christianburg, Virginia on April 12, 1865.

First Commander: Ezekiel F. Clay (Lieutenant Colonel)

Field Officers: Peter M. Everett (Major)

John B. Holladay (Major)

Assignments: District of Abingdon, Department of Southwestern Virginia (November 1862-January 1863)

District of Abingdon, Department of East Tennessee (January-July 1863)

Preston's Brigade, Army of East Tennessee, Department of Tennessee (July-August 1863)

Tyler's Brigade, Armstrong's Division, Wheeler's Cavalry Corps, Army of Tennessee (October-November 1863)

Tyler's-Hodge's Brigade, Armstrong's Division, Wheeler's-Martin's Cavalry Corps, Department of East Tennessee (November 1863-January 1864)

Hodge's Brigade, Jones' Division, Cavalry Corps, Department of East Tennessee (March-April 1864)

Giltner's Cavalry Brigade, Department of Western Virginia and East Tennessee (April-September 1864)

Cosby's Cavalry Brigade, Department of Western Virginia and East Tennessee (September 1864-April 1865)

Battles: *vs.* Carter's East Tennessee and Southwest Virginia Raid (December 20, 1862-January 5, 1863)

Snow Hill [skirmish] (June 4, 1863)

Everett's Raid into Eastern Kentucky (June 13-23, 1863)
Wheeler's Sequatchie Raid (September-October 1863)

29. KENTUCKY 3RD (JESSEE'S) CAVALRY BATTALION, MOUNTED RIFLES

Organization: Organized with three companies in mid-1862. It was later increased to six companies. Redesignated as the 6th Confederate Cavalry Battalion on September 29, 1863.

First Commander: George M. Jessee (Major)

Field Officer: Allen L. McAfee (Major)

Assignment: Department of East Tennessee (September 1862-September 1863)

Battle: Big Creek Gap (September 10, 1862)

30. KENTUCKY 3RD SPECIAL CAVALRY BATTALION

Organization: Organized from the remnants of John Hunt Morgan's old command on November 10, 1864. Disbanded by Brigadier General John Echols, commanding Department of Southwestern Virginia and East Tennessee, at Christianburg, Virginia on April 12, 1865. [NOTE: Part of this command joined President Jefferson Davis' escort on his flight from Richmond.]

First Commander: Joseph T. Tucker (Colonel)

Assignment: Duke's Cavalry Brigade, Department of Western Virginia and East Tennessee (December 1864-April 1865)

Further Reading: Duke, Basil, *A History of Morgan's Cavalry*.

31. KENTUCKY 3RD CAVALRY REGIMENT

Organization: Organized in the fall of 1862. Merged into the 1st Cavalry Regiment on March 2, 1863.

First Commander: J. Russell Butler (Colonel)

Field Officers: Jack Allen (Lieutenant Colonel)

James Q. Chenoweth (Major)

J. W. Griffith (Lieutenant Colonel)

Assignments: Scott's Cavalry Brigade, Department of East Tennessee (October-November 1862)

Unattached, Department of East Tennessee (November 1862)

Buford's Cavalry Brigade, Army of Tennessee (December 1862)

Buford's Brigade, Wheeler's Cavalry Division, Army of Tennessee (December 1862-March 1863)

Battle: Murfreesboro (December 31, 1862-January 3, 1863)

32. KENTUCKY 3RD (GANO'S) CAVALRY REGIMENT

See: KENTUCKY 7TH CAVALRY REGIMENT

33. KENTUCKY 4TH SPECIAL CAVALRY BATTALION

Organization: Organized from the remnants of John Hunt Morgan's old command on November 10, 1864. Disbanded by Brigadier General John Echols, commanding Department of Southwestern Virginia and East Tennessee, at Christianburg, Virginia on April 12, 1865. [NOTE: Part of this command joined President Jefferson Davis' escort on his flight from Richmond.]

First Commander: W. R. Messick (Major [acting])

Field Officer: Thomas B. Webber (Major)

Assignment: Duke's Cavalry Brigade, Department of Western Virginia and East Tennessee (November 1864-April 1865)

Further Reading: Duke, Basil, *A History of Morgan's Cavalry*.

34. KENTUCKY 4TH CAVALRY REGIMENT

Organization: Organized at Mosgrove, near Owenton on September 10, 1862. Surrendered at Mount Sterling on April 30, 1865.

First Commander: Henry L. Giltner (Colonel)

Field Officers: Nathan Parker (Major)

Moses T. Pryor (Lieutenant Colonel)

William R. Ray (Major)

Assignments: 1st Brigade [Abingdon], Department of East Tennessee (February-July 1863)

Preston's Brigade, Army of East Tennessee, Department of Tennessee (July-August 1863)

Williams' Cavalry Brigade, Ransom's Division, Department of Western Virginia and East Tennessee (October-November 1863)

Williams'-Giltner's-Carter's Cavalry Brigade, Ransom's Division, Department of Southwestern Virginia and East Tennessee (November 1863-February 1864)

Giltner's Brigade, Cavalry, Department of East Tennessee (February-March 1864)

Giltner's Brigade, Vaughn's Division, Ransom's Cavalry Corps, Department of East Tennessee (March-April 1864)

Giltner's Brigade, Cavalry, Department of East Tennessee (April-June 1864)

Giltner's Cavalry Brigade, Department of Southwestern Virginia and East Tennessee (June 1864-April 1865)

Battles: Blue Springs (October 10, 1863)

Rogersville (November 6, 1863)

Laurel Gap (October 1, 1864)

Saltville (October 2, 1864)
Further Reading: Mosgrove, George Dallas, *Kentucky Cavaliers in Dixie: Reminiscences of a Confederate Cavalryman.*

35. KENTUCKY 4TH CAVALRY REGIMENT, MOUNTED RIFLES

See: KENTUCKY 9TH CAVALRY REGIMENT

36. KENTUCKY 5TH CAVALRY REGIMENT

Organization: Organized ca. September 9, 1862. Captured during Morgan's Ohio Raid in July 1863.
First Commander: D. Howard Smith (Colonel)
Field Officers: Thomas Y. Brent, Jr. (Major)
Churchill G. Campbell (Lieutenant Colonel)
Preston Thompson (Lieutenant Colonel)
Assignments: Buford's Cavalry Brigade, Army of the Mississippi, Department #2 (September-November 1862)
Buford's Cavalry Brigade, Army of Tennessee (November-December 1862)
Buford's Brigade, Wheeler's Cavalry Division, Army of Tennessee (December 1862-March 1863)
Duke's Brigade, Morgan's Cavalry Division, Army of Tennessee (March 1863)
Duke's Brigade, Morgan's Division, Wheeler's Cavalry Corps, Army of Tennessee (March-July 1863)
Battles: Perryville (October 8, 1862)
Murfreesboro (December 31, 1862-January 3, 1863)
Milton (March 20, 1863)
Morgan's Ohio Raid (July 2-26, 1863)
Further Reading: Smith, Sydney K., *Life, Army Record, and Public Services of D. Howard Smith.* Duke, Basil, *A History of Morgan's Cavalry.*

37. KENTUCKY 6TH CAVALRY REGIMENT

Organization: Organization begun at Stanford on September 8, 1862. Captured during Morgan's Ohio Raid in July 1863.
First Commander: J. Warren Grigsby (Colonel)
Field Officers: William G. Bullitt (Major)
Thomas W. Napier (Lieutenant Colonel)
Assignments: Buford's Cavalry Brigade, Army of the Mississippi, Department #2 (September-November 1862)
Buford's Cavalry Brigade, Army of Tennessee (November-December 1862)
Buford's Brigade, Wheeler's Cavalry Division, Army of Tennessee (December 1862-March 1863)
Duke's Brigade, Morgan's Cavalry Division, Army of Tennessee (March 1863)

Duke's Brigade, Morgan's Division, Wheeler's Cavalry Corps, Army of Tennessee (March-July 1863)

Battles: Perryville (October 8, 1862)

Murfreesboro (December 31, 1862-January 3, 1863)

Milton (March 20, 1863)

Morgan's Ohio Raid (July 2-26, 1863)

Further Reading: Duke, Basil, *A History of Morgan's Cavalry*.

38. KENTUCKY 7TH CAVALRY REGIMENT

Also Known As: 3rd Cavalry Regiment

Organization: Organized September 1, 1862. Captured during Morgan's Ohio Raid in July 1863.

First Commander: Richard M. Gano (Colonel)

Field Officers: J. M. Huffman (Lieutenant Colonel)

M. D. Logan (Major, Lieutenant Colonel)

Theophilus Steele (Major)

Assignments: Morgan's Cavalry Brigade, Department of East Tennessee (September-November 1862)

Morgan's Cavalry Brigade, Army of Tennessee (November-December 1862)

Cluke's-Johnson's Brigade, Morgan's Cavalry Division, Army of Tennessee (December 1862-March 1863)

Johnson's Brigade, Morgan's Division, Wheeler's Cavalry Corps, Army of Tennessee (March-July 1863)

Battles: Kentucky Campaign (August-October 1862)

Lexington [Gano's Squadron] (October 18, 1862)

Hartsville (December 7, 1862)

Morgan's Christmas Raid (December 21, 1862-January 1, 1863)

Muldraugh's Hill Trestle (December 28, 1862)

Morgan's Ohio Raid (July 2-26, 1863)

Further Reading: Duke, Basil, *A History of Morgan's Cavalry*.

39. KENTUCKY 7TH (CHENAULT'S) CAVALRY REGIMENT

See: KENTUCKY 11TH CAVALRY REGIMENT

40. KENTUCKY 8TH CAVALRY REGIMENT

Organization: Organized on September 10, 1862. Captured during Morgan's Ohio Raid in July 1863.

First Commander: Roy S. Cluke (Colonel)

Field Officers: Robert S. Bullock (Major)

Cicero Coleman (Lieutenant Colonel)

Assignments: Morgan's Cavalry Brigade, Department of East Tennessee (October-November 1862)
Morgan's Cavalry Brigade, Army of Tennessee (November-December 1862)
Cluke's-Johnson's Brigade, Morgan's Cavalry Division, Army of Tennessee (December 1862-March 1863)
Johnson's Brigade, Morgan's Division, Wheeler's Cavalry Corps, Army of Tennessee (March-July 1863)
Battles: Hartsville (December 7, 1862)
Morgan's Christmas Raid (December 21, 1862-January 1, 1863)
Elizabethtown (December 27, 1862)
Muldraugh's Hill Trestle (December 28, 1862)
Mount Sterling (March 22, 1863)
Expedition to Monticello (April 26-May 12, 1863)
Morgan's Ohio Raid (July 2-26, 1863)
Further Reading: Duke, Basil, *A History of Morgan's Cavalry*.

41. KENTUCKY 9TH CAVALRY BATTALION

See: KENTUCKY BRECKINRIDGE'S CAVALRY BATTALION

42. KENTUCKY 9TH CAVALRY REGIMENT

Also Known As: 4th Mounted Rifles Regiment
Organization: Orgnized by the consolidation of Stoner's and Breckinridge's Cavalry Battalions at Alexandria, Tennessee on December 17, 1862. Surrendered at Washington, Georgia on May 10, 1865.
First Commander: William C. P. Breckinridge (Colonel)
Field Officers: John P. Austin (Major)
William E. Jones (Major)
Robert G. Stoner (Lieutenant Colonel)
Assignments: Breckinridge's Brigade, Morgan's Cavalry Division, Army of Tennessee (December 1862-March 1863)
Breckinridge's-Duke's Brigade, Morgan's Division, Wheeler's Cavalry Corps, Army of Tennessee (March-October 1863)
Grigsby's Brigade, Kelly's Division, Wheeler's Cavalry Corps, Army of Tennessee (October 1863-July 1864)
Grigsby's-Williams' Brigade, Humes' Division, Wheeler's Cavalry Corps, Army of Tennessee (July-August 1864)
Williams' Brigade, Kelly's-Dibrell's Division, Wheeler's Cavalry Corps, Army of Tennessee (August-November 1864)
Williams'-Breckinridge's Brigade, Humes'-Dibrell's Division, Wheeler's Cavalry Corps, Department of South Carolina, Georgia, and Florida (November 1864-January 1865)

Kentucky Brigade, Iverson's Division, Wheeler's Cavalry Corps, Department of South Carolina, Georgia, and Florida (January-February 1865)
Kentucky Brigade, Humes' Division, Wheeler's Cavalry Corps, Army of Tennessee (February 1865)
Kentucky Brigade, Humes'-Dibrell's Division, Wheeler's Cavalry Corps, Hampton's Cavalry Command (February-April 1865)
Kentucky Brigade, Dibrell's Division, Wheeler's Cavalry Corps, Hampton's Cavalry Command, Army of Tennessee (April 1865)
Kentucky Brigade, Dibrell's Division, President Davis' Escort (April-May 1865)
Battles: Glasgow (December 24, 1862)
Morgan's Christmas Raid (December 21, 1862-January 1, 1863)
Muldraugh's Hill Trestle (December 28, 1862)
New Haven (December 30, 1862)
Milton (March 20, 1863)
Mount Sterling (March 22, 1863)
near Woodbury [skirmish] (May 25, 1863)
Tullahoma Campaign (June-July 1863)
Chattanooga Siege (September-November 1863)
Chattanooga (November 23-25, 1863)
Taylor's Ridge (November 27, 1863)
Charleston (December 27, 1863)
Atlanta Campaign (May-September 1864)
Dug Gap (May 8, 1864)
Sugar Valley (May 9, 1864)
Snake Creek Gap (May 9-10, 1864)
Resaca (May 14-15, 1864)
Cassville (May 19-22, 1864)
Cartersville (May 20, 1864)
Allatoona (May 30, 1864)
Marietta (June 1, 1864)
Rosswell's Ferry (June 10, 1864)
Noonday Creek (June 21, 1864)
Peach Tree Creek (July 20, 1864)
Atlanta (July 22, 1864)
Atlanta Siege (July-September 1864)
Jug Tavern (August 3, 1864)
Strawberry Plains (August 24, 1864)
Saltville (October 2, 1864)
Savannah Campaign (November-December 1864)
Carolinas Campaign (February-April 1865)
Columbia (February 16-17, 1865)

Monroe's Crossroads (March 9-10, 1865)
Bentonville (March 19-21, 1865)
Further Reading: Austin, J. P., *The Blue and the Gray.*

43. KENTUCKY 10TH CAVALRY BATTALION

See: KENTUCKY 13TH CAVALRY REGIMENT

44. KENTUCKY 10TH CAVALRY BATTALION, MOUNTED RIFLES

See: KENTUCKY 13TH CAVALRY REGIMENT

45. KENTUCKY 10TH CAVALRY REGIMENT, MOUNTED RIFLES

See: KENTUCKY 13TH CAVALRY REGIMENT

46. KENTUCKY 10TH (JOHNSON'S) CAVALRY REGIMENT

See: KENTUCKY 10TH CAVALRY REGIMENT, PARTISAN RANGERS

47. KENTUCKY 10TH (MAY'S) CAVALRY REGIMENT

See: KENTUCKY 14TH CAVALRY REGIMENT

48. KENTUCKY 10TH CAVALRY REGIMENT, PARTISAN RANGERS

Also Known As: 10th Cavalry Regiment
Organization: Organized in August 1862. Most of the regiment was captured during Morgan's Ohio Raid in July 1863.
First Commander: Adam R. Johnson (Colonel)
Field Officers: Robert M. Martin (Lieutenant Colonel)
Washington G. Owen (Major)
Assignments: Morgan's Cavalry Brigade, Army of Tennessee (November 1862-February 1863)
Morgan's Brigade, Wheeler's Cavalry Division, Army of Tennessee (February-March 1863)
Cluke's Brigade, Morgan's Division, Wheeler's Cavalry Corps, Army of Tennessee (March-July 1863)
Department of Southwestern Kentucky (September 1864-April 1865)
Battles: Morgan's Christmas Raid (December 21, 1862-January 1, 1863)
Muldraugh's Hill Trestle (December 28, 1862)
near Auburn [skirmish] (February 15, 1863)
Vaught's Hill, near Milton (March 20, 1863)
Celina (April 19, 1863)
Morgan's Ohio Raid (July 2-26, 1863)

Further Reading: Duke, Basil, *A History of Morgan's Cavalry.*

49. KENTUCKY 11TH CAVALRY REGIMENT

Also Known As: 7th (Chenault's) Cavalry Regiment

Organization: Organized on August 10, 1862. Mustered into Confederate service at Richmond, Kentucky on September 10, 1862. Captured during Morgan's Ohio Raid in July 1863. The remnants were merged into the 3rd Special Cavalry Battalion on November 10, 1864.

First Commander: David W. Chenault (Colonel)

Field Officers: James B. McCreary (Major, Lieutenant Colonel)

Joseph T. Tucker (Lieutenant Colonel, Major)

Assignments: Morgan's Cavalry Brigade, Army of Kentucky, Department #2 (August-October 1862)

Morgan's Cavalry Brigade, Army of Tennessee (November-December 1862)

Breckinridge's Brigade, Morgan's Cavalry Division, Army of Tennessee (December 1862-March 1863)

Breckinridge's Brigade, Morgan's Division, Army of Tennessee (March-July 1863)

Battles: Hartsville (December 7, 1862)

Morgan's Christmas Raid (December 21, 1862-January 1, 1863)

Muldraugh's Hill Trestle (December 28, 1862)

Boston (December 29, 1862)

Pegram's Kentucky Raid (March 22-April 1, 1863)

Expedition to Monticello (April 26-May 12, 1863)

Greasy Creek (May 8-9, 1863)

Morgan's Ohio Raid (July 2-26, 1863)

Green River Bridge (July 4, 1863)

Lebanon (July 5, 1863)

Buffington Island (July 19, 1863)

Further Reading: Duke, Basil, *A History of Morgan's Cavalry.*

50. KENTUCKY 11TH CAVALRY REGIMENT, MOUNTED RIFLES

See: KENTUCKY 13TH CAVALRY REGIMENT

51. KENTUCKY 12TH CAVALRY REGIMENT

Also Known As: 1st Kentucky and Tennessee Mounted Rifles

Organization: Organization begun at Tupelo, Mississippi in April 1863. Organization completed on September 15, 1863. Field consolidation with the Infantry Regiment (Mounted) and Sypert's Cavalry Battalion in early 1865. Surrendered at Gainesville, Alabama on May 10, 1865.

First Commander: William W. Faulkner (Colonel)

Field Officers: William D. Lannom (Lieutenant Colonel)
John M. Malone (Major)
Thomas S. Tate, Jr. (Major)
Assignments: Slemons' Brigade, 5th Military District, Department of Mississippi and East Louisiana [battalion] (May-June 1863)
McCulloch's Brigade, Chalmers' Division, Forrest's Cavalry Corps, Department of Mississippi and East Louisiana (January 1864)
McCulloch's Brigade, Chalmers' Division, Forrest's Cavalry Corps, Department of Alabama, Mississippi, and East Louisiana (January 1864)
Thompson's-Crossland's-Lyon's Brigade, Buford's Division, Forrest's Cavalry Corps, Department of Alabama, Mississippi, and East Louisiana (February-November 1864)
Lyon's-Crossland's Brigade, Buford's Division, Forrest's Cavalry Corps, Army of Tennessee (November 1864-January 1865)
Crossland's Brigade, Forrest's Cavalry Corps, Department of Alabama, Mississippi, and East Louisiana (February-May 1865)
Battles: near Commerce (June 17, 1863)
on the Coldwater River (June 19, 1863)
Okolona (February 22, 1864)
Brice's Crossroads (June 10, 1864)
Tupelo (July 14, 1864)
Forrest's Middle Tennessee Raid (September-October 1864)
Spring Hill (November 29, 1864)
Franklin (November 30, 1864)
Nashville (December 15-16, 1864)
Wilson's Raid (March 22-April 24, 1865)
Selma (April 2, 1865)
Further Reading: George, Henry, *History of the Third, Seventh, Eighth and Twelfth Kentucky*, C.S.A.

52. KENTUCKY 13TH CAVALRY REGIMENT

Also Known As: 10th Mounted Rifles
10th Infantry Regiment
10th Cavalry Battalion
10th Mounted Rifles Battalion
11th Mounted Rifles
11th Mounted Infantry Regiment
Organization: Organized on November 2, 1862. Disbanded by Brigadier General John Echols, commanding Department of Southwestern Virginia and East Tennessee, at Christianburg, Virginia on April 12, 1865.
First Commander: Benjamin F. Caudill (Colonel)

Field Officers: David J. "Henry" Caudill (Lieutenant Colonel)
John Thomas Chenoweth (Major)
Assignments: District of Abingdon, Department of East Tennessee (February-July 1863)
Preston's Brigade, Army of East Tennessee, Department of Tennessee (July-August 1863)
Williams' Cavalry Brigade, Ransom's Division, Department of Western Virginia and East Tennessee (October-November 1863)
Williams'-Giltner's Cavalry Brigade, Department of East Tennessee (January-February 1864)
Giltner's Brigade, Cavalry, Department of East Tennessee (February-March 1864)
Giltner's Brigade, Vaughn's Division, Ransom's Cavalry Corps, Department of East Tennessee (March-April 1864)
Giltner's Cavalry Brigade, Department of Southwestern Virginia and East Tennessee (April 1864-April 1865)
Battles: Knoxville Siege (November-December 1863)
Rogersville (November 6, 1863)
Jonesville (January 3, 1864)
Laurel Gap (October 1, 1864)
Saltville (October 2, 1864)

53. KENTUCKY 14TH CAVALRY REGIMENT

Also Known As: 10th (May's) Cavalry Regiment
Organization: Organized by the increase of May's Kentucky and Virginia Mounted Rifles Battalion to a regiment of 11 companies ca. July 1863. Disbanded by Brigadier General John Echols, commanding Department of Southwestern Virginia and East Tennessee, at Christianburg, Virginia on April 12, 1865.
First Commander: Andrew J. May (Colonel)
Field Officers: George R. Diamond (Lieutenant Colonel, Colonel)
William R. Lee (Major)
Edwin Trimble (Lieutenant Colonel, Colonel)
Assignments: Williams' Cavalry Brigade, Department of Western Virginia (July-October 1863)
Williams' Cavalry Brigade, Ransom's Division, Department of Western Virginia and East Tennessee (October-November 1863)
Williams'-Giltner's Cavalry Brigade, Department of East Tennessee (January-February 1864)
Giltner's Brigade, Cavalry, Department of East Tennessee (February-March 1864)

Giltner's Brigade, Vaughn's Division, Ransom's Cavalry Corps, Department of East Tennessee (March-April 1864)

Giltner's Cavalry Brigade, Department of Southwestern Virginia and East Tennessee (April 1864-April 1865)

Battles: Walker's Mountain, near Wytheville (July 18, 1863)

Blue Springs (October 10, 1863)

Knoxville Siege (November-December 1863)

Cedar Bluffs [skirmish] (September 30, 1864)

Flat Top Mountain (October 1, 1864)

Saltville (October 2, 1864)

54. KENTUCKY 14TH (MORGAN'S [R. C.]) CAVALRY REGIMENT

See: KENTUCKY MORGAN'S [R. C.] CAVALRY REGIMENT

55. KENTUCKY 15TH CAVALRY REGIMENT

Also Known As: 2nd (Woodward's) Cavalry Regiment

Organization: Organized on April 7, 1862. Company H was a Louisiana company. Surrendered at Washington, Georgia on May 10, 1865.

First Commander: Thomas G. Woodward (Lieutenant Colonel, Colonel)

Field Officer: Thomas W. Lewis (Major)

Assignments: Unattached, Breckinridge's Division, 1st Corps, Army of Tennessee [Company D] (November-December 1862)

Cosby's Brigade, Martin's Division, Van Dorn's Cavalry Corps, Army of Tennessee (March 1863)

Dibrell's-Armstrong's Brigade, Forrest's Cavalry Division, Army of Tennessee (July-August 1863)

Armstrong's-Wheeler's Brigade, Armstrong's Division, Forrest's Cavalry Corps, Army of Tennessee (August-October 1863)

Grigsby's Brigade, Kelly's Division, Wheeler's Cavalry Corps, Army of Tennessee (October 1863-July 1864)

Grigsby's-Williams' Brigade, Humes' Division, Wheeler's Cavalry Corps, Army of Tennessee (July-August 1864)

Williams' Brigade, Kelly's-Dibrell's Division, Wheeler's Cavalry Corps, Army of Tennessee (August-November 1864)

Williams'-Breckinridge's Brigade, Humes'-Dibrell's Division, Wheeler's Cavalry Corps, Department of South Carolina, Georgia, and Florida (November 1864-January 1865)

Kentucky Brigade, Iverson's Division, Wheeler's Cavalry Corps, Department of South Carolina, Georgia, and Florida (January-February 1865)

Kentucky Brigade, Humes' Division, Wheeler's Cavalry Corps, Army of Tennessee (February 1865)

Kentucky Brigade, Humes'-Dibrell's Division, Wheeler's Cavalry Corps, Hampton's Cavalry Command (February-April 1865)
Kentucky Brigade, Dibrell's Division, Wheeler's Cavalry Corps, Hampton's Cavalry Command, Army of Tennessee (April 1865)
Kentucky Brigade, Dibrell's Division, President Davis' Escort (April-May 1865)
Battles: New Providence [skirmish] (September 6, 1862)
Riggin's Hill [skirmish] (September 7, 1862)
Forrest's West Tennessee Raid (December 15, 1862-January 3, 1863)
Thompson's Station (March 5, 1863)
Chickamauga (September 19-20, 1863)
Chattanooga Siege (September-November 1863)
Chattanooga (November 23-25, 1863)
Taylor's Ridge (November 27, 1863)
Charleston (December 27, 1863)
Atlanta Campaign (May-September 1864)
Dug Gap (May 8, 1864)
Sugar Valley (May 9, 1864)
Snake Creek Gap (May 9-10, 1864)
Resaca (May 14-15, 1864)
Cassville (May 19-22, 1864)
Cartersville (May 20, 1864)
Allatoona (May 30, 1864)
Marietta (June 1, 1864)
Rosswell's Ferry (June 10, 1864)
Noonday Creek (June 21, 1864)
Peach Tree Creek (July 20, 1864)
Atlanta (July 22, 1864)
Atlanta Siege (July-September 1864)
Jug Tavern (August 3, 1864)
Strawberry Plains (August 24, 1864)
Saltville (October 2, 1864)
Savannah Campaign (November-December 1864)
Carolinas Campaign (February-April 1865)
Columbia (February 16-17, 1865)
Monroe's Crossroads (March 9-10, 1865)
Bentonville (March 19-21, 1865)

56. KENTUCKY BRECKINRIDGE'S CAVALRY BATTALION

Also Known As: 9th Cavalry Battalion

Organization: Organized with five companies in August 1862. Consolidated with Stoner's Cavalry Battalion and designated as the 9th Cavalry Regiment at Alexandria, Tennessee on December 17, 1862.
First Commander: William C. P. Breckinridge (Major)
Assignments: Morgan's Cavalry Brigade, Army of Kentucky, Department #2 (August-October 1862)
Morgan's Cavalry Brigade, Department of East Tennessee (October-November 1862)
Morgan's Cavalry Brigade, Army of Tennessee (November-December 1862)
Morgan's Brigade, Wheeler's Cavalry Division, Army of Tennessee (December 1862)
Battle: Lexington (October 18, 1862)
Further Reading: Ramage, James A., *Rebel Raider, The Life of General John Hunt Morgan.*

57. KENTUCKY CHENOWETH'S CAVALRY REGIMENT

Organization: Organized ca. October 1864. Surrender by Colonel J. Q. A. Chenoweth, commanding Department of Western Kentucky at Paris, Tennessee on May 4, 1865.
First Commander: James Q. A. Chenoweth (Colonel)
Field Officer: W. H. Jones (Major [acting])
Assignment: Department of Western Kentucky (October 1864-May 1865)

58. KENTUCKY HOLLIS' CAVALRY REGIMENT

Organization: Organized ca. October 1864. This unit does not appear in the *Official Records*. Surrender by Colonel J. Q. A. Chenoweth, commanding Department of Western Kentucky at Paris, Tennessee on May 4, 1865.
First Commander: William Hollis (Colonel)
Field Officer: James Waller (Major)
Assignment: Department of Western Kentucky (October 1864-May 1865)

59. KENTUCKY KING'S CAVALRY BATTALION

See: KENTUCKY 1ST (KING'S) CAVALRY BATTALION

60. KENTUCKY MAY'S CAVALRY BATTALION, MOUNTED RIFLES

Organization: Organized companies from Kentucky and Virginia in early 1863. Company F was assigned on February 28, 1863. Increased to a regiment and designated as the 14th Cavalry Regiment [AKA: 10th (May's) Cavalry Regiment] ca. July 1863.
First Commander: Andrew J. May (Major)

Assignment: Williams' Cavalry Brigade, Department of Western Virginia (April-July 1863)

61. KENTUCKY MORGAN'S [R. C.] CAVALRY REGIMENT

Also Known As: 14th (Morgan's [R. C.]) Cavalry Regiment
Organization: Organized in mid-1863. The regiment was captured during Morgan's Ohio Raid in July 1863.
First Commander: Richard C. Morgan (Colonel)
Assignment: Morgan's Division, Wheeler's Cavalry Corps, Army of Tennessee (July 1863)
Battle: Morgan's Ohio Raid (July 2-26, 1863)

62. KENTUCKY MORGAN'S CAVALRY SQUADRON

Organization: Organized with three companies at Bowling Green on October 27, 1861. Company D was assigned in the spring of 1862. Merged into the 2nd Cavalry Regiment in June 1862.
First Commander: John Hunt Morgan (Captain)
Assignments: Hindman's Brigade, Hardee's Division, Central Army of Kentucky, Department #2 (December 1861-February 1862)
Breckinridge's Brigade, Reserve, Central Army of Kentucky, Department #2 (February-March 1862)
Unattached, Army of the Mississippi, Department #2 (March-June 1862)
Battles: Expedition to Bacon Creek Bridge (December 5-8, 1861)
Operations near Greensburg and Lebanon (January 28-February 2, 1862)
Scout to Nashville (February 26, 1862)
near Nashville [detachment] (March 8, 1862)
Operations about Gallatin (March 15-18, 1862)
Shiloh (April 6-7, 1862)
Morgan's Middle Tennessee Raid (April-May 1862)
Pulaski (May 1, 1862)
Lebanon (May 5, 1862)
Cave City (May 11, 1862)
Further Reading: Thompson, Edward Porter, *History of the Orphan Brigade.* Davis, William C., *The Orphan Brigade: The Kentucky Confederates Who Couldn't Go Home.*

63. KENTUCKY MORRIS' CAVALRY REGIMENT, MOUNTED RIFLES

Organization: Organized in the summer of 1863. Apparently never completed to complete its organization and was disbanded in the fall of 1863.
First Commander: John D. Morris (Colonel)

Assignment: Williams' Cavalry Brigade, Department of Western Virginia (July-September 1863)
Battle: Wytheville (July 18, 1863)

64. KENTUCKY PATTON'S CAVALRY BATTALION, PARTISAN RANGERS

Organization: Failed to complete its organization. This unit does not appear in the *Official Records*. However, Lieutenant Colonel Oliver A. Patton is listed by the Union authorities as having been captured in Morgan County, Kentucky on October 15, 1863, possibly while trying to recruit his battalion.
First Commander: Oliver A. Patton (Lieutenant Colonel)

65. KENTUCKY STONER'S CAVALRY BATTALION

Organization: Organized with five companies September/October 1862. Consolidated with Breckinridge's Cavalry Battalion and designated as the 9th Cavalry Regiment at Alexandria, Tennessee on December 17, 1862.
First Commander: Robert G. Stoner (Major)
Assignments: Morgan's Cavalry Brigade, Army of Kentucky, Department #2 (October 1862)
Morgan's Cavalry Brigade, Department of East Tennessee (October-November 1862)
Morgan's Cavalry Brigade, Army of Tennessee (December 1862)
Morgan's Brigade, Wheeler's Cavalry Division, Army of Tennessee (December 1862)
Breckinridge's Brigade, Morgan's Cavalry Division, Army of Tennessee (December 1862)

66. KENTUCKY SYPERT'S CAVALRY REGIMENT

Organization: Organized in the fall of 1864. Field consolidation with the 12th Cavalry Regiment and the 8th Infantry Regiment (Mounted) briefly in early 1865. Surrendered at Columbus, Mississippi on May 6, 1865.
First Commander: Leonidas A. Sypert (Colonel)
Field Officers: L. D. Hockersmith (Major)
Robert B. Storey (Lieutenant Colonel)
Presley N. Garr (Major)
Assignment: Department of Western Kentucky (October 1864-May 1865)

INFANTRY

67. Kentucky 1st Infantry Battalion

Organization: Organized with four companies in April 1861. Consolidated with Taylor's Infantry Battalion and designated as the 1st Infantry Regiment at Manassas Junction, Virginia on August 7, 1861, per S.O. #117, Adjutant and Inspector General's Office.

First Commander: Blanton Duncan (Lieutenant Colonel)

Field Officer: Thomas Claiborne (Major)

Assignments: Bartow's Brigade, Army of the Shenandoah (June-July 1861)

Bartow's-D. R. Jones' Brigade, 2nd Corps, Army of the Potomac (July-August 1861)

68. Kentucky 1st Infantry Regiment

Organization: Organized by the consolidation of the 1st Infantry Battalion (four companies) and Taylor's Infantry Battalion (six companies) at Manassas Junction, Virginia on August 7, 1861, per S.O. #117, Adjutant and Inspector General's Office. Reorganized on April 30, 1862. Mustered out at Richmond, Virginia on May 13-14, 1862.

First Commander: Thomas H. Taylor (Colonel)

Field Officers: Benjamin M. Anderson (Major)

Edward Crossland (Major, Lieutenant Colonel)

William P. Johnston (Lieutenant Colonel)

Assignments: D. R. Jones' Brigade, 2nd Corps, Army of the Potomac (August-October 1861)

D. R. Jones' Brigade, 2nd Corps, Potomac District, Department of Northern Virginia (October 1861-February 1862)

D. R. Jones' Brigade, G. W. Smith's Division, Potomac District, Department of Northern Virginia (February-April 1862)

D. R. Jones'-Semmes' Brigade, Toombs' Division, Magruder's Command, Department of Northern Virginia (April-May 1862)

Battles: Mason's Hill [Company A] (September 28, 1861)
Dranesville (December 20, 1861)

69. KENTUCKY 2ND INFANTRY REGIMENT

Organization: Organized at Camp Boone, Montgomery County, Tennessee on July 13, 1861. Mustered into Confederate service at Camp Boone, Montgomery County, Tennessee on July 16, 1861. Surrendered at Fort Donelson on February 16, 1862. Exchanged on August 5, 1862. Mounted at Barnesville, Georgia on September 4, 1864. Surrendered at Washington, Georgia on May 6, 1865.

First Commander: James M. Hawes (Colonel)

Field Officers: Roger W. Hanson (Colonel)
James W. Hewitt (Major, Lieutenant Colonel)
Robert A. Johnson (Lieutenant Colonel, Colonel)
William P. Johnston (Major)
Philip L. Lee (Major, Lieutenant Colonel)
Hervey McDowell (Major)
James W. Moss (Major, Lieutenant Colonel, Colonel)

Assignments: Central Geographical Division of Kentucky, Department #2 (September-October 1861)
Kentucky Brigade, Buckner's Division, Central Army of Kentucky, Department #2 (October 1861-February 1862)
Baldwin's Brigade, Buckner's Division, Fort Donelson, Department #2 (February 1862)
Kentucky Brigade, Army of Middle Tennessee, Department #2 (October-November 1862)
Kentucky Brigade, Breckinridge's Division, 1st Corps, Army of Tennessee (November-December 1862)
Kentucky Brigade, Breckinridge's Division, 2nd Corps, Army of Tennessee (December 1862-May 1863)
Kentucky Brigade, Breckinridge's Division, Department of the West (May-July 1863)
Kentucky Brigade, Breckinridge's Division, Department of Mississippi and East Louisiana (July-August 1863)
Kentucky Brigade, Breckinridge's Division, 2nd Corps, Army of Tennessee (August 1863-February 1864)
Kentucky Brigade, Bate's Division, 1st Corps, Army of Tennessee (February-September 1864)
Kentucky Brigade, Jackson's Cavalry Division, Army of Tennessee (September 1864)

Kentucky Brigade, Iverson's Division, Wheeler's Cavalry Corps, Army of Tennessee (September-November 1864)
Kentucky Brigade, Iverson's-Young's Division, Wheeler's Cavalry Corps, Department of South Carolina, Georgia, and Florida (November 1864-February 1865)
Kentucky Brigade, Humes' Division, Wheeler's Cavalry Corps, Army of Tennessee (February 1865)
Kentucky Brigade, Humes'-Dibrell's Division, Wheeler's Cavalry Corps, Hampton's Cavalry Command (February-April 1865)
Kentucky Brigade, Dibrell's Division, Wheeler's Cavalry Corps, Hampton's Cavalry Command, Army of Tennessee (April 1865)
Kentucky Brigade, Dibrell's Division, President Davis' Escort (April-May 1865)
Battles: Fort Donelson (February 12-16, 1862)
Hartsville (December 7, 1862)
Murfreesboro (December 31, 1862-January 3, 1863)
Chickamauga (September 19-20, 1863)
Chattanooga Siege (September-November 1863)
Chattanooga (November 23-25, 1863)
Atlanta Campaign (May-September 1864)
Rocky Face Ridge (May 5-11, 1864)
Resaca (May 14-15, 1864)
Adairsville (May 15-18, 1864)
New Hope Church (May 25-June 4, 1864)
Dallas (June 25-27, 1864)
Kennesaw Mountain (June 27, 1864)
Peach Tree Creek (July 20, 1864)
Atlanta (July 22, 1864)
Ezra Church (July 28, 1864)
Atlanta Siege (July-September 1864)
Utoy Creek (August 5-7, 1864)
Jonesboro (August 31-September 1, 1864)
Savannah Campaign (November-December 1864)
Carolinas Campaign (February-April 1865)
Further Reading: Davis, William C., *The Orphan Brigade: The Kentucky Confederates Who Couldn't Go Home*. Thompson, Edward Porter, *History of the First Kentucky Brigade*.

70. KENTUCKY 3RD INFANTRY REGIMENT

Organization: Organized at Camp Boone, Montgomery County, Tennessee on July 5, 1861. 1st Company F became the 1st Artillery Battery at Bowling Green on September 20, 1861. Companies L and M were created by the assignment of Company E, 12th and Company F, 22nd Tennessee Infantry Regiments on May 15, 1862. Company N was subsequently assigned. Mounted on March 10, 1864. Surrendered at Meridian, Mississippi on May 4, 1865.

First Commander: Lloyd Tilghman (Colonel)

Field Officers: Benjamin M. Anderson (Major, Lieutenant Colonel)

T. T. Barnett (Major, Lieutenant Colonel)

James H. Bowman (Major)

Gustavus A. C. Holt (Lieutenant Colonel, Colonel)

Alfred Johnston (Major, Lieutenant Colonel)

William P. Johnston (Major)

Al. McGoodwin (Major)

Albert P. Thompson (Colonel)

Assignments: Central Geographical Division of Kentucky, Department #2 (September-October 1861)

Kentucky Brigade, Buckner's Division, Central Army of Kentucky, Department #2 (October 1861-February 1862)

Kentucky Brigade, Reserve, Central Army of Kentucky, Department #2 (February-March 1862)

Kentucky Brigade, Reserve Corps, Army of the Mississippi, Department #2 (March-June 1862)

Kentucky Brigade, Breckinridge's Division, District of the Mississippi, Department #2 (June-July 1862)

Thompson's Brigade, Ruggles' Division, Breckinridge's Command, District of the Mississippi, Department #2 (July-August 1862)

Rust's Brigade, Lovell's Division, District of the Mississippi, Department #2 (October 1862)

Baldwin's Brigade, Tilghman's Division, 1st Corps, Army of the Department of Mississippi and East Louisiana (October 1862-January 1863)

Rust's Brigade, Loring's Division, Department of Mississippi and East Louisiana (January-February 1863)

Rust's Brigade, 3rd Military District, Department of Mississippi and East Louisiana (March 1863)

Buford's Brigade, 3rd Military District, Department of Mississippi and East Louisiana (March-April 1863)

Buford's Brigade, Loring's Division, Department of Mississippi and East Louisiana (April-May 1863)

Buford's Brigade, Loring's Division, Department of the West (May-July 1863)

Buford's Brigade, Loring's Division, Department of Mississippi and East Louisiana (July 1863-January 1864)

Buford's Brigade, Loring's Division, Department of Alabama, Mississippi, and East Louisiana (January-March 1864)

Thompson's-Crossland's-Lyon's-Crossland's Brigade, Buford's Division, Forrest's Cavalry Corps, Department of Alabama, Mississippi, and East Louisiana (March-November 1864)
Crossland's Brigade, Buford's Division, Forrest's Cavalry Corps, Army of Tennessee (November 1864-January 1865)
Crossland's Brigade, Forrest's Cavalry Corps, Department of Alabama, Mississippi, and East Louisiana (March-May 1865)
Battles: Shiloh (April 6-7, 1862)
Corinth Campaign (April-June 1862)
Vicksburg Bombardments (May 18-July 27, 1862)
Baton Rouge (August 5, 1862)
Coffeeville (December 5, 1862)
Chickasaw Bayou (December 27-29, 1862)
Vicksburg Campaign (April-July 1863)
Champion Hill (May 16, 1863)
Paducah (March 25, 1864)
Meridian Campaign (February-March 1864)
Fort Pillow (April 12, 1864)
Brice's Crossroads (June 10, 1864)
Johnsonville (November 3-5, 1864)
Franklin-Nashville Campaign (November 1864-December 1864)
Wilson's Raid (March 22-April 24, 1865)
Further Reading: Davis, William C., *The Orphan Brigade: The Kentucky Confederates Who Couldn't Go Home*. George, Henry, *History of the Third, Seventh, Eighth and Twelfth Kentucky, C.S.A.*

71. KENTUCKY 4TH INFANTRY REGIMENT

Organization: Organized at Camp Burnett, Montgomery County, Tennessee on September 13, 1861. Company B served in Graves' Artillery Battery and was captured at Fort Donelson on February 16, 1862. Company B was exchanged in September 1862. Mounted at Barnsville, Georgia on September 14, 1864. Surrendered at Washington, Georgia on May 6, 1865.
First Commander: Robert P. Trabue (Colonel)
Field Officers: John A. Adair (Major, Lieutenant Colonel)
Andrew R. Hynes (Lieutenant Colonel)
Joseph H. Millett (Major)
Thomas B. Monroe, Jr. (Major)
Joseph P. Nuckols (Major, Lieutenant Colonel, Colonel)
Willis S. Roberts (Major)
John Bird Rogers (Major)
Thomas W. Thompson (Major, Lieutenant Colonel, Colonel)

Assignments: Central Geographical Division of Kentucky, Department #2 (September-October 1861)

Kentucky Brigade, Buckner's Division, Central Army of Kentucky, Department #2 (October 1861-February 1862)

Kentucky Brigade, Reserve, Central Army of Kentucky, Department #2 (February-March 1862)

Kentucky Brigade, Reserve Corps, Army of the Mississippi, Department #2 (March-April 1862)

Hawes' Brigade, Breckinridge's Division, Army of the Mississippi, Department #2 (April-June 1862)

Hawes' Brigade, Breckinridge's Division, District of the Mississippi, Department #2 (June-July 1862)

Helm's Brigade, Clarks' Division, Breckinridge's Command, District of the Mississippi, Department #2 (July-August 1862)

Kentucky Brigade, Army of Middle Tennessee, Department #2 (October-November 1862)

Kentucky Brigade, Breckinridge's Division, 1st Corps, Army of Tennessee (November-December 1862)

Kentucky Brigade, Breckinridge's Division, 2nd Corps, Army of Tennessee (December 1862-May 1863)

Kentucky Brigade, Breckinridge's Division, Department of the West (May-July 1863)

Kentucky Brigade, Breckinridge's Division, Department of Mississippi and East Louisiana (July-August 1863)

Kentucky Brigade, Breckinridge's Division, 2nd Corps, Army of Tennessee (August 1863-February 1864)

Kentucky Brigade, Bate's Division, 1st Corps, Army of Tennessee (February-September 1864)

Kentucky Brigade, Jackson's Cavalry Division, Army of Tennessee (September 1864)

Kentucky Brigade, Iverson's Division, Wheeler's Cavalry Corps, Army of Tennessee (September-November 1864)

Kentucky Brigade, Iverson's-Young's Division, Wheeler's Cavalry Corps, Department of South Carolina, Georgia, and Florida (November 1864-February 1865)

Kentucky Brigade, Humes' Division, Wheeler's Cavalry Corps, Army of Tennessee (February 1865)

Kentucky Brigade, Humes'-Dibrell's Division, Wheeler's Cavalry Corps, Hampton's Cavalry Command (February-April 1865)

Kentucky Brigade, Dibrell's Division, Wheeler's Cavalry Corps, Hampton's Cavalry Command, Army of Tennessee (April 1865)

Kentucky Brigade, Dibrell's Division, President Davis' Escort (April-May 1865)
Battles: Fort Donelson [Company B] (February 12-16, 1862)
Shiloh (April 6-7, 1862)
Corinth Campaign (April-June 1862)
Vicksburg Bombardments (May 18-July 27, 1862)
Baton Rouge (August 5, 1862)
Murfreesboro (December 31, 1862-January 3, 1863)
Chickamauga (September 19-20, 1863)
Chattanooga Siege (September-November 1863)
Chattanooga (November 23-25, 1863)
Atlanta Campaign (May-September 1864)
Rocky Face Ridge (May 5-11, 1864)
Resaca (May 14-15, 1864)
Adairsville (May 15-18, 1864)
New Hope Church (May 25-June 4, 1864)
Dallas (June 25-27, 1864)
Kennesaw Mountain (June 27, 1864)
Peach Tree Creek (July 20, 1864)
Atlanta (July 22, 1864)
Ezra Church (July 28, 1864)
Atlanta Siege (July-September 1864)
Utoy Creek (August 5-7, 1864)
Jonesboro (August 31-September 1, 1864)
Savannah Campaign (November-December 1864)
Carolinas Campaign (February-April 1865)
Further Reading: Davis, William C., *The Orphan Brigade: The Kentucky Confederates Who Couldn't Go Home*. Thompson, Edward Porter, *History of the First Kentucky Brigade*.

72. KENTUCKY 5TH INFANTRY REGIMENT

Organization: Organized on October 22, 1861. Reorganized for the war on October 20, 1862. Consolidated into eight companies on November 18, 1862. Companies A and B, Desha's Infantry Battalion were assigned as 3rd Companies I and K, respectively, of this regiment on August 22, 1863. Mounted at Barnsville, Georgia on September 4, 1864. Surrendered at Washington, Georgia on May 6, 1865.
First Commander: John S. Williams (Colonel)
Field Officers: George W. Connor (Major, Lieutenant Colonel)
Hiram Hawkins (Major, Lieutenant Colonel, Colonel)
Andrew J. May (Lieutenant Colonel, Colonel)
William Mynheir (Major)

Assignments: Marshall's Brigade, Army of Eastern Kentucky (November 1861-May 1862)

District of Abingdon (May 1862)

District of Abingdon, Department of Southwestern Virginia (May-November 1862)

District of Abingdon, Department of Western Virginia (November 1862-January 1863)

District of Abingdon, Department of East Tennessee (January-August 1863)

Kelly's Brigade, Preston's Division, Buckner's Corps, Army of Tennessee (August-September 1863)

Kelly's Brigade, Preston's Division, Longstreet's Corps, Army of Tennessee (September-October 1863)

Kelly's Brigade, Buckner's Division, 1st Corps, Army of Tennessee (October-November 1863)

Kentucky Brigade, Breckinridge's Division, 2nd Corps, Army of Tennessee (November 1863-February 1864)

Kentucky Brigade, Bate's Division, 1st Corps, Army of Tennessee (February-September 1864)

Kentucky Brigade, Jackson's Cavalry Division, Army of Tennessee (September 1864)

Kentucky Brigade, Iverson's Division, Wheeler's Cavalry Corps, Army of Tennessee (September-November 1864)

Kentucky Brigade, Iverson's-Young's Division, Wheeler's Cavalry Corps, Department of South Carolina, Georgia, and Florida (November 1864-February 1865)

Kentucky Brigade, Humes' Division, Wheeler's Cavalry Corps, Army of Tennessee (February 1865)

Kentucky Brigade, Humes'-Dibrell's Division, Wheeler's Cavalry Corps, Hampton's Cavalry Command (February-April 1865)

Kentucky Brigade, Dibrell's Division, Wheeler's Cavalry Corps, Hampton's Cavalry Command, Army of Tennessee (April 1865)

Kentucky Brigade, Dibrell's Division, President Davis' Escort (April-May 1865)

Battles: Ivy Mountain (November 8, 1861)

Piketon (November 9, 1861)

Middle Creek (January 10, 1862)

Wolf Creek (May 15, 1862)

Princeton (May 15-17, 1862)

Chickamauga (September 19-20, 1863)

Chattanooga Siege (September-November 1863)

Chattanooga (November 23-25, 1863)

Atlanta Campaign (May-September 1864)

Rocky Face Ridge (May 5-11, 1864)
Resaca (May 14-15, 1864)
Adairsville (May 15-18, 1864)
New Hope Church (May 25-June 4, 1864)
Dallas (June 25-27, 1864)
Kennesaw Mountain (June 27, 1864)
Peach Tree Creek (July 20, 1864)
Atlanta (July 22, 1864)
Ezra Church (July 28, 1864)
Atlanta Siege (July-September 1864)
Utoy Creek (August 5-7, 1864)
Jonesboro (August 31-September 1, 1864)
Savannah Campaign (November-December 1864)
Carolinas Campaign (February-April 1865)
Further Reading: Davis, William C., *The Orphan Brigade: The Kentucky Confederates Who Couldn't Go Home*. Thompson, Edward Porter, *History of the First Kentucky Brigade*.

73. KENTUCKY 5TH (HUNT'S) INFANTRY REGIMENT

See: KENTUCKY 9TH INFANTRY REGIMENT

74. KENTUCKY 6TH INFANTRY REGIMENT

Organization: Organized at Cave City on September 10, 1861. Reorganized with eight companies on April 26, 1862. Mounted at Barnesville, Georgia on September 17, 1864. Surrendered at Washington, Georgia on May 6, 1865.
First Commander: Joseph H. Lewis (Colonel)
Field Officers: William L. Clarke (Major, Lieutenant Colonel)
Martin H. Cofer (Lieutenant Colonel, Colonel)
Thomas H. Hays (Major)
George W. Maxson (Major)
Assignments: Kentucky Brigade, Buckner's Division, Central Army of Kentucky, Department #2 (October 1861-February 1862)
Kentucky Brigade, Reserve, Central Army of Kentucky, Department #2 (February-March 1862)
Kentucky Brigade, Reserve Corps, Army of the Mississippi, Department #2 (March-June 1862)
Kentucky Brigade, Breckinridge's Division, District of the Mississippi, Department #2 (June-July 1862)
Thompson's Brigade, Ruggles' Division, Breckinridge's Command, District of the Mississippi, Department #2 (July-August 1862)

Kentucky Brigade, Army of Middle Tennessee, Department #2 (October-November 1862)

Kentucky Brigade, Breckinridge's Division, 1st Corps, Army of Tennessee (November-December 1862)

Kentucky Brigade, Breckinridge's Division, 2nd Corps, Army of Tennessee (December 1862-May 1863)

Kentucky Brigade, Breckinridge's Division, Department of the West (May-July 1863)

Kentucky Brigade, Breckinridge's Division, Department of Mississippi and East Louisiana (July-August 1863)

Kentucky Brigade, Breckinridge's Division, 2nd Corps, Army of Tennessee (August 1863-February 1864)

Kentucky Brigade, Bate's Division, 1st Corps, Army of Tennessee (February-September 1864)

Kentucky Brigade, Jackson's Cavalry Division, Army of Tennessee (September 1864)

Kentucky Brigade, Iverson's Division, Wheeler's Cavalry Corps, Army of Tennessee (September-November 1864)

Kentucky Brigade, Iverson's-Young's Division, Wheeler's Cavalry Corps, Department of South Carolina, Georgia, and Florida (November 1864-February 1865)

Kentucky Brigade, Humes' Division, Wheeler's Cavalry Corps, Army of Tennessee (February 1865)

Kentucky Brigade, Humes'-Dibrell's Division, Wheeler's Cavalry Corps, Hampton's Cavalry Command (February-April 1865)

Kentucky Brigade, Dibrell's Division, Wheeler's Cavalry Corps, Hampton's Cavalry Command, Army of Tennessee (April 1865)

Kentucky Brigade, Dibrell's Division, President Davis' Escort (April-May 1865)

Battles: Shiloh (April 6-7, 1862)

Corinth Campaign (April-June 1862)

Vicksburg Bombardments (May 18-July 27, 1862)

Baton Rouge (August 5, 1862)

Murfreesboro (December 31, 1862-January 3, 1863)

Jackson Siege (July 1863)

Chickamauga (September 19-20, 1863)

Chattanooga Siege (September-November 1863)

Chattanooga (November 23-25, 1863)

Atlanta Campaign (May-September 1864)

Rocky Face Ridge (May 5-11, 1864)

Resaca (May 14-15, 1864)

Adairsville (May 15-18, 1864)

New Hope Church (May 25-June 4, 1864)
Dallas (June 25-27, 1864)
Kennesaw Mountain (June 27, 1864)
Peach Tree Creek (July 20, 1864)
Atlanta (July 22, 1864)
Ezra Church (July 28, 1864)
Atlanta Siege (July-September 1864)
Utoy Creek (August 5-7, 1864)
Jonesboro (August 31-September 1, 1864)
Savannah Campaign (November-December 1864)
Carolinas Campaign (February-April 1865)
Further Reading: Davis, William C., *The Orphan Brigade: The Kentucky Confederates Who Couldn't Go Home*. Thompson, Edward Porter, *History of the First Kentucky Brigade*.

75. KENTUCKY 7TH INFANTRY REGIMENT

Organization: Organized at Camp Burnett, near Clinton, Hickman County in September 1861. 1st Company K became Company E, 13th Arkansas Infantry Regiment. 2nd Company K was formerly Company C, 2nd Confederate Infantry Regiment. Reorganized at Corinth, Mississippi on May 20, 1862. Mounted on March 1, 1864. Surrendered at Columbus, Mississippi on May 6, 1865.
First Commander: Charles Wickliffe (Colonel)
Field Officers: Edward Crossland (Colonel)
Henry S. Hale (Major)
William D. Lannom (Lieutenant Colonel)
L. J. Sherrill (Lieutenant Colonel)
W. J. N. Welborn (Major)
Assignments: 2nd Brigade, Cheatham's Division, 1st Geographical Division, Department #2 (November 1861-March 1862)
Stephens' Brigade, 1st Grand Division, Army of the Mississippi, Department #2 (March 1862)
Stephens' Brigade, Cheatham's Division, 1st Grand Division, Army of the Mississippi, Department #2 (March 1862)
Stephens'-Maney's Brigade, Cheatham's Division, 1st Corps, Army of the Mississippi, Department #2 (March-April 1862)
Preston's Brigade, Reserve Corps, Army of the Mississippi, Department #2 (April-June 1862)
Preston's Brigade, Breckinridge's Division, District of the Mississippi, Department #2 (June-July 1862)

Thompson's Brigade, Ruggles' Division, Breckinridge's Command, District of the Mississippi, Department #2 (July-August 1862)
Rust's Brigade, Lovell's Division, District of the Mississippi, Department #2 (October 1862)
Thompson's Brigade, Rust's Division, 1st Corps, Army of the Department of Mississippi and East Louisiana (October 1862-January 1863)
Rust's Brigade, Loring's Division, Department of Mississippi and East Louisiana (January-February 1863)
Rust's Brigade, 3rd Military District, Department of Mississippi and East Louisiana (March 1863)
Buford's Brigade, 3rd Military District, Department of Mississippi and East Louisiana (March-April 1863)
Buford's Brigade, Loring's Division, Department of Mississippi and East Louisiana (April-May 1863)
Buford's Brigade, Loring's Division, Department of the West (May-July 1863)
Buford's Brigade, Loring's Division, Department of Mississippi and East Louisiana (July 1863-January 1864)
Buford's Brigade, Loring's Division, Department of Alabama, Mississippi, and East Louisiana (January-March 1864)
Thompson's-Crossland's-Lyon's-Crossland's Brigade, Buford's Division, Forrest's Cavalry Corps, Department of Alabama, Mississippi, and East Louisiana (March-November 1864)
Crossland's Brigade, Buford's Division, Forrest's Cavalry Corps, Army of Tennessee (November 1864-January 1865)
Crossland's Brigade, Forrest's Cavalry Corps, Department of Alabama, Mississippi, and East Louisiana (March-May 1865)
Battles: Shiloh (April 6-7, 1862)
Corinth Campaign (April-June 1862)
Vicksburg Bombardments (May 18-July 27, 1862)
Baton Rouge (August 5, 1862)
Corinth (October 3-4, 1862)
Murfreesboro (December 31, 1862-January 3, 1863)
Vicksburg Campaign (April-July 1863)
Raymond (May 12, 1863)
Champion Hill (May 16, 1863)
Jackson Siege (July 1863)
Meridian Campaign (February-March 1864)
Paducah (March 25, 1864)
Brice's Crossroads (June 10, 1864)
Tupelo (July 14, 1864)
Spring Hill (November 29, 1864)

Franklin (November 30, 1864)
Nashville (December 15-16, 1864)
Wilson's Raid (March 22-April 24, 1865)
Plantersville (April 1, 1865)
Ebenezer Church (April 1, 1865)
Selma (April 2, 1865)
Further Reading: George, Henry, *History of the Third, Seventh, Eighth and Twelfth Kentucky*, C.S.A.

76. KENTUCKY 8TH INFANTRY REGIMENT

Organization: Organized with nine companies at Hopkinsville in October 1861. Surrendered at Fort Donelson on February 16, 1862. Exchanged at Vicksburg, Warren County, Mississippi on September 13, 1862. Reorganized on September 25, 1862. Company B, 40th Tennessee Regiment, an Arkansas company was assigned on October 1, 1862. Mounted on March 10, 1864. Field consolidation with the 12th Cavalry Regiment and Sypert's Cavalry Battalion in early 1865. Surrendered at Columbus, Mississippi on May 6, 1865.
First Commander: Henry C. Burnett (Colonel)
Field Officers: Jabez Bingham (Major)
Robert W. Henry (Major)
Hylan B. Lyon (Lieutenant Colonel, Colonel)
R. R. Ross (Lieutenant Colonel)
Absalom R. Shacklett (Lieutenant Colonel)
Assignments: Clark's Brigade, Central Army of Kentucky, Department #2 (December 1861-February 1862)
Davidson's Brigade, Johnson's Division, Fort Donelson, Department #2 (February 1862)
Rust's Brigade, Lovell's Division, District of the Mississippi, Department #2 (October 1862)
Baldwin's Brigade, Tilghman's Division, 1st Corps, Army of the Department of Mississippi and East Louisiana (October 1862-January 1863)
Rust's Brigade, Loring's Division, Department of Mississippi and East Louisiana (January-March 1863)
Buford's Brigade, 3rd Military District, Department of Mississippi and East Louisiana (March-April 1863)
Buford's Brigade, Loring's Division, Department of Mississippi and East Louisiana (April 1863-January 1864)
Buford's Brigade, Loring's Division, Department of Alabama, Mississippi, and East Louisiana (January-March 1864)

Thompson's-Crossland's-Lyon's-Crossland's Brigade, Buford's Division, Forrest's Cavalry Corps, Forrest's Cavalry Corps, Department of Alabama, Mississippi, and East Louisiana (March-November 1864)
Crossland's Brigade, Buford's Division, Forrest's Cavalry Corps, Army of Tennessee (November-December 1864)
Crossland's Brigade, Forrest's Cavalry Corps, Department of Alabama, Mississippi, and East Louisiana (March-May 1865)
Battles: Fort Donelson (February 12-16, 1862)
Coffeeville (December 5, 1862)
Vicksburg Campaign (April-July 1863)
Champion Hill (May 16, 1863)
Big Black River Bridge (May 17, 1863)
Vicksburg Siege [detachment] (May-July 1863)
Jackson Siege (July 1863)
Meridian Campaign (February-March 1864)
Paducah (March 25, 1864)
Brice's Crossroads (June 10, 1864)
Tupelo (July 14, 1864)
Johnsonville (November 3-5, 1864)
Spring Hill (November 29, 1864)
Franklin (November 30, 1864)
Wilson's Raid (March 22-April 24, 1865)
Ebenezer Church (April 1, 1865)
Murfreesboro (December 5-7, 1864)
Columbia (December 20, 1864)
Selma (April 2, 1865)
Further Reading: George, Henry, *History of the Third, Seventh, Eighth and Twelfth Kentucky*, C.S.A.

77. KENTUCKY 9TH INFANTRY REGIMENT

Also Known As: 5th Infantry Regiment
Organization: Organized with eight companies as the 5th Infantry Regiment at Camp Boone, Montgomery County, Tennessee on October 3, 1861. Company K, a Texas unit, was assigned on December 1, 1861. Companies E and F became Companies A and B, respectively, of the 23rd Tennessee Infantry Battalion in April 1862. Company K was merged into Company H on April 25, 1862. Thus the regiment was reduced to only six companies. Mounted at Barnsville, Georgia in September 1864. Surrendered at Washington, Georgia on May 6, 1865.
First Commander: Thomas H. Hunt (Colonel)
Field Officers: John W. Caldwell (Major, Lieutenant Colonel, Colonel)

A. Casseday (Lieutenant Colonel)
Benjamin Desha (Major)
Robert A. Johnston (Lieutenant Colonel)
John C. Wickliffe (Major, Lieutenant Colonel)

Assignments: Central Geographical Division of Kentucky, Department #2 (October 1861)

Kentucky Brigade, Buckner's Division, Central Army of Kentucky, Department #2 (October 1861-February 1862)

Kentucky Brigade, Reserve, Central Army of Kentucky, Department #2 (February-March 1862)

Kentucky Brigade, Reserve Corps, Army of the Mississippi, Department #2 (March-June 1862)

Kentucky Brigade, Breckinridge's Division, District of the Mississippi, Department #2 (June-July 1862)

Helm's Brigade, Clark's Division, Breckinridge's Command, District of the Mississippi, Department #2 (July-August 1862)

Kentucky Brigade, Army of Middle Tennessee, Department #2 (October-November 1862)

Kentucky Brigade, Breckinridge's Division, 1st Corps, Army of Tennessee (November-December 1862)

Kentucky Brigade, Breckinridge's Division, 2nd Corps, Army of Tennessee (December 1862-May 1863)

Kentucky Brigade, Breckinridge's Division, Department of the West (May-July 1863)

Kentucky Brigade, Breckinridge's Division, Department of Mississippi and East Louisiana (July-August 1863)

Kentucky Brigade, Breckinridge's Division, 2nd Corps, Army of Tennessee (August 1863-February 1864)

Kentucky Brigade, Bate's Division, 1st Corps, Army of Tennessee (February-September 1864)

Kentucky Brigade, Jackson's Cavalry Division, Army of Tennessee (September 1864)

Kentucky Brigade, Iverson's Division, Wheeler's Cavalry Corps, Army of Tennessee (September-November 1864)

Kentucky Brigade, Iverson's-Young's Division, Wheeler's Cavalry Corps, Department of South Carolina, Georgia, and Florida (November 1864-February 1865)

Kentucky Brigade, Humes' Division, Wheeler's Cavalry Corps, Army of Tennessee (February 1865)

Kentucky Brigade, Humes'-Dibrell's Division, Wheeler's Cavalry Corps, Hampton's Cavalry Command (February-April 1865)

Kentucky Brigade, Dibrell's Division, Wheeler's Cavalry Corps, Hampton's Cavalry Command, Army of Tennessee (April 1865)
Kentucky Brigade, Dibrell's Division, President Davis' Escort (April-May 1865)
Battles: Whippoorwill Creek [detachment] (Dec. 1, 1861)
Shiloh (April 6-7, 1862)
Corinth Campaign (April-June 1862)
Vicksburg Bombardments (May 18-July 27, 1862)
Baton Rouge (August 5, 1862)
Hartsville (December 7, 1862)
Murfreesboro (December 31, 1862-January 3, 1863)
Jackson Siege (July 1863)
Chickamauga (September 19-20, 1863)
Chattanooga Siege (September-November 1863)
Chattanooga (November 23-25, 1863)
Atlanta Campaign (May-September 1864)
Rocky Face Ridge (May 5-11, 1864)
Resaca (May 14-15, 1864)
Adairsville (May 15-18, 1864)
New Hope Church (May 25-June 4, 1864)
Dallas (June 25-27, 1864)
Kennesaw Mountain (June 27, 1864)
Peach Tree Creek (July 20, 1864)
Atlanta (July 22, 1864)
Ezra Church (July 28, 1864)
Atlanta Siege (July-September 1864)
Utoy Creek (August 5-7, 1864)
Jonesboro (August 31-September 1, 1864)
Savannah Campaign (November-December 1864)
Carolinas Campaign (February-April 1865)
Further Reading: Davis, William C., *The Orphan Brigade: The Kentucky Confederates Who Couldn't Go Home*. Thompson, Edward Porter, *History of the First Kentucky Brigade.*

78. KENTUCKY 10TH INFANTRY REGIMENT

See: KENTUCKY 13TH CAVALRY REGIMENT

79. KENTUCKY 11TH MOUNTED INFANTRY REGIMENT

See: KENTUCKY 13TH CAVALRY REGIMENT

80. KENTUCKY DESHA'S INFANTRY BATTALION

Organization: Organized by the detachment of two companies from the 9th Infantry Regiment and the assignment of additional companies on May 27, 1863, per S.O. #126, Adjutant and Inspector General's Office. The companies were ordered to organize as a battalion at Abingdon, Virginia. Apparently disbanded in late 1863.

First Commander: Joseph Desha (Major [acting])

Assignments: District of Abingdon, Department of East Tennessee (June-July 1863)

Gracie's Brigade, Army of East Tennessee, Department of Tennessee (July-August 1863)

81. KENTUCKY TAYLOR'S INFANTRY BATTALION

Organization: Organized with six companies at Nashville, Tennessee ca. April 23, 1861. Consolidated with the 1st Infantry Battalion and designated as the 1st Infantry Regiment at Manassas Junction, Virginia on August 7, 1861, per S.O. #117, Adjutant and Inspector General's Office.

First Commander: Thomas H. Taylor (Lieutenant Colonel)

Field Officer: Edward Crossland (Major)

Assignments: Harper's Ferry, Virginia (May-June 1861)

Bartow's Brigade, Army of the Shenandoah (June-July 1861)

Bartow's-D. R. Jones' Brigade, 2nd Corps, Army of the Potomac (July-August 1861)

82. KENTUCKY WHITE'S INFANTRY BATTALION

Organization: Organized in the fall of 1861. Apparently disbanded in late 1861.

First Commander: D. M. White (Lieutenant Colonel)

Assignment: Tilghman's Brigade [Hopkinsville], Unattached, Central Army of Kentucky, Department #2 (October-November 1861)

MARYLAND

MARYLAND UNITS

Maryland never seceded from the Union.

Many Marylanders served in Confederate units from other states, principally Virginia. There were attempts to detach them from these other organizations and organize the "Maryland Line;" however, these efforts were short-lived.

Note: The index for the Maryland units begins on page 217.

ARTILLERY

1. MARYLAND 1ST ARTILLERY BATTERY

Organization: Organized on May 29, 1861. It was armed with four 12-lb. Napoleons from August 20, 1862 to December 28, 1864. Surrendered at Appomattox Court House, Virginia on April 9, 1865.

First Commander: R. Snowden Andrews (Captain)

Captain: William F. Dement

Assignments: Unattached, Department of Fredericksburg (September-October 1861)

French's Brigade, Aquia District, Department of Northern Virginia (October 1861-March 1862)

Pettigrew's Brigade, G. W. Smith's-Whiting's Division, Department of Northern Virginia (April-May 1862)

Artillery Battalion, A. P. Hill's Division, Army of Northern Virginia (May-June 1862)

Artillery Battalion, A. P. Hill's Division, 1st Corps, Army of Northern Virginia (June-July 1862)

Artillery Battalion, Ewell's-Early's Division, 2nd Corps, Army of Northern Virginia (July 1862-July 1863)

Andrews' Battalion, Artillery, 2nd Corps, Army of Northern Virginia (July 1863-March 1864)

Maryland Line, Department of Richmond (April-June 1864)

McIntosh's Battalion, Artillery, 3rd Corps, Army of Northern Virginia (September-December 1864)

Smith's Battalion, Artillery, 3rd Corps, Army of Northern Virginia (December 1864-April 1865)

Battles: Evansport (March 7, 1862)

Seven Days Battles (June 25-July 1, 1862)

Mechanicsville (June 26, 1862)

Gaines' Mill (June 27, 1862)

Malvern Hill (July 1, 1862)

Cedar Mountain (August 9, 1862)
Bristoe and Manasass Junction (August 26, 1862)
2nd Bull Run (August 28-30, 1862)
Harpers Ferry (September 12-15, 1862)
Fredericksburg (December 13, 1862)
Chancellorsville (May 1-4, 1863)
2nd Winchester (June 14-15, 1863)
Gettysburg (July 1-3, 1863)
Mine Run Campaign (November-December 1863)
Petersburg Siege (June 1864-April 1865)
Turkey Creek (July 12, 1864)
White Sulphur Springs (Aug. 26-27, 1864)
Squirrel Level Road (September 30, 1864)
Appomattox Court House (April 9, 1865)

Further Reading: Goldsborough, William Worthington, *The Maryland Line in the Confederate States Army, 1861-1865.*

2. MARYLAND 2ND ARTILLERY BATTERY

Nickname: Baltimore Light Artillery

Organization: Organized at Richmond, Virginia ca. October 1861. It was armed with one 3" Rifle, one 12-lb. Howitzer, and two Blakeley Rifles in August and September 1862. Converted to horse artillery ca. June 1863. It was armed with four 10-lb. Parrotts on July 1-3, 1863. Four guns were captured at Maurytown, Virginia on October 8, 1864. Surrendered at Appomattox Court House, Virginia on April 9, 1865.

First Commander: John B. Brockenbrough (Captain)

Captain: William H. Griffin

Assignments: Elzey's Brigade, E. K. Smith's-Ewell's Division, Potomac District, Department of Northern Virginia (January-March 1862)

Elzey's Brigade, Ewell's Division, Department of Northern Virginia (March-May 1862)

Maryland Line, Ewell's Division, Valley District, Department of Northern Virginia (May-June 1862)

Maryland Line, Ewell's Division, 2nd Corps, Army of Northern Virginia (June-July 1862)

Artillery Battalion, Ewell's Division, 2nd Corps, Army of Northern Virginia (July-August 1862)

Artillery Battalion, Jackson's Division, 2nd Corps, Army of Northern Virginia (August-November 1862)

Maryland Line, Department of Northern Virginia (November 1862-June 1863)

Horse Artillery Battalion, Cavalry Division, Army of Northern Virginia (June-November 1863)
Maryland Line, Department of Richmond (November 1863-May 1864)
Breathed's Battalion, Horse Artillery, Cavalry Corps, Army of Northern Virginia (May-June 1864)
Horse Artillery Battalion, Lomax's Cavalry Division, Valley District, Department of Northern Virginia (June 1864-March 1865)
Breathed's Battalion, Horse Artillery, Cavalry Corps, Army of Northern Virginia (March-April 1865)

Battles: Shenandoah Valley Campaign (May-June 1862)
Front Royal (May 23, 1862)
1st Winchester (May 25, 1862)
Harrisonburg (June 6, 1862)
Cross Keys (June 8, 1862)
Seven Days Battles (June 25-July 1, 1862)
Gaines' Mill (June 27, 1862)
Malvern Hill (July 1, 1862)
Cunningham's Ford (August 21, 1862)
2nd Bull Run (August 28-30, 1862)
Harpers Ferry (September 12-15, 1862)
Antietam (September 17, 1862)
2nd Winchester (June 14-15, 1863)
Millville (June 21, 1863)
Harrisburg (June 30, 1863)
Gettysburg (July 1-3, 1863)
Bristoe Campaign (October 1863)
Mine Run Campaign (November-December 1863)
Yellow Tavern (May 11, 1864)
Maurytown (October 8, 1864)
Tom's Brook (October 9, 1864)
Cedar Creek (October 19, 1864)
Petersburg Siege (June 1864-April 1865)
Appomattox Court House (April 9, 1865)

Further Reading: Goldsborough, William Worthington, *The Maryland Line in the Confederate States Army, 1861-1865.*

3. MARYLAND 3RD ARTILLERY BATTERY

Organization: Organized at Ashland, Virginia in September 1861. Mustered into Confederate service at Richmond, Virginia on January 14, 1862. One section captured upon the destruction of the CSS *Queen of the West* on April 14, 1863. Battery surrendered at Vicksburg, Warren County, Mississippi on

July 4, 1863. Paroled at Vicksburg, Warren County, Mississippi on July 12, 1863. Declared exchanged on September 12, 1863. Reorganized at Decatur, Georgia and redesignated as the Stephens Georgia Light Artillery Battery in October 1863.

First Commander: Henry B. Latrobe (Captain)

Captains: Ferdinand O. Claiborne

John B. Rowan

Assignments: Leadbetter's Brigade, District of East Tennessee, Department #2 (February-March 1862)

Reynolds' Brigade, Department of East Tennessee (March-July 1862)

Reynolds' Brigade, Stevenson's Division, Department of East Tennessee (July-October 1862)

Reynolds' Brigade, Heth's Division, Department of East Tennessee (October-December 1862)

Reynolds' Brigade, Stevenson's Division, 2nd Military District, Department of Mississippi and East Louisiana (January-February 1863)

Aboard the CSS *Queen of the West* [section] (February-April 1863)

Artillery Battalion, Stevenson's Division, 2nd Military District, Department of Mississippi and East Louisiana (April 1863)

Reynolds' Brigade, Stevenson's Division, Department of Mississippi and East Louisiana (April-July 1863)

Battles: CSS *Queen of the West* vs. the *USS Indianola* [section] (February 24, 1863)

Deer Creek [detachment] (March 21, 1863)

Destruction of the CSS *Queen of the West* [section] (April 14, 1863)

Vicksburg Campaign (May-July 1863)

near Greenville, Mississippi vs. *USS Minnesota* (May 4, 1863)

Champion Hill (May 16, 1863)

Island #82, Mississippi River [section] (May 18, 1863)

Vicksburg Siege (May-July 1863)

Jackson Siege [detachment] (July 10-17, 1863)

4. MARYLAND 4TH ARTILLERY BATTERY

Nickname: Chesapeake Artillery

Organization: Organized in the spring of 1862. It was armed with two 10-lb. Parrotts and one 3" Rifle in August and September 1862. It was armed with one 10-lb. Parrott and two 3" Rifles on December 28, 1864. Surrendered at Appomattox Court House, Virginia on April 9, 1865.

First Commander: William D. Brown (Captain)

Captain: Walter S. Chew

Assignments: Early's Brigade, Ewell's Division, 2nd Corps, Army of Northern Virginia (July-August 1862)
Artillery Battalion, Ewell's-Early's Division, 2nd Corps, Army of Northern Virginia (August 1862-May 1863)
Artillery Battalion, Johnson's Division, 2nd Corps, Army of Northern Virginia (May-July 1863)
Andrews'-Braxton's Battalion, Artillery, 2nd Corps, Army of Northern Virginia (July 1863-March 1864)
Maryland Line, Department of Richmond (May-June 1864)
McIntosh's Battalion, Artillery, 3rd Corps, Army of Northern Virginia (September 1864-April 1865)
Battles: Cedar Mountain (August 9, 1862)
Bristoe and Manassas Junction (August 26, 1862)
2nd Bull Run (August 28-30, 1862)
Harpers Ferry (September 12-15, 1862)
Fredericksburg (December 13, 1862)
Chancellorsville (May 1-4, 1863)
2nd Winchester (June 14-15, 1863)
Gettysburg (July 1-3, 1863)
Bristoe Campaign (October 1863)
Mine Run Campaign (November-December 1863)
Petersburg Siege (June 1864-April 1865)
Petersburg Final Assault (April 2, 1865)
Fort Gregg (April 2, 1865)
Appomattox Court House (April 9, 1865)
Further Reading: Goldsborough, William Worthington, *The Maryland Line in the Confederate States Army, 1861-1865.*

5. MARYLAND BALTIMORE LIGHT ARTILLERY BATTERY

See: MARYLAND 2ND ARTILLERY BATTERY

6. MARYLAND CHESAPEAKE ARTILLERY BATTERY

See: MARYLAND 4TH ARTILLERY BATTERY

CAVALRY

7. Maryland 1st Cavalry Battalion

Organization: Organized with four companies at Winchester, Virginia on November 25, 1862. Company A consisted of the Maryland members of Company K, 1st Virginia Cavalry Regiment. Companies E and F were assigned ca. August 1863. Company K, 1st Virginia Cavalry Regiment was assigned as Company K of this battalion in July 1864. Disbanded at Cloverdale, Botetourt County, Virginia on April 28, 1865.

First Commander: Ridgely Brown (Major, Lieutenant Colonel)

Field Officers: Gustavus W. Dorsey (Lieutenant Colonel)

Robert C. Smith (Major)

Assignments: Maryland Line (December 1862-February 1863)

Jones' Brigade, Cavalry Division, Army of Northern Virginia (February-June 1863)

F. Lee's Brigade, Cavalry Division, Army of Northern Virginia (June-September 1863)

Lomax's Brigade, F. Lee's Division, Cavalry Corps, Army of Northern Virginia (September-November 1863)

Maryland Line, Department of Richmond (November 1863-June 1864)

Jones'-Johnson's Brigade, Ransom's-Lomax's Cavalry Division, Valley District, Department of Northern Virginia (June 1864)

Jackson's-Davidson's Brigade, Lomax's Cavalry Division, Valley District, Department of Northern Virginia (July 1864-March 1865)

Payne's Brigade, F. Lee's-Munford's Division, Cavalry Corps, Army of Northern Virginia (April 1865)

Battles: Expedition to Moorefield and Petersburg (January 2-5, 1863)

Jones' and Imboden's West Virginia Raid (April 1863)

Greenland Gap (April 25, 1863)

Fairmont (April 29, 1863)

Bridgeport (April 30, 1863)

Middleburg (June 19, 1863)

near Winchester [skirmish] (June 25, 1863)
Gettysburg (July 1-3, 1863)
Monterey Gap [detachment] (July 4, 1863)
Hagerstown (July 6-13, 1863)
Kilpatrick-Dahlgren Raid (February-March 1864)
New Market (May 15, 1864)
Pollard's Farm (May 27, 1864)
South Anna River (June 1, 1864)
Trevilian Station (June 11-12, 1864)
Moorefield (August 7, 1864)
3rd Winchester (September 19, 1864)
Fisher's Hill (September 22, 1864)
Cedar Creek (October 19, 1864)
Waynesborough (March 2, 1865)
Appomattox Court House (April 9, 1865)
Further Reading: Goldsborough, William Worthington, *The Maryland Line in the Confederate States Army, 1861-1865.*

8. MARYLAND 2ND CAVALRY BATTALION

Organization: Organized with three companies ca. May 27, 1863. Increased to six companies. In existence into 1865.
First Commander: Harry W. Gilmor (Major)
Assignments: Imboden's Cavalry Brigade, Valley District, Department of Northern Virginia (December 1863-May 1864)
Jackson's-Davidson's Brigade, Lomax's Cavalry Division, Valley District, Department of Northern Virginia (July-December 1864)
Battles: Bath (September 7, 1863)
Gilmor's Raid on the Baltimore and Ohio Railroad (February 11, 1864)
New Market (May 15, 1864)
Monocacy (July 9, 1864)
Moorefield (August 7, 1864)
3rd Winchester (September 19, 1864)
Fisher's Hill (September 22, 1864)
Cedar Creek (October 19, 1864)
Further Reading: Gilmor, Harry, *Four Years in the Saddle.* Goldsborough, William Worthington, *The Maryland Line in the Confederate States Army, 1861-1865.*

9. MARYLAND DAVIS' CAVALRY BATTALION

Organization: Organized at Richmond, Virginia in the spring of 1864. Disbanded and reduced to one company, which became Company M, 23rd

Virginia Cavalry Regiment later in 1864. This unit does not appear in the *Official Records*. Apparently a temporary field organization.

First Commander: Thomas Sturgis Davis (Major)

Assignment: Northwest Virginia Brigade, Department of Northern Virginia (May 1864)

Battle: New Market (May 15, 1864)

INFANTRY

10. MARYLAND 1ST INFANTRY BATTALION

See: MARYLAND 2ND INFANTRY REGIMENT

11. MARYLAND 1ST INFANTRY REGIMENT

Organization: Organized with eight companies on June 17, 1861. Later increased to 10 companies. Mustered out of Confederate service on August 17, 1862.

First Commander: Arnold Elzey (Colonel)

Field Officers: Edward R. Dorsey (Major, Lieutenant Colonel)

Bradley T. Johnson (Major, Lieutenant Colonel, Colonel)

George H. Stewart (Lieutenant Colonel, Colonel)

Assignments: Elzey's-E. K. Smith's Brigade, Army of the Shenandoah (June-July 1861)

E. K. Smith's Brigade, 2nd Corps, Army of the Potomac (July-October 1861)

Elzey's Brigade, 2nd Corps, Potomac District, Department of Northern Virginia (October 1861-January 1862)

Elzey's Brigade, E. K. Smith's-Ewell's Division, Potomac District, Department of Northern Virginia (January-March 1862)

Elzey's Brigade, Ewell's Division, Department of Northern Virginia (March-May 1862)

Maryland Line, Ewell's Division, Valley District, Department of Northern Virginia (May-June 1862)

Stewart's Brigade, Ewell's Division, Valley District, Department of Northern Virginia (June 1862)

Maryland Line, Ewell's Division, 2nd Corps, Army of Northern Virginia (June-August 1862)

Battles: Hall's Hill [two companies] (1861)

1st Bull Run (July 21, 1861)

near Munson's Hill (August 31, 1861)
Sangster's Station (March 9, 1862)
Shenandoah Valley Campaign (May-June 1862)
Front Royal (May 23, 1862)
1st Winchester (May 25, 1862)
Harrisonburg (June 6, 1862)
Cross Keys (June 8, 1862)
Port Republic (June 9, 1862)
Seven Days Battles (June 25-July 1, 1862)
Gaines' Mill (June 27, 1862)
Malvern Hill (July 1, 1862)
Further Reading: Booth, George Wilson, *Personal Reminiscences of a Maryland Soldier*. Goldsborough, William Worthington, *The Maryland Line in the Confederate States Army, 1861-1865.*

12. MARYLAND 2ND INFANTRY REGIMENT

Also Known As: 1st Infantry Battalion
Organization: Organized from six independent compnies on November 8, 1862, per S.O. #262, Adjutant and Inspector General's Office. Later increased to eight companies. Surrendered at Appomattox Court House, Virginia on April 9, 1865.
First Commander: James R. Herbert (Major, Lieutenant Colonel)
Field Officers: J. Parren Crane (Major)
William W. Goldsborough (Major)
Assignments: Maryland Line, Department of Northern Virginia (December 1862-January 1863)
Stewart's Brigade, Johnson's Division, 2nd Corps, Army of Northern Virginia (June-November 1863)
Maryland Line, Department of Richmond (November 1863-June 1864)
Walker's Brigade, Heth's Division, 3rd Corps, Army of Northern Virginia (August 1864-February 1865)
McComb's Brigade, Heth's Division, 3rd Corps, Army of Northern Virginia (February-April 1865)
Battles: Expedition to Moorefield and Petersburg (January 2-5, 1863)
2nd Winchester (June 14-15, 1863)
Gettysburg (July 1-3, 1863)
Bristoe Campaign (October 1863)
Mine Run Campaign (November-December 1863)
Cold Harbor (June 1-3, 1864)
White Oak Swamp (June 13, 1864)
Petersburg Siege (June 1864-April 1865)

Weldon Railroad (August 18-21, 1864)
Pegram's Farm (October 1, 1864)
Squirrel Level Road (September 30, 1864)
Jones' Farm (September 30, 1864)
1st Pegram's Farm (October 1, 1864)
Harman Road (October 2, 1864)
Hatcher's Run (February 5-7, 1865)
Appomattox Court House (April 9, 1865)

Further Reading: Booth, George Wilson, *Personal Reminiscences of a Maryland Soldier*. McKim, Randolph Harrison, A *Soldiers' Recollections: Leaves from the Diary of a Young Confederate*.

MISSOURI

MISSOURI UNITS

Missouri never seceded from the Union. It was, however, admitted to the Confederacy on August 19, 1861. The remanants of the secessionist legislature voted the state into the Confederacy on October 31, 1861.

The units of the Missouri State Guard are treated in a seperate sub-chapter at the end of this chapter since they were organized into permanent divisions based upon geographical districts. Their records are somewhat sketchy. They generally disbanded as most of their members transferred to Confederate service and formed new organizations. In a few cases an entire unit transferred to the Confederate service en masse.

Note: The index for the Missouri units begins on page 221.

ARTILLERY

1. MISSOURI 1ST ARTILLERY BATTERY

Organization: Organized on December 28, 1861. It was armed with four 10-lb. Parrotts from May 1 to July 4, 1863. Battery surrendered at Vicksburg, Warren County, Mississippi on July 4, 1863. Paroled at Vicksburg, Warren County, Mississippi in July 1863. Declared exchanged on September 12, 1863. Apparently never reorganized after its exchange.

First Commander: William Wade (Captain)

Captain: Richard C. Walsh

Assignments: Little's Brigade, Confederate Volunteers, Missouri State Guard, Trans-Mississippi District, Department #2 (January-March 1862)

Little's Brigade, Price's Division, Trans-Mississippi District, Department #2 (March-April 1862)

Little's-Gates' Brigade, Price's-Little's Division, Army of the West, Department #2 (April-July 1862)

Little's-Gates' Brigade, Little's-Hébert's-Green's Division, Price's Corps, Army of West Tennessee, Department #2 (September-October 1862)

Hebert's Brigade, Bowen's Division, Price's Corps, Army of West Tennessee, Department of Mississippi and East Louisiana (October 1862)

Missouri Brigade, Bowen's Division, Price's Corps, Army of West Tennessee, Department of Mississippi and East Louisiana (October-December 1862)

Missouri Brigade, Bowen's Division, Price's Corps, Army of North Mississippi, Department of Mississippi and East Louisiana (December 1862-January 1863)

Missouri Brigade, Price's Division, Army of the Department of Mississippi and East Louisiana (January 1863)

Missouri Brigade, Forney's-Bowen's Division, 2nd Military District, Department of Mississippi and East Louisiana (April 1863)

Missouri Brigade, Bowen's Division, Department of Mississippi and East Louisiana (April-July 1863)

Battles: Flat Creek (February 15, 1862)

Pea Ridge (March 7-8, 1862)
Corinth Campaign (April-June 1862)
Iuka (September 19, 1862)
Corinth (October 3-4, 1862)
Grand Gulf (March 19, 1863)
Grand Gulf (March 31, 1863)
Grand Gulf (April 29, 1863)
Vicksburg Campaign (May-July 1863)
Champion's Hill (May 16, 1863)
Big Black River Bridge (May 17, 1863)
Vicksburg Campaign (May-July 1863)

Further Reading: Bevier, R. S., *History of the First and Second Missouri Confederate Brigades 1861-1865*. Anderson, Ephraim McD., *Memoirs: Historical and Personal; Including the Campaigns of the First Missouri Confederate Brigade*.

2. MISSOURI 1ST (BLEDSOE'S, H. M.) ARTILLERY BATTERY

Organization: Organized by the change of designation of Bledsoe's Artillery Battery, 8th Division, Missouri State Guard on April 21, 1862. Mustered into Confederate service on April 21, 1861. It was armed with three guns on May 14, 1863. It received four 12-lb. Napoleons on November 12, 1863. These were captured at Missionary Ridge on November 25, 1863. It was reported as without guns on December 14, 1863. It was armed with four 12-lb. Napoleons from March 29, 1864 to April 1, 1864. No record after February 1865 when it was reported as leaving Montgomery, Alabama.

First Commander: Hiram M. Bledsoe (Captain)

Assignments: Frost's-Clark's Artillery Brigade, Price's Division, Army of the West, Department #2 (April-May 1862)

Clark's Artillery Brigade, Army of the West, Department #2 (May-June 1862)

Moore's Brigade, Maury's Division, Army of the West, Department #2 (June-August 1862)

Moore's Brigade, Maury's Division, Price's Corps, Army of West Tennessee, Department #2 (August-October 1862)

Moore's Brigade, Maury's Division, Price's Corps, Army of West Tennessee, Department of Mississippi and East Louisiana (October-December 1862)

Moore's Brigade, Maury's Division, 2nd Corps, Army of North Mississippi, Department of Mississippi and East Louisiana (December 1862-January 1863)

Artillery, Maury's Division, 2nd Military District, Department of Mississippi and East Louisiana (January 1863)

Light Artillery, 3rd Military District, Department of Mississippi and East Louisiana (January-February 1863)
Gregg's Brigade, 3rd Military District, Department of Mississippi and East Louisiana (March-May 1863)
Gregg's Brigade, Department of the West (May-June 1863)
Gregg's Brigade, Walker's Division, Department of the West (June-July 1863)
Gregg's Brigade, Walker's Division, Department of Mississippi and East Louisiana (July-August 1863)
Gregg's Brigade, Department of Mississippi and East Louisiana (August-September 1863)
Gregg's Brigade, Johnson's Provisional Division, Army of Tennessee (September 1863)
Gregg's Brigade, Walker's Division, 1st Corps, Army of Tennessee (September 1863)
Gregg's Brigade, Walker's Division, Longstreet's Corps, Army of Tennessee (September-October 1863)
Artillery Battalion, Walker's Division, Longstreet's Corps, Army of Tennessee (October-November 1863)
Artillery Battalion, Walker's Division, 1st Corps, Army of Tennessee (November 1863-February 1864)
Martin's Battalion, Artillery, 1st Corps, Army of Tennessee (February-September 1864)
Hotchkiss' Battalion, Artillery, 1st Corps, Army of Tennessee (September 1864-January 1865)

Battles: Wilson's Creek (August 10, 1861)
Pea Ridge (March 7-8, 1862)
Corinth Campaign (April-June 1862)
Corinth (October 3-4, 1862)
*vs.*Steele's Greenville Expedition (April 2-14, 1863)
Thomas' Plantation [two sections] (April 7, 1863)
Vicksburg Campaign (May-July 1863)
Raymond (May 12, 1863)
Jackson (May 14, 1864)
Jackson Siege (July 1863)
Chickamauga (September 19-20, 1863)
Chattanooga Siege (September-November 1863)
Chattanooga (November 23-25, 1863)
Atlanta Campaign (May-September 1864)
Atlanta Siege (July-September 1864)
Nashville (December 15-16, 1864)
Hollow Tree Gap, near Franklin (December 17, 1864)

3. MISSOURI 1ST FIELD ARTILLERY BATTERY

Organization: Organized in late 1862. It was armed with four guns in August and September 1863. Designated as 1st Missouri Field Artillery Battery on November 19, 1864, per S.O. #290, Trans-Mississippi Department. It was armed with four 6-lb. Smoothbores on May 26, 1865. Surrendered by General E. K. Smith, commanding Trans-Mississippi Department, on May 26, 1865.

First Commander: Westley Roberts (Captain)

Captain: Samuel T. Ruffner

Assignments: Shaver's Brigade, Parsons' Division, 1st Corps, Trans-Mississippi Department (December 1862)

Frost's Brigade, Hindman's Division, District of Arkansas, Trans-Mississippi Department (January-February 1863)

Clark's Brigade, Frost's Division, District of Arkansas, Trans-Mississippi Department (May-June 1863)

Shelby's Brigade, Marmaduke's Cavalry Division, District of Arkansas, Trans-Mississippi Department (July-September 1863)

Marmaduke's-Greene's Brigade, Marmaduke's Cavalry Division, District of Arkansas, Trans-Mississippi Department (October 1863)

Drayton's-Clark's Brigade, Price's-Drayton's Division, District of Arkansas, Trans-Mississippi Department (December 1863-March 1864)

Clark's Brigade, Parsons' Missouri Division, District of Arkansas, Trans-Mississippi Department (March-April 1864)

Clark's Brigade, Parsons' Missouri Division, Detachment District of Arkansas, District of West Louisiana, Trans-Mississippi Department (April 1864)

Clark's Brigade, Parsons' Missouri Division, District of Arkansas, Trans-Mississippi Department (April-September 1864)

5th [Blocher's] Artillery Battalion, 2nd Corps, Trans-Mississippi Department (September 1864-May 1865)

Battles: *vs.* Steele's Little Rock Expedition (August 1-September 14, 1863)

Pine Bluff (October 25, 1863)

Red River Campaign (March-May 1864)

Camden Expedition (March-May 1864)

Jenkins' Ferry (April 30, 1864)

4. MISSOURI 2ND ARTILLERY BATTERY

Nickname: Clark Artillery

Organization: Organized by the transfer to Confederate service of Clark's Artillery Battery, 4th Division, Missouri State Guard in early 1862. Reorganized on April 26, 1862. It was armed with four 10-lb. Parrotts on July 5-23, 1863. It was armed with two 3" Rifles and two 12-lb. Howitzers from November 28, 1863 to January 5, 1864. It was armed with four 3" Rifles ca. May 1, 1864.

Surrendered by Lieutenant General Richard Taylor, commanding the Department of Alabama, Mississippi, and East Louisiana, at Citronelle, Alabama on May 4, 1865.

First Commander: Samuel Churchill Clark (Captain)

Captain: Houston King

Assignments: Little's Brigade, Confederate Volunteers, Missouri State Guard, Trans-Mississippi District, Department #2 (March-April 1862)

Steen's Brigade, Price's Division, Trans-Mississippi District, Department #2 (March-April 1862)

Green's Brigade, Price's-Little's Division, Army of the West, Department #2 (April-July 1862)

Hébert's Brigade, Little's-Hébert's Division, Price's Corps, Army of West Tennessee, Department #2 (September-October 1862)

Hébert's Brigade, Hébert's-Bowen's Division, Price's Corps, Army of West Tennessee, Department of Mississippi and East Louisiana (October 1862)

Green's Brigade, Bowen's Division, Price's Corps, Army of West Tennessee, Department of Mississippi and East Louisiana (October-December 1862)

Green's Brigade, Bowen's Division, Army of North Mississippi, Department of Mississippi and East Louisiana (December 1862-January 1863)

Artillery, Van Dorn's Cavalry Corps, Department of Mississippi and East Louisiana (January-February 1863)

Artillery, Jackson's Division, Van Dorn's Cavalry Corps, Army of Tennessee (February-May 1863)

Artillery, Jackson's Cavalry Division, Army of Tennessee (May 1863)

Artillery, Jackson's Cavalry Division, Department of the West (June-July 1863)

Artillery, Jackson's Cavalry Division, Department of Mississippi and East Louisiana (July 1863)

Cosby's Brigade, Jackson's Cavalry Division, Department of Mississippi and East Louisiana (July-August 1863)

Whitfield's Brigade, Jackson's Cavalry Division, Department of Mississippi and East Louisiana (September 1863)

Cosby's Brigade, Jackson's Division, Lee's Cavalry Corps, Department of Mississippi and East Louisiana (November-December 1863)

Ross' Brigade, Jackson's Division, Lee's Cavalry Corps, Department of Mississippi and East Louisiana (December 1863-January 1864)

Ross' Brigade, Jackson's Division, Lee's Cavalry Corps, Department of Alabama, Mississippi, and East Louisiana (January-March 1864)

Starke's Brigade, Jackson's Division, Lee's Cavalry Corps, Department of Alabama, Mississippi, and East Louisiana (April-May 1864)

Artillery Battalion, Jackson's Cavalry Division, Army of Mississippi (May-July 1864)

Artillery Battalion, Jackson's Cavalry Division, Army of Tennessee (July-November 1864)

Artillery Battalion, Jackson's Division, Forrest's Cavalry Corps, Army of Tennessee (November 1864-February 1865)

[Sub-]District of South Mississippi & East Louisiana, District of Mississippi and East Mississippi, Department of Alabama, Mississippi, and East Louisiana (February-April 1865)

Battles: Pea Ridge (March 7-8, 1862)

Corinth Campaign (April-June 1862)

Iuka (September 19, 1862)

Corinth (October 3-4, 1862)

Thompson's Station (March 5, 1863)

Vicksburg Campaign (May-July 1863)

Jackson Siege (July 1863)

Meridian Campaign (February-March 1864)

Atlanta Campaign (May-September 1864)

Atlanta Siege (July-September 1864)

Franklin-Nashville Campaign (November 1864-January 1865)

Further Reading: Bevier, R. S., *History of the First and Second Missouri Confederate Brigades 1861-1865*. Anderson, Ephraim McD., *Memoirs: Historical and Personal; Including the Campaigns of the First Missouri Confederate Brigade*.

5. MISSOURI 2ND FIELD ARTILLERY BATTERY

Organization: Organized in mid-1862. It was armed with two guns on September 29, 1862. It was armed with two 10-lb. Parrotts and two 6-lb. Smoothbores on April 17-May 2, 1863. It was armed with four guns on May 20, 1864 to November 19, 1864. Designated as the 2nd Missouri Field Battery on November 19, 1864, per S.O. #290, Trans-Mississippi Department. It was armed with two 3.80" Rifles and two 12-lb. Howitzers on May 26, 1865. Surrendered by General E. K. Smith, commanding Trans-Mississippi Department, on May 26, 1865.

First Commander: Joseph Bledsoe (Captain)

Captain: Richard A. Collins

Assignments: Cooper's Division, District of Arkansas, Trans-Mississippi Department (September-October 1862)

Shelby's Brigade, Marmaduke's Cavalry Division, 1st Corps, Trans-Mississippi Department (November 1862-January 1863)

Shelby's Brigade, Marmaduke's Cavalry Division, District of Arkansas, Trans-Mississippi Department (April 1863-May 1864)

Shelby's Brigade, Shelby's Cavalry Division, Army of Missouri, Trans-Mississippi Department (August-September 1864)

2nd [Pratt's] Horse Artillery Battalion, Cavalry Corps, Trans-Mississippi Department (September 1864-May 1865)

Battles: Newtonia (September 30, 1862)

Cane Hill (November 28, 1862)

Prairie Grove (December 7, 1862)

Marmaduke's Expedition into Missouri (December 31, 1862-January 25, 1863)

Springfield [detachment] (January 8, 1863)

Hartville [detachment] (January 11, 1863)

Marmaduke's Expedition into Missouri (April 17-May 2, 1863)

Helena (July 4, 1863)

vs. Steele's Little Rock Expedition (August 1-September 14, 1863)

Bayou Meto (August 27, 1863)

Bayou Fourche (September 10, 1863)

Fall of Little Rock (September 10, 1863)

Shelby's Raid in Arkansas and Missouri [section] (September 22-October 26, 1863)

Camden Expedition (March-May 1864)

Prairie d'Ane (April 9-10, 1864)

Marks' Mills (April 25, 1864)

Price's Missouri Raid (August-October 1864)

6. MISSOURI 3RD ARTILLERY BATTERY

Nickname: St. Louis Artillery

Organization: Organized in early 1862. Battery surrendered at Vicksburg, Warren County, Mississippi on July 4, 1863. Paroled at Vicksburg, Warren County, Mississippi in July 1863. Declared exchanged on September 12, 1863. Field consolidation, under the name of the 3rd Missouri Battery, with the Jackson (Mo.) Artillery from late 1863 or early 1864 to May 4, 1865. The consolidated battery was armed with four 20-lb. Parrotts from May 19, 1864 to February 21, 1865. Surrendered by Lieutenant General Richard Taylor, commanding the Department of Alabama, Mississippi, and East Louisiana, at Citronelle, Alabama on May 4, 1865.

First Commander: Emmett MacDonald (Captain)

Captain: William E. Dawson

Assignments: Hebert's Brigade, Price's Division, Trans-Mississippi District, Department #2 (March-April 1862)

Hébert's Brigade, Price's-Little's Division, Army of the West, Department #2 (April-July 1862)

Hébert's Brigade, Little's-Hébert's-Green's Division, Price's Corps, Army of West Tennessee, Department #2 (September-October 1862)
Hébert's Brigade, Bowen's Division, Price's Corps, Army of West Tennessee, Department of Mississippi and East Louisiana (October 1862)
Green's Brigade, Bowen's Division, Price's Corps, Army of West Tennessee, Department of Mississippi and East Louisiana (October-December 1862)
Green's Brigade, Bowen's Division, Price's Corps, Army of North Mississippi, Department of Mississippi and East Louisiana (December 1862-January 1863)
Green's Brigade, Price's Division, Army of the Department of Mississippi and East Louisiana (January 1863)
Green's Brigade, Forney's-Bowen's Division, 2nd Military District, Department of Mississippi and East Louisiana (April 1863)
Green's Brigade, Bowen's Division, Department of Mississippi and East Louisiana (April-July 1863)
Cantey's Brigade, Department of the Gulf (December 1863-January 1864)
Truehart's Artillery Battalion, District of the Gulf, Department of Alabama, Mississippi, and East Louisiana (April-May 1864)
Fuller's-Higgins' Artillery Brigade, District of the Gulf, Department of Alabama, Mississippi, and East Louisiana (June 1864)
Truehart's Artillery Battalion, Higgins' Brigade, District of the Gulf, Department of Alabama, Mississippi, and East Louisiana (August 1864)
Liddell's Brigade, District of the Gulf, Department of Alabama, Mississippi, and East Louisiana (September-October 1864)
Semple's Artillery Battalion, District of the Gulf, Department of Alabama, Mississippi, and East Louisiana (October-November 1864)
Burnet's Command, District of the Gulf, Department of Alabama, Mississippi, and East Louisiana (November 1864)
Semple's Artillery Battalion, District of the Gulf, Department of Alabama, Mississippi, and East Louisiana (December 1864-February 1865)
Burnet's Command, Artillery Reserves, etc., District of the Gulf, Department of Alabama, Mississippi, and East Louisiana (March-April 1865)
Burnet's Command, Department of Alabama, Mississippi, and East Louisiana (April-May 1865)

Battles: Pea Ridge (March 7-8, 1862)
Corinth Campaign (April-June 1862)
Iuka (September 19, 1862)
Corinth (October 3-4, 1862)
Grand Gulf (April 29, 1863)
Vicksburg Campaign (May-July 1863)
Champion's Hill (May 16, 1863)

Big Black River Bridge (May 17, 1863)
Vicksburg Siege (May-July 1863)
Mobile (March 17-April 12, 1865)

7. MISSOURI 3RD FIELD ARTILLERY BATTERY

Organization: Organized from Gorham's Battery, 6th Division, Missouri State Guard in March, 1862. Designated as the 3rd Missouri Field Artillery Battery on November 19, 1864, per S.O. #290, Trans-Mississippi Department. It was armed with four 12-lb. Howitzers on May 26, 1865. Surrendered by General E. K. Smith, commanding Trans-Mississippi Department, on May 26, 1865.

First Commander: James C. Gorham (Captain)

Captains: Charles B. Tilden
A. A. LeSeuer

Assignments: Frost's Artillery Brigade, Price's Division, Trans-Mississippi District, Department #2 (March-April 1862)
Frost's-Clark's Artillery Brigade, Army of the West, Department #2 (April-May 1862)
Steen's Brigade, Parsons' Division, 1st Corps, Trans-Mississippi Department (December 1862-January 1863)
Parsons'-Burns' Brigade, Hindman's-Price's-Drayton's-Price's Division, District of Arkansas, Trans-Mississippi Department (February 1863-March 1864)
Burns' Brigade, Missouri [Parsons'] Division, District of Arkansas, Trans-Mississippi Department (March-April 1864)
Burns' Brigade, Missouri [Parsons'] Division, Detachment District of Arkansas, District of West Louisiana, Trans-Mississippi Department (April 1864)
Burns' Brigade, Missouri [Parsons'] Division, District of Arkansas, Trans-Mississippi Department (April-September 1864)
5th [Blocher's] Artillery Battalion, 2nd Corps, Trans-Mississippi Department (September 1864-May 1865)

Battles: Corinth Campaign (April-June 1862)
Helena (July 4, 1863)
Red River Campaign (March-May 1864)
Camden Expedition (March-May 1864)
Jenkins' Ferry (April 30, 1864)

8. MISSOURI 4TH FIELD ARTILLERY BATTERY

Organization: Organized in early 1864. It was armed with four 6-lb. Smoothbores from May 19 to November 19, 1864. Designated as the 4th Missouri Field Artillery Battery on November 19, 1864 per S.O. #290, Trans- Mississippi

Department. It was serving as heavy artillery on May 26, 1865. Surrendered by General E. K. Smith, commanding Trans-Mississippi Department, on May 26, 1865.

First Commander: S. S. Harris (Captain)

Assignments: Marmaduke's Brigade, Marmaduke's Cavalry Division, District of Arkansas, Trans-Mississippi Department (April-September 1864)

2nd [Pratt's] Horse Artillery Battalion, Cavalry Corps, Trans-Mississippi Department (September 1864-May 1865)

Battles: Camden Expedition (March-May 1864)

Poison Spring (April 18, 1864)

Jenkins' Ferry (April 30, 1864)

Lake Chicot (June 6, 1864)

Price's Missouri Raid (August-October 1864)

9. MISSOURI 10TH ARTILLERY BATTERY

Organization: Organized on April 1, 1862. It was armed with two 6-lb. Smoothbores and two 12-lb. Howitzers on May 19, 1862. The Orleans Guard (Louisiana) Artillery Battery was merged into this battery in July 1862. It was armed with four 12-lb. Howitzers from March 29, 1864 to April 1, 1864. Probably surrendered or dispersed at Columbus, Georgia on April 16, 1865 [the battery flag was captured at that time].

First Commander: Overton Barret (Captain)

Assignments: L. M. Walker's Brigade, 2nd Corps, Army of the Mississippi, Department #2 (June-July 1862)

Powel's Brigade, Jones'-Anderson's Division, Army of the Mississippi, Department #2 (July 1862)

Powel's Brigade, Anderson's Division, Left Wing, Army of the Mississippi, Department #2 (August-November 1862)

Powel's Brigade, Anderson's Division, 2nd Corps, Army of Tennessee (November-December 1862)

Anderson's-Manigault's Brigade, Withers' Division, 1st Corps, Army of Tennessee (December 1862-May 1863)

Reserve Artillery, Army of Tennessee (July-November 1863)

Robertson's Battalion, Reserve Artillery, Army of Tennessee (November 1863-April 1864)

Waddell's Battalion, Reserve Artillery, Army of Tennessee (April-July 1864)

Waddell's Battalion, Artillery, 3rd Corps, Army of Tennessee (July-August 1864)

Waddell's Battalion, Macon, Georgia, Department of Tennessee (September 1864)

District of Georgia, Department of Tennessee and Georgia (September 1864-April 1865)
Battles: Corinth Campaign (April-June 1862)
Perryville (October 8, 1862)
Murfreesboro (December 31, 1862-January 3, 1863)
Tullahoma Campaign (June 1863)
Chickamauga (September 19-20, 1863)
Chattanooga Siege (September-November 1863)
Chattanooga (November 23-25, 1863)
Atlanta Campaign (May-September 1864)
Atlanta Siege (July-September 1864)
Wilson's Raid (March 22-April 24, 1865)
Columbus (April 16, 1865)

10. MISSOURI BELL'S ARTILLERY BATTERY

See: MISSOURI PRAIRIE GUN ARTILLERY BATTERY

11. MISSOURI BLEDSOE'S, H. M. ARTILLERY BATTERY

See: MISSOURI 1ST (BLEDSOE'S, H. M.) ARTILLERY BATTERY

12. MISSOURI BLEDSOE'S, J. ARTILLERY BATTERY

See: MISSOURI 2ND FIELD ARTILLERY BATTERY

13. MISSOURI BOWMAN'S ARTILLERY BATTERY

See: MISSOURI BOWMAN'S ARTILLERY BATTERY, 1ST DIVISION, MISSOURI STATE GUARD

14. MISSOURI CLARK'S ARTILLERY BATTERY

See: MISSOURI 2ND ARTILLERY BATTERY

15. MISSOURI COLLINS' ARTILLERY BATTERY

See: MISSOURI 2ND FIELD ARTILLERY BATTERY

16. MISSOURI DAWSON'S ARTILLERY BATTERY

See: MISSOURI ST. LOUIS ARTILLERY BATTERY

17. MISSOURI GORHAM'S ARTILLERY BATTERY

See: MISSOURI 3RD FIELD ARTILLERY BATTERY; MISSOURI GORHAM'S ARTILLERY BATTALION, 6TH DIVISION, MISSOURI STATE GUARD

18. MISSOURI GRISWOLD'S ARTILLERY BATTERY

Organization: Organized in late 1863. No further record after November 1863.

First Commander: D. B. Griswold (Captain)

Assignment: Marmaduke's-Greene's Brigade, Marmaduke's Cavalry Division, District of Arkansas, Trans-Mississippi Department (October-November 1863)

Battle: Pine Bluff (October 25, 1863)

19. MISSOURI GUIBOR'S ARTILLERY BATTERY

Organization: Organized by the transfer of Guibor's Artillery Battery, 6th Division, Missouri State Guard to Confederate service in early 1862. Brown's (Louisiana) Battery merged into this battery on June 30, 1862. It was armed with four 6-lb. Smoothbores from April 29 to July 4, 1863. Battery surrendered at Vicksburg, Warren County, Mississippi on July 4, 1863. Paroled at Vicksburg, Warren County, Mississippi in July 1863. Declared exchanged on September 12, 1863. It was armed with four 12-lb. Napoleons from November 28, 1863 to May 19, 1864. Apparently disbanded and the men assigned to other batteries in early 1865.

First Commander: Henry Guibor (Captain)

Assignments: Frost's Artillery Brigade, Price's Division, Trans-Mississippi District, Department #2 (March-April 1862)

Frost's-Clark's Artillery Brigade, Price's Division, Army of the West, Department #2 (April-May 1862)

Clarks' Artillery Brigade, Army of the West, Department #2 (May-June 1862)

Reserve Artillery, Department #2 (June-July 1862)

Green's Brigade, Little's-Hebert's-Green's Division, Price's Corps, Army of West Tennessee, Department #2 (September-October 1862)

Green's Brigade, Bowen's Division, Price's Corps, Army of West Tennessee, Department of Mississippi and East Louisiana (October-December 1862)

Green's Brigade, Bowen's Division, Price's Corps, Army of North Mississippi, Department of Mississippi and East Louisiana (December 1862-January 1863)

Missouri Brigade, Price's Division, Army of the Department of Mississippi and East Louisiana (January 1863)

Missouri Brigade, Forney's-Bowen's Division, 2nd Military District, Department of Mississippi and East Louisiana (April 1863)

Missouri Brigade, Bowen's Division, Department of Mississippi and East Louisiana (April-July 1863)

Missouri Brigade, Department of Mississippi and East Louisiana (November 1863-January 1864)

Missouri Brigade, Department of the Gulf (January-February 1864)
Artillery Battalion, French's Division, Department of Alabama, Mississippi, and East Louisiana (February-May 1864)
Artillery Battalion, French's Division, Army of Mississippi (May-July 1864)
Storrs' Battalion, Artillery, 3rd Corps, Army of Tennessee (July 1864-January 1865)
Battles: Corinth Campaign (April-June 1862)
Iuka (September 19, 1862)
Corinth (October 3-4, 1862)
Grand Gulf (March 19, 1863)
Grand Gulf (March 31, 1863)
Grand Gulf (April 29, 1863)
Vicksburg Campaign (May-July 1863)
Port Gibson (May 1, 1863)
Champion's Hill (May 16, 1863)
Big Black River Bridge (May 17, 1863)
Vicksburg Siege (May-July 1863)
Atlanta Campaign (May-September 1864)
Atlanta Siege (July-September 1864)
Franklin-Nashville Campaign (November 1864-January 1865)
Nashville (December 15-16, 1864)
Further Reading: Bevier, R. S., *History of the First and Second Missouri Confederate Brigades 1861-1865*. Anderson, Ephraim McD., *Memoirs: Historical and Personal; Including the Campaigns of the First Missouri Confederate Brigade*.

20. MISSOURI HAMILTON'S ARTILLERY BATTERY

See: MISSOURI PRAIRIE GUN ARTILLERY BATTERY

21. MISSOURI HARRIS' [1ST] ARTILLERY BATTERY

See: MISSOURI HARRIS' ARTILLERY BATTERY, 1ST DIVISION, MISSOURI STATE GUARD

22. MISSOURI HARRIS' [2ND] ARTILLERY BATTERY

See: MISSOURI 4TH FIELD ARTILLERY BATTERY

23. MISSOURI JACKSON ARTILLERY BATTERY

Organization: Organized early 1862. Battery surrendered at Vicksburg, Warren County, Mississippi on July 4, 1863. Paroled at Vicksburg, Warren County, Mississippi in July 1863. Declared exchanged on September 12, 1863. Field consolidation with the 3rd [or St. Louis] Missouri Artillery Battery from late

1863 or early 1864 to May 4, 1865. NOTE: It was usually referred to as the 3rd Battery or St. Louis Artillery despite Captain Lowe being in command much of the time. The consolidated battery was armed with four 20-lb. Parrotts from May 19, 1864 to February 21, 1865. Surrendered by Lieutenant General Richard Taylor, commanding the Department of Alabama, Mississippi, and East Louisiana, at Citronelle, Alabama on May 4, 1865.

First Commander: William Lucas (Captain)

Captain: Schuyler Lowe

Assignments: Slack's Brigade, Confederate Volunteers, Missouri State Guard, Trans-Mississippi District, Department #2 (March 1862)

Green's Brigade, Price's Division, Trans-Mississippi District, Department #2 (March-April 1862)

Cabell's Brigade, Maury's Division, Army of the West, Department #2 (April-July 1862)

Martin's Brigade, Hébert's-Green's Division, Price's Corps, Army of West Tennessee, Department #2 (October 1862)

Hébert's Brigade, Bowen's Division, Price's Corps, Army of West Tennessee, Department of Mississippi and East Louisiana (October 1862)

Cravens' Brigade, Bowen's Division, Price's Corps, Army of West Tennessee, Department of Mississippi and East Louisiana (October-December 1862)

Cravens' Brigade, Bowen's Division, Price's Corps, Army of North Mississippi, Department of Mississippi and East Louisiana (December 1862-January 1863)

Green's Brigade, Price's Division, Army of the Department of Mississippi and East Louisiana (January 1863)

Green's Brigade, Forney's-Bowen's Division, 2nd Military District, Department of Mississippi and East Louisiana (April 1863)

Green's Brigade, Bowen's Division, Department of Mississippi and East Louisiana (April-July 1863)

Cantey's Brigade, Department of the Gulf (December-January 1864)

Truehart's Artillery Battalion, District of the Gulf, Department of Alabama, Mississippi, and East Louisiana (April-May 1864)

Fuller's-Higgins' Artillery Brigade, District of the Gulf, Department of Alabama, Mississippi, and East Louisiana (June 1864)

Truehart's Artillery Battalion, Higgins' Brigade, District of the Gulf, Department of Alabama, Mississippi, and East Louisiana (August 1864)

Liddell's Brigade, District of the Gulf, Department of Alabama, Mississippi, and East Louisiana (September-October 1864)

Semple's Artillery Battalion, District of the Gulf, Department of Alabama, Mississippi, and East Louisiana (October-November 1864)

Burnet's Command, District of the Gulf, Department of Alabama, Mississippi, and East Louisiana (November 1864)

Semple's Artillery Battalion, District of the Gulf, Department of Alabama, Mississippi, and East Louisiana (December 1864-February 1865)

Unattached, Burnet's Command, Artillery Reserves, etc., District of the Gulf, Department of Alabama, Mississippi, and East Louisiana (March-April 1865)

Battles: Pea Ridge (March 7-8, 1862)

Corinth Campaign (April-June 1862)

Vicksburg Campaign (May-July 1863)

Champion's Hill (May 16, 1863)

Big Black River Bridge (May 17, 1863)

Vicksburg Siege (May-July 1863)

Mobile (March 17-April 12, 1865)

24. MISSOURI KELLY'S ARTILLERY BATTERY

Organization: Organized by the transfer of Kelly's Artillery Battery, 5th Division, Missouri State Guard to Confederate service ca. March 1862. Apparently disbanded ca. June 1862.

First Commander: E. V. Kelly (Captain)

Assignments: Frost's Artillery Brigade, Price's Division, Trans-Mississippi District, Department #2 (March-April 1862)

Frost's-Clark's Artillery Brigade, Price's Division, Army of the West, Department #2 (April-May 1862)

Battle: Corinth Campaign (April-June 1862)

25. MISSOURI KING'S ARTILLERY BATTERY

See: MISSOURI 2ND ARTILLERY BATTERY

26. MISSOURI KNEISLEY'S ARTILLERY BATTERY

Organization: Organized by the transfer of Kneisley's Artillery Battery, 2nd Division, Missouri State Guard to Confederate service ca. March 1862. Apparently disbanded in the spring of 1862.

First Commander: J. W. Kneisley (Captain)

Assignments: Frost's Artillery Brigade, Price's Division, Trans-Mississippi District, Department #2 (March-April 1862)

Frost's-Clark's Artillery Brigade, Price's Division, Army of the West, Department #2 (March-May 1862)

Battle: Corinth Campaign (April-June 1862)

27. MISSOURI LANDIS' ARTILLERY BATTERY

Organization: Organized ca. December 8, 1861. It was armed with four Howitzers on March 17, 1862. It was armed with four guns from April 29 to July 4, 1863. Battery surrendered at Vicksburg, Warren County, Mississippi on July 4, 1863. Paroled at Vicksburg, Warren County, Mississippi in July 1863. Declared exchanged on September 12, 1863. Apparently never reorganized after its exchange.

First Commander: John C. Landis (Captain)

Assignments: Green's Brigade, Price's Division, Confederate Volunteers, Trans-Mississippi District, Department #2 (March 1862)

Frost's Artillery Brigade, Price's Division, Trans-Mississippi District, Department #2 (March-April 1862)

Frost's-Clarks' Artillery Brigade, Price's Division, Army of the West, Department #2 (April-May 1862)

Clarks' Artillery Brigade, Army of the West, Department #2 (May-July 1862)

Green's Brigade, Little's-Hébert's-Green's Division, Price's Corps, Army of West Tennessee, Department #2 (September-October 1862)

Green's Brigade, Bowen's Division, Price's Corps, Army of West Tennessee, Department of Mississippi and East Louisiana (October-December 1862)

Missouri Brigade, Bowen's Division, Army of North Mississippi, Department of Mississippi and East Louisiana (December 1862-January 1863)

Missouri Brigade, Price's Division, Army of the Department of Mississippi and East Louisiana (January 1863)

Missouri Brigade, Forney's-Bowen's Division, 2nd Military District, Department of Mississippi and East Louisiana (April 1863)

Missouri Brigade, Bowen's Division, Department of Mississippi and East Louisiana (April-July 1863)

Battles: Pea Ridge (March 7-8, 1862)

Corinth Campaign (April-June 1862)

Iuka (September 19, 1862)

Corinth Campaign (April-June 1862)

Grand Gulf (March 19, 1863)

Grand Gulf (March 31, 1863)

Grand Gulf (April 29, 1863)

Vicksburg Campaign (May-July 1863)

Port Gibson [section] (May 1, 1863)

Champion's Hill (May 16, 1863)

Big Black River Bridge (May 17, 1863)

Vicksburg Siege (May-July 1863)

Further Reading: Bevier, R. S., *History of the First and Second Missouri Confederate Brigades 1861-1865*. Anderson, Ephraim McD., *Memoirs: Historical and Personal; Including the Campaigns of the First Missouri Confederate Brigade*.

28. MISSOURI LESEUER'S ARTILLERY BATTERY

See: MISSOURI 3RD FIELD ARTILLERY BATTERY

29. MISSOURI LOWE'S ARTILLERY BATTERY

See: MISSOURI JACKSON ARTILLERY BATTERY

30. MISSOURI LUCAS' ARTILLERY BATTERY

See: MISSOURI JACKSON ARTILLERY BATTERY

31. MISSOURI MACDONALD'S, EMMETT ARTILLERY BATTERY

See: MISSOURI ST. LOUIS ARTILLERY BATTERY

32. MISSOURI MACDONALD'S, ROBERT ARTILLERY BATTERY

See: MISSOURI MACDONALD'S ARTILLERY BATTERY, 1ST DIVISION, MISSOURI STATE GUARD

33. MISSOURI PRAIRIE GUN ARTILLERY BATTERY

Organization: Organized in the spring of 1863. It was armed with four guns on July 4, 1863. Apparently broken up after Lieutenant Bell's death on August 27, 1863.

First Commander: James L. Hamilton (Lieutenant)

Captain: C. O. Bell

Assignment: Marmaduke's-Greene's-Marmaduke's Brigade, Marmaduke's Cavalry Division, District of Arkansas, Trans-Mississippi Department (May-August 1863)

Battles: Helena (July 4, 1863)

vs. Steele's Little Rock Expedition (August 1-September 14, 1863)

Bayou Meto (August 27, 1863)

34. MISSOURI ROBERTS' ARTILLERY BATTERY

See: MISSOURI 1ST FIELD ARTILLERY BATTERY

35. MISSOURI RUFFNER'S ARTILLERY BATTERY

See: MISSOURI 1ST FIELD ARTILLERY BATTERY

36. MISSOURI ST. LOUIS ARTILLERY BATTERY

See: MISSOURI 3RD ARTILLERY BATTERY

37. MISSOURI TILDEN'S ARTILLERY BATTERY

See: MISSOURI 3RD FIELD ARTILLERY BATTERY

38. MISSOURI TULL'S ARTILLERY BATTERY

Organization: Organized in early 1862. Apparently disbanded in the spring of 1862.

First Commander: Francis S. Tull (Captain)

Assignments: Artillery, McCulloch's Division, Army of the West, Department #2 (March 1862)

Frost's Artillery Brigade, Price's Division, Trans-Mississippi District, Department #2 (March-April 1862)

Frost's-Clark's Artillery Brigade, Price's Division, Army of the West, Department #2 (April-May 1862)

Battles: Pea Ridge (March 7-8, 1862)

Corinth Campaign (April-June 1862)

39. MISSOURI WADE'S ARTILLERY BATTERY

See: MISSOURI 1ST ARTILLERY BATTERY

40. MISSOURI WALSH'S ARTILLERY BATTERY

See: MISSOURI 1ST ARTILLERY BATTERY

CAVALRY

41. MISSOURI 1ST (ELLIOTT'S) CAVALRY BATTALION

Also Known As: 10th Cavalry Battalion

Organization: Organized in late 1862. Increased to a regiment and designated as the 1st (Elliott's) Cavalry Regiment in the spring of 1864.

First Commander: Benjamin Elliott (Major, Lieutenant Colonel)

Field Officers: Washington McDaniel (Major)

Thomas H. Walton (Major)

Assignments: Shelby's Brigade, Marmaduke's Division, 1st Corps, Trans-Mississippi Department (November-December 1862)

Shelby's Brigade, Marmaduke's Division, District of Arkansas, Trans-Mississippi Department (January 1863-May 1864)

Battles: Cane Hill (November 28, 1862)

Prairie Grove (December 7, 1862)

Marmaduke's Expedition into Missouri (December 31, 1862-January 25, 1863)

White Springs (January 2, 1863)

Springfield (January 8, 1863)

Hartville (January 11, 1863)

Marmaduke's Expedition into Missouri (April 17-May 2, 1863)

Helena (July 4, 1863)

Little Rock (September 10, 1863)

Shelby's Raid in Arkansas and Missouri (September 22-October 26, 1863)

Camden Expedition (March-May 1864)

Marks' Mills (April 25, 1864)

42. MISSOURI 1ST CAVALRY BATTALION, INDIAN BRIGADE

Organization: Organized in the spring of 1864. Surrendered by General E. K. Smith, commanding Trans-Mississippi Department, on May 26, 1865.

First Commander: Thomas R. Livingston (Major)

Field Officers: J. F. Pickler (Major)

Andrew J. Piercey (Major)

Assignments: Shelby's Brigade, Marmaduke's Cavalry Division, District of Arkansas, Trans-Mississippi Department (May-September 1864)

District of the Indian Territory, Trans-Mississippi Department (April-May 1865)

Battles: Carthage (July 21, 1864)

near Enterprise [skirmish] (August 7, 1864)

43. MISSOURI 1ST CAVALRY REGIMENT

Organization: Organized from the Missouri State Guard on December 30, 1861. Dismounted in April 1862. Regiment surrendered at Vicksburg, Warren County, Mississippi on July 4, 1863. Paroled at Vicksburg, Warren County, Mississippi in July 1863. Declared exchanged on September 12, 1863. Field consolidation with the 3rd Cavalry Regiment from September 1863 to April 1865. Surrendered by Lieutenant Richard Taylor, commanding the Department of Alabama, Mississippi, and East Louisiana, at Meridian, Mississippi on May 4, 1865.

First Commander: Elijah Gates (Colonel)

Field Officers: Richard B. Chiles (Lieutenant Colonel)

C. B. Cleveland (Lieutenant Colonel)

Robert R. Lawther (Major)

George W. Lay (Major, Lieutenant Colonel)

William D. Maupin (Lieutenant Colonel)

William C. Parker (Major)

Assignments: Little's Brigade, Confederate Volunteers, Missouri State Guard, Trans-Mississippi District, Department #2 (January-April 1862)

Little's-Gates' Brigade, Price's-Little's Division, Army of the West, Department #2 (April-July 1862)

Gates' Brigade, Little's-Hébert's-Green's Division, Price's Corps, Army of West Tennessee, Department #2 (July-October 1862)

Green's Brigade, Bowen's Division, Army of West Tennessee, Department of Mississippi and East Louisiana (October-November 1862)

Missouri Brigade, Bowen's Division, Price's Corps, Army of West Tennessee, Department of Mississippi and East Louisiana (November-December 1862)

Missouri Brigade, Bowen's Division, 2nd Corps, Army of North Mississippi, Department of Mississippi and East Louisiana (December 1862-January 1863)

Missouri Brigade, Price's Division, Army of the Department of Mississippi and East Louisiana (January-February 1863)

Missouri Brigade, Forney's-Bowen's Division, 2nd Military District, Department of Mississippi and East Louisiana (February-April 1863)

Missouri Brigade, Bowen's Division, Department of Mississippi and East Louisiana (April-July 1863)
Missouri Brigade, Department of Mississippi and East Louisiana (November-December 1863)
Missouri Brigade, Department of the Gulf (January-February 1864)
Missouri Brigade, French's Division, Department of Alabama, Mississippi, and East Louisiana (February-May 1864)
Missouri Brigade, French's Division, Army of Mississippi (May-July 1864)
Missouri Brigade, French's Division, 3rd Corps, Army of Tennessee (July 1864-January 1865)
Missouri Brigade, French's Division, District of the Gulf, Department of Alabama, Mississippi, and East Louisiana (February-April 1865)
Missouri Brigade, French's Division, Department of Alabama, Mississippi, and East Louisiana (April 1865)
Battles: Pea Ridge (March 7-8, 1862)
Corinth Campaign (April-June 1862)
Iuka (September 19, 1862)
Corinth (October 3-4, 1862)
Vicksburg Campaign (May-July 1863)
Champion's Hill (May 16, 1863)
Big Black River Bridge (May 17, 1863)
Vicksburg Siege (May-July 1863)
Meridian Campaign (February-March 1864)
Atlanta Campaign (May-September 1864)
New Hope Church (May 25-June 4, 1864)
Lattimer's Mills (June 20, 1864)
Kennesaw Mountain (June 27, 1864)
Smyrna Campground (July 4, 1864)
Chattahoochee River (July 5-17, 1864)
Atlanta (July 22, 1864)
Atlanta Siege (July-September 1864)
Jonesboro (August 31-September 1, 1864)
Lovejoy's Station (September 2-5, 1864)
Allatoona (October 5, 1864)
Franklin (November 30, 1864)
Mobile (March 17-April 12, 1865)
Fort Blakely (April 1-9, 1865)
Further Reading: Bevier, R. S., *History of the First and Second Missouri Confederate Brigades 1861-1865*. Anderson, Ephraim McD., *Memoirs: Historical and Personal; Including the Campaigns of the First Missouri Confederate Brigade.*

44. MISSOURI 1ST (ELLIOTT'S) CAVALRY REGIMENT

Also Known As: 10th (Elliott's) Cavalry Battalion

Organization: Organized by the increase of the 1st Cavalry Battalion to a regiment mid-1864. Surrendered by General E. K. Smith, commanding Trans-Mississippi Department, on May 26, 1865.

First Commander: Benjamin Elliott (Colonel)

Assignments: Shelby's Brigade, Marmaduke's-Shelby's Division, District of Arkansas, Trans-Mississippi Department (August-December 1864)

1st Missouri Cavalry Brigade, 1st Missouri Cavalry Division, Cavalry Corps, Trans-Mississippi Department (December 1864-May 1865)

Battles: Camden Expedition (March-May 1864)

Jenkins' Ferry (April 30, 1864)

Price's Missouri Raid (August-October 1864)

45. MISSOURI 1ST NORTHEAST CAVALRY REGIMENT

Organization: Organized in mid-1862. Apparently disbanded in late 1862.

First Commander: Joseph C. Porter (Colonel)

Field Officers: William C. Blanton (Lieutenant Colonel)

Elliott D. Majors (Major)

Battles: near Memphis [skirmish] (July 18, 1862)

Florida [skirmish] (July 22, 1862)

Brown's Spring [skirmish] (July 27, 1862)

Moore's Mill (July 28, 1862)

Panther Creek [skirmish] (August 8, 1862)

Portland (October 16, 1862)

California House [skirmish] (October 18, 1862)

near Uniontown [skirmish] (October 18, 1862)

46. MISSOURI 2ND CAVALRY REGIMENT

Organization: Organized by the increase of the 4th Cavalry Battalion to a regiment in August 1862. Surrendered by Lieutenant General Richard Taylor, commanding the Department of Alabama, Mississippi, and East Louisiana, at Citronelle, Alabama on May 4, 1865.

First Commander: Robert McCulloch (Colonel)

Field Officers: William H. Couzens (Major)

George B. Harper (Lieutenant Colonel)

Samuel M. Hyams, Jr. (Lieutenant Colonel)

Robert A. McCulloch (Major, Lieutenant Colonel)

A. B. Sharp (Major)

John J. Smith (Major)

Assignments: Cavalry, Department #2 (August 1862)

Armstrong's Cavalry Brigade, Price's Corps, Army of West Tennessee, Department #2 (September-October 1862)
Armstrong's-Jackson's Cavalry Brigade, 1st Corps, Army of West Tennessee, Department of Mississippi and East Louisiana (October 1862-January 1863)
2nd Brigade, Jackson's Division, Van Dorn's Cavalry Corps, Department of Mississippi and East Louisiana (January-February 1863)
Escort, Forney's-Bowen's Division, 2nd Military District, Department of Mississippi and East Louisiana [one company] (April 1863)
McCulloch's Cavalry Brigade, Department of Mississippi and East Louisiana (February-April 1863)
McCulloch's Cavalry Brigade, 5th Military District, Department of Mississippi and East Louisiana (April-July 1863)
5th Military District, Department of Mississippi and East Louisiana (August-September 1863)
Chalmers' Cavalry Brigade, Department of Mississippi and East Louisiana (September-October 1863)
McCulloch's Brigade, Chalmers' Cavalry Division, Department of Mississippi and East Louisiana (October-November 1863)
McCulloch's Brigade, Chalmers' Division, Lee's Cavalry Corps, Department of Mississippi and East Louisiana (November 1863-January 1864)
McCulloch's Brigade, Chalmers' Division, Forrest's Cavalry Corps, Department of Mississippi and East Louisiana (January 1864)
McCulloch's-Wade's-McCulloch's Brigade, Chalmers' Division, Forrest's Cavalry Corps, Department of Alabama, Mississippi, and East Louisiana (January-September 1864)
McCulloch's Cavalry Brigade, District of the Gulf, Department of Alabama, Mississippi, and East Louisiana (September-December 1864)
Forrest's Cavalry Corps, Department of Alabama, Mississippi, and East Louisiana (March-May 1865)
Battles: Iuka (September 19, 1862)
Corinth (October 3-4, 1862)
Coffeeville (December 5, 1862)
Holly Springs (December 20, 1862)
Vicksburg Campaign (May-July 1863)
Colliersville (November 3, 1863)
Yazoo Pass (February 16-19, 1863)
near Charleston, on the Coldwater River (March 15, 1863)
Chalmers' Raid in West Tennessee and North Mississippi (October 4-17, 1863)
Chickasawha Bridge [skirmish] (December 10, 1863)
A. J. Smith's 1st Mississippi Invasion (July 5-21, 1864)
Tupelo (July 14-15, 1864)

A. J. Smith's 2nd Mississippi Invasion (August 1864)
Forrest's Memphis Raid (August 21, 1864)
Wilson's Raid (March 22-April 24, 1865)

47. MISSOURI 2ND (JEANS') CAVALRY REGIMENT

See: MISSOURI 12TH CAVALRY REGIMENT

48. MISSOURI 2ND NORTHEAST CAVALRY REGIMENT

Organization: Organized in 1862. This unit does not appear in the *Official Records*. Apparently disbanded in 1862.
First Commander: Cyrus Franklin (Colonel)
Field Officers: Frisby H. McCullough (Lieutenant Colonel)
Raphael Smith (Major)

49. MISSOURI 3RD CAVALRY BATTALION

Also Known As: 6th Cavalry Battalion
Organization: Organized in the spring of 1862. Dismounted in the spring of 1862. Increased to a regiment and designated as the 3rd Cavalry Regiment in late 1862.
First Commander: Leonidas C. Campbell (Lieutenant Colonel)
Field Officers: Thomas J. McQuidy (Major)
D. Todd Samuel (Major, Lieutenant Colonel)
Assignments: Green's Brigade, Little's Division, Army of the West, Department #2 (June-July 1862)
Green's Brigade, Price's Division, Army of West Tennessee, Department #2 (August-October 1862)
Green's Brigade, Price's Division, Army of West Tennessee, Department of Mississippi and East Louisiana (October 1862)
Battles: Corinth (October 3-4, 1862)
Hatchie Bridge (October 5, 1862)
Further Reading: Bevier, R. S., *History of the First and Second Missouri Confederate Brigades 1861-1865*. Anderson, Ephraim McD., *Memoirs: Historical and Personal; Including the Campaigns of the First Missouri Confederate Brigade*.

50. MISSOURI 3RD CAVALRY BATTALION

Organization: Organized in mid-1863. Apparently disbanded in 1863.
Assignment: Greene's Brigade, Marmaduke's Cavalry Division, District of Arkansas, Trans-Mississippi Department (July 1863)
Battle: Helena (July 4, 1863)

51. MISSOURI 3RD CAVALRY REGIMENT

Organization: Organized by the increase of the 3rd Cavalry Battalion to a regiment in late 1862. Regiment surrendered at Vicksburg, Warren County, Mississippi on July 4, 1863. Paroled at Vicksburg, Warren County, Mississippi in July 1863. Declared exchanged on September 12, 1863. Field consolidation with the 1st Cavalry Regiment from September 1863 to April 1865. Surrendered by Lieutenant Richard Taylor, commanding the Department of Alabama, Mississippi, and East Louisiana, at Meridian, Mississippi on May 4, 1865.

First Commander: Colton Greene (Colonel)

Field Officers: L. A. Campbell (Major, Lieutenant Colonel)
Leonidas C. Campbell (Lieutenant Colonel)
Thomas J. McQuidy (Major)
D. Todd Samuel (Major, Lieutenant Colonel)
James Surridge (Major)

Assignments: Little's Brigade, Confederate Volunteers, Missouri State Guard, Trans-Mississippi District, Department #2 (January-April 1862)

Little's-Gates' Brigade, Price's-Little's Division, Army of the West, Department #2 (April-July 1862)

Gates' Brigade, Little's-Hébert's-Green's Division, Price's Corps, Army of West Tennessee, Department #2 (July-October 1862)

Green's Brigade, Bowen's Division, Army of West Tennessee, Department of Mississippi and East Louisiana (October-November 1862)

Missouri Brigade, Bowen's Division, Price's Corps, Army of West Tennessee, Department of Mississippi and East Louisiana (November-December 1862)

Missouri Brigade, Bowen's Division, 2nd Corps, Army of North Mississippi, Department of Mississippi and East Louisiana (December 1862-January 1863)

Missouri Brigade, Price's Division, Army of the Department of Mississippi and East Louisiana (January-February 1863)

Missouri Brigade, Forney's-Bowen's Division, 2nd Military District, Department of Mississippi and East Louisiana (February-April 1863)

Missouri Brigade, Bowen's Division, Department of Mississippi and East Louisiana (April-July 1863)

Missouri Brigade, Department of Mississippi and East Louisiana (November-December 1863)

Missouri Brigade, Department of the Gulf (January-February 1864)

Missouri Brigade, French's Division, Department of Alabama, Mississippi, and East Louisiana (February-May 1864)

Missouri Brigade, French's Division, Army of Mississippi (May-July 1864)

Missouri Brigade, French's Division, 3rd Corps, Army of Tennessee (July 1864-January 1865)

Missouri Brigade, French's Division, District of the Gulf, Department of Alabama, Mississippi, and East Louisiana (February-April 1865)
Missouri Brigade, French's Division, Department of Alabama, Mississippi, and East Louisiana (April 1865)
Battles: Pea Ridge (March 7-8, 1862)
Corinth Campaign (April-June 1862)
Iuka (September 19, 1862)
Corinth (October 3-4, 1862)
Vicksburg Campaign (May-July 1863)
Champion's Hill (May 16, 1863)
Big Black River Bridge (May 17, 1863)
Vicksburg Siege (May-July 1863)
Meridian Campaign (February-March 1864)
Atlanta Campaign (May-September 1864)
New Hope Church (May 25-June 4, 1864)
Lattimer's Mills (June 20, 1864)
Kennesaw Mountain (June 27, 1864)
Smyrna Campground (July 4, 1864)
Chattahoochee River (July 5-17, 1864)
Atlanta (July 22, 1864)
Atlanta Siege (July-September 1864)
Jonesboro (August 31-September 1, 1864)
Lovejoy's Station (September 2-5, 1864)
Allatoona (October 5, 1864)
Franklin (November 30, 1864)
Mobile (March 17-April 12, 1865)
Fort Blakely (April 1-9, 1865)
Further Reading: Bevier, R. S., *History of the First and Second Missouri Confederate Brigades 1861-1865*. Anderson, Ephraim McD., *Memoirs: Historical and Personal; Including the Campaigns of the First Missouri Confederate Brigade*.

52. MISSOURI 3RD NORTHEAST CAVALRY REGIMENT

Organization: This unit does not appear in the *Official Records*.
Field Officer: Raphael Smith (Major)

53. MISSOURI 4TH CAVALRY BATTALION

Organization: Organized on April 27, 1862. Increased to a regiment and designated as the 2nd Cavalry Regiment in August 1862.
First Commander: Robert McCulloch (Lieutenant Colonel)
Field Officer: John J. Smith (Major)

Assignments: Green's Brigade, Price's Division, Army of the West, Department #2 (April-May 1862)
Cavalry, Army of the Mississippi, Department #2 (May-June 1862)
Cavalry, Department #2 (June-August 1862)
Battles: Corinth Campaign (April-June 1862)
Booneville (May 30, 1862)

54. MISSOURI 4TH CAVALRY REGIMENT

Organization: Organized in late 1862. Surrendered by General E. K. Smith, commanding Trans-Mississippi Department, on May 26, 1865.
First Commander: John Q. Burbridge (Colonel)
Field Officers: William I. Preston (Lieutenant Colonel)
Dennis Smith (Major)
Assignments: White's Brigade, Churchill's Division, 2nd Corps, Trans-Mississippi Department (December 1862)
Porter's Brigade, Marmaduke's Cavalry Division, District of Arkansas, Trans-Mississippi Department (December 1862-January 1863)
Burbridge's Brigade, Marmaduke's Cavalry Division, District of Arkansas, Trans-Mississippi Department (April-June 1863)
Marmaduke's-Clark's-Greene's Brigade, Marmaduke's Cavalry Division, Army of Missouri, Trans-Mississippi Department (September 1864)
2nd Missouri Cavalry Brigade, 1st Missouri Cavalry Division, Cavalry Corps, Trans-Mississippi Department (September 1864-May 1865)
Battles: Marmaduke's Expedition into Missouri (April 17-May 2, 1863)
Hartville (January 11, 1863)
Scout from Pocahontas, Arkansas to Patterson, Missouri (August 1863)
Little Rock (September 10, 1863)
Pine Bluff (October 25, 1863)
Camden Expedition (March-May 1864)
Poison Spring (April 18, 1864)
Jenkins' Ferry (April 30, 1864)
Greene's Operations on the west bank of the Mississippi River (May 24-June 4, 1864)
Lake Chicot (June 6, 1864)
Price's Missouri Raid (August-October 1864)
Fort Davidson, Pilot Knob (September 27, 1864)
Cuba (September 29, 1864)
Boonville (October 11, 1864)
Glasgow (October 15, 1864)
Little Blue (October 21, 1864)
Independence (October 22, 1864)

Big Blue (October 23, 1864)
Mine Creek (October 25, 1864)

55. MISSOURI 5TH CAVALRY REGIMENT

Also Known As: 1st Cavalry Regiment

Organization: Organized along the Missouri River in August 1862. Company D served for a time as escort to Brigadier General John S. Marmaduke. Surrendered by General E. K. Smith, commanding Trans-Mississippi Department, on May 26, 1865.

First Commander: Joseph O. Shelby (Colonel)

Field Officers: Y. H. Blackwell (Lieutenant Colonel)
B. Frank Gordon (Major, Lieutenant Colonel, Colonel)
George P. Gordon (Major)
George R. Kirtley (Major)

Assignments: Cooper's-Shelby's Brigade, Cooper's Division, Indian Territory, District of Arkansas, Trans-Mississippi Department (September-October 1862)
Shelby's Cavalry Brigade, Marmaduke's Cavalry Division, 1st Corps, Trans-Mississippi Department (November 1862-January 1863)
Shelby's Brigade, Marmaduke's Cavalry Division, District of Arkansas, Trans-Mississippi Department (January 1863-September 1864)
Shelby's-Shanks'-Thompson's Brigade, Shelby's Cavalry Division, Army of Missouri, Trans-Mississippi Department (September 1864)
1st Missouri Cavalry Brigade, 1st Missouri Cavalry Division, Cavalry Corps, Trans-Mississippi Department (September 1864-May 1865)

Battles: Coon Creek, near Lamar [skirmish] (August 24, 1862)
Newtonia (September 30, 1862)
Newtonia (October 4, 1862)
Cane Hill (November 28, 1862)
Prairie Grove (December 7, 1862)
Marmaduke's Expedition into Missouri (December 31, 1862-January 25, 1863)
Springfield (January 8, 1863)
Hartville (January 11, 1863)
Helena (July 4, 1863)
Brownsville [skirmish] (August 25, 1863)
Bayou Meto (August 27, 1863)
Little Rock (September 10, 1863)
Shelby's Raid in Arkansas and Missouri (September 22-October 26, 1863)
Camden Expedition (March-May 1864)
Marks' Mills (April 25, 1864)
Ashley's and Jones' Stations, near Devall's Bluff (August 24, 1864)

Price's Missouri Raid (August-October 1864)

56. MISSOURI 6TH CAVALRY BATTALION

See: MISSOURI 3RD CAVALRY BATTALION

57. MISSOURI 6TH CAVALRY REGIMENT

Organization: Organized in mid-1862. Designated as the 11th Cavalry Regiment in December 1862.

First Commander: John T. Coffee (Colonel)

Field Officers: John T. Crisp (Lieutenant Colonel)

M. J. B. Young (Major)

Assignments: Shelby's Brigade, Marmaduke's Cavalry Division, District of Arkansas, Trans-Mississippi Department (September-December 1862)

Shelby's Brigade, Marmaduke's Cavalry Division, 1st Corps, Trans-Mississippi Department (December 1862)

Battles: near Neosho [skirmish] (May 31, 1862)

Montevallo [skirmish] (August 5, 1862)

near Montevallo [skirmish] (August 7, 1862)

Lone Jack (August 16, 1862)

Coon Creek, near Lamar [skirmish] (August 24, 1862)

Cane Hill (November 28, 1862)

Prairie Grove (December 7, 1862)

58. MISSOURI 6TH (THOMPSON'S) CAVALRY REGIMENT

See: MISSOURI 11TH CAVALRY REGIMENT

59. MISSOURI 7TH CAVALRY REGIMENT

Also Known As: 10th Cavalry Regiment

Organization: Organized by the increase of Kitchen's Cavalry Battalion to a regiment on July 9, 1863. Surrendered by General E. K. Smith, commanding Trans-Mississippi Department, on May 26, 1865.

First Commander: Solomon G. Kitchen (Colonel)

Field Officers: J. F. Davies (Lieutenant Colonel)

Jesse Ellison (Lieutenant Colonel)

James A. Walker (Major)

Assignments: Greene's-Burbridge's Brigade, Marmaduke's Cavalry Division, District of Arkansas, Trans-Mississippi Department (April-September 1864)

Marmaduke's-Clark's-Greene's Brigade, Marmaduke's Cavalry Division, Army of Missouri, Trans-Mississippi Department (September 1864)

2nd (Clark's) Missouri Cavalry Brigade, 1st Missouri (Marmaduke's) Cavalry Division, Cavalry Corps, Trans-Mississippi Department (September 1864-May 1865)

Battles: Camden Expedition (March-May 1864)
Jenkins' Ferry (April 30, 1864)
Greene's Operations on the west bank of the Mississippi River (May 24-June 4, 1864)
Capture of *USS Clara Eames* (May 30, 1864)
Worthington's Landing [skirmish] (June 5, 1864)
Lake Chicot (June 6, 1864)
Sunnyside Landing [skirmish] (June 7, 1864)
Price's Missouri Raid (August-October 1864)
near California (October 9, 1864)
Boonville (October 11, 1864)
Glasgow (October 15, 1864)
Blue Mills (October 21, 1864)
Independence (October 22, 1864)
Big Blue (October 23, 1864)
Osage River (October 5, 1864)

60. MISSOURI 8TH CAVALRY REGIMENT

Organization: Organized in late 1862. Surrendered by General E. K. Smith, commanding Trans-Mississippi Department, on May 26, 1865.

First Commander: William L. Jeffers (Colonel)

Field Officers: James Parrott (Major)
Samuel J. Ward (Lieutenant Colonel)

Assignments: Porter's-Greene's-Marmaduke's-Greene's Brigade, Marmaduke's Cavalry Division, District of Arkansas, Trans-Mississippi Department (December 1862-September 1864)

Marmaduke's-Clark's-Greene's-Clark's Brigade, Marmaduke's Cavalry Division, Army of Missouri, Trans-Mississippi Department (September 1864)

2nd Missouri Cavalry Brigade, 1st Missouri Cavalry Division, Cavalry Corps, Trans-Mississippi Department (September 1864-May 1865)

Battles: Marmaduke's Expedition into Missouri (December 31, 1862-January 25, 1863)
Hartville (January 11, 1863)
Helena (July 4, 1863)
Bayou Meto (August 27, 1863)
Little Rock (September 10, 1863)
Pine Bluff (October 25, 1863)
Red River Campaign (March-May 1864)

Campti [skirmish] (April 4, 1864)
Camden Expedition (March-May 1864)
Poison Spring [detachment] (April 18, 1864)
Jenkins' Ferry (April 30, 1864)
Greene's Operations on the west bank of the Mississippi River (May 24-June 4, 1864)
Worthington's Landing (June 5, 1864)
Lake Chicot (June 6, 1864)
Sunnyside Landing (June 7, 1864)
Price's Missouri Raid (August-October 1864)
Union [skirmish] (October 1, 1864)
Boonville (October 11, 1864)
Glasgow (October 15, 1864)
Osage River (October 5, 1864)

61. MISSOURI 10TH CAVALRY BATTALION

See: MISSOURI 11TH CAVALRY BATTALION

62. MISSOURI 10TH (ELLIOTT'S) CAVALRY BATTALION

See: MISSOURI 1ST (ELLIOTT'S) CAVALRY BATTALION

63. MISSOURI 10TH CAVALRY REGIMENT

Organization: Organized by the increase of the 11th Cavalry Battalion to a regiment in the fall of 1863. Surrendered by General E. K. Smith, commanding Trans-Mississippi Department, on May 26, 1865.
First Commander: Robert R. Lawther (Colonel)
Field Officers: George W. C. Bennett (Major)
Merritt L. Young (Lieutenant Colonel)
Assignments: Post of Camden, District of Arkansas, Trans-Mississippi Department (October 1863)
Unattached, Price's Division, District of Arkansas, Trans-Mississippi Department (November 1863)
Marmaduke's-Greene's Brigade, Marmaduke's Cavalry Division, District of Arkansas, Trans-Mississippi Department (December 1863-September 1864)
Marmaduke's Brigade, Marmaduke's Cavalry Division, Army of Missouri, Trans-Mississippi Department (September 1864)
2nd Missouri Cavalry Brigade, 1st Missouri Cavalry Division, Cavalry Corps, Trans-Mississippi Department (September 1864-May 1865)
Battles: Ozark and on White River, near Forsyth (August 1-4, 1862)
Pine Bluff (October 25, 1863)
Camden Expedition (March-May 1864)

Jenkins' Ferry (April 30, 1864)
Greene's Operations on the west bank of the Mississippi River (May 24-June 4, 1864)
Worthington's Landing (June 5, 1864)
Lake Chicot (June 6, 1864)
Sunnyside Landing (June 7, 1864)
Price's Missouri Raid (August-October 1864)
Pilot Knob (September 27, 1864)
Leesburg [skirmish] (September 28, 1864)
Union [skirmish] (October 1, 1864)
Hermann [skirmish] (October 3, 1864)
California [skirmish] (October 9, 1864)
Boonville (October 11, 1864)
Glasgow (October 15, 1864)
Little Blue (October 16, 1864)
Big Blue (October 23, 1864)
Marais des Cynes (October 25, 1864)
Newtonia (October 28, 1864)

64. MISSOURI 10TH (ELLIOTT'S) CAVALRY REGIMENT

See: MISSOURI 1ST (ELLIOTT'S) CAVALRY REGIMENT

65. MISSOURI 10TH (KITCHEN'S) CAVALRY REGIMENT

See: MISSOURI 7TH CAVALRY REGIMENT

66. MISSOURI 11TH CAVALRY BATTALION

Also Known As: 10th Cavalry Battalion

Organization: Organized by the reduction of MacDonald's Cavalry Regiment in early 1863. Increased to a regiment and designated as the 10th Cavalry Regiment in the fall of 1863.

First Commander: Merritt L. Young (Lieutenant Colonel)

Field Officer: George W. C. Bennett (Major)

Assignment: Marmaduke's-Greene's-Marmaduke's Brigade, Marmaduke's Cavalry Division, District of Arkansas, Trans-Mississippi Department (April-October 1863)

Battles: Marmaduke's Expedition into Missouri (April 17-May 2, 1863)
Taylor's Creek [skirmish] (May 11, 1863)
Helena (July 4, 1863)
vs. Steele's Little Rock Expedition (August 1-September 14, 1863)
near Bayou Meto [skirmish] (August 26, 1863)
Pine Bluff (October 25, 1863)

67. MISSOURI 11TH CAVALRY REGIMENT

Also Known As: 6th Cavalry Regiment

Organization: Originally organized as the 6th Cavalry Regiment [q.v.]. Redesignated as the 11th Cavalry Regiment in December 1862. Surrendered by General E. K. Smith, commanding Trans-Mississippi Department, on May 26, 1865.

First Commander: Gideon W. Thompson (Colonel)

Field Officers: Jeremiah C. Cravens (Major)
James C. Hooper (Lieutenant Colonel)
George W. Nichols (Major)
Moses W. Smith (Major, Colonel)

Assignments: Shelby's Brigade, Marmaduke's Cavalry Division, District of Arkansas, Trans-Mississippi Department (December 1862-September 1864)
Shelby's Brigade, Shelby's Cavalry Division, Army of Missouri, Trans-Mississippi Department (September 1864)
1st Missouri Cavalry Brigade, 1st Missouri Cavalry Division, District of Arkansas, Trans-Mississippi Department (September 1864-May 1865)

Battles: Marmaduke's Expedition into Missouri (December 31, 1862-January 25, 1863)
Marmaduke's Expedition into Missouri (April 17-May 2, 1863)
Springfield (January 8, 1863)
Hartville (January 11, 1863)
Helena (July 4, 1863)
Bayou Meto (August 27, 1863)
Little Rock (September 10, 1863)
Shelby's Raid in Arkansas and Missouri (September 22-October 26, 1863)
Camden Expedition (March-May 1864)
Marks' Mills (April 25, 1864)
Price's Missouri Raid (August-October 1864)

68. MISSOURI 12TH CAVALRY REGIMENT

Also Known As: 2nd Cavalry Regiment

Nickname: Jackson County Cavalry

Organization: Organized in the summer of 1862. Surrendered by General E. K. Smith, commanding Trans-Mississippi Department, on May 26, 1865.

First Commander: Upton Hays (Colonel)

Field Officers: Samuel Bowman (Major)
William H. Erwin (Lieutenant Colonel)
Charles A. Gilkey (Major, Lieutenant Colonel)
Beal G. Jeans (Lieutenant Colonel, Colonel)
David Shanks (Major, Lieutenant Colonel, Colonel)

H. J. Vivien (Major)

Assignments: Cooper's Division, District of Arkansas, Trans-Mississippi Department (September 1862)

Shelby's Brigade, Marmaduke's Cavalry Division, 1st Corps, Trans-Mississippi Department (September-December 1862)

Shelby's Brigade, Marmaduke's Cavalry Division, District of Arkansas, Trans-Mississippi Department (December 1862-September 1864)

Shelby's Brigade, Marmaduke's Cavalry Division, Army of Missouri, Trans-Mississippi Department (September 1864)

1st Missouri Cavalry Brigade, 1st Missouri Cavalry Division, Cavalry Corps, Trans-Mississippi Department (September 1864-May 1865)

Battles: Newtonia (September 30, 1862)

Cane Hill (November 28, 1862)

Prairie Grove (December 7, 1862)

Marmaduke's Expedition into Missouri (December 31, 1862-January 25, 1863)

Springfield (January 8, 1863)

Hartville (January 11, 1863)

Marmaduke's Expedition into Missouri (April 17-May 2, 1863)

vs. Steele's Little Rock Expedition (August 1-September 14, 1863)

Pine Bluff (October 25, 1863)

Camden Expedition (March-May 1864)

Helena (July 4, 1863)

Marks' Mills (April 25, 1864)

Ashley's and Jones' Stations, near Devall's Bluff (August 24, 1864)

Price's Missouri Raid (August-October 1864)

69. MISSOURI 14TH CAVALRY BATTALION

Also Known As: Wood's Partisan Rangers Battalion

Organization: Organized with eight companies in the fall of 1863. Surrendered by General E. K. Smith, commanding Trans-Mississippi Department, on May 26, 1865.

First Commander: Robert C. Wood (Major)

Assignments: Unattached, Marmaduke's Cavalry Division, District of Arkansas, Trans-Mississippi Department (October-November 1863)

Unattached, District of the Indian Territory, Trans-Mississippi Department (November 1863)

Unattached, Marmaduke's Cavalry Division, District of Arkansas, Trans-Mississippi Department (December 1863-January 1864)

Marmaduke's-Greene's-Clark's Brigade, Marmaduke's Cavalry Division, District of Arkansas, Trans-Mississippi Department (April-May 1864)

Unattached, Marmaduke's Cavalry Division, District of Arkansas, Trans-Mississippi Department (August-September 1864)
Unattached, Marmaduke's Cavalry Division, Army of Missouri, Trans-Mississippi Department (September 1864)
1st Missouri Cavalry Brigade, 1st Missouri Cavalry Division, Cavalry Corps, Trans-Mississippi Department (September 1864-May 1865)
Battles: Pine Bluff (October 25, 1863)
Camden Expedition (March-May 1864)
Jenkins' Ferry (April 30, 1864)
Price's Missouri Raid (August-October 1864)

70. MISSOURI 15TH CAVALRY REGIMENT

Organization: Organized by the increase of Reves' Cavalry Battalion to a regiment in the summer of 1864. Apparently never completed its organization and was disbanded in the fall of 1864.
First Commander: Timothy Reves (Colonel)
Assignment: McCray's Brigade, Fagan's Cavalry Division, Army of Missouri, Trans-Mississippi Department (August-October 1864)
Battle: Price's Missouri Raid (August-October 1864)

71. MISSOURI BUSTER'S CAVALRY BATTALION

See: MISSOURI CLARKSON'S-BUSTER'S INFANTRY BATTALION

72. MISSOURI CEARNAL'S CAVALRY BATTALION

Organization: Organized in early 1862. Apparently disbanded in the spring of 1862.
First Commander: James T. Cearnal (Lieutenant Colonel)
Assignment: Escort, Confederate Volunteers, Missouri State Guard, Trans-Mississippi District, Department #2 (March 1862)
Battle: Pea Ridge (March 7-8, 1862)

73. MISSOURI CLARK'S CAVALRY BATTALION

Organization: Organized in early 1862. Apparently increased to a regiment and designated as Clark's Cavalry Regiment in the spring of 1862.
First Commander: H. E. Clark (Colonel)
Assignment: Army of the West, Department #2 (May 1862)
Battle: Corinth Campaign (April-June 1862)

74. MISSOURI CLARK'S CAVALRY REGIMENT

Organization: Organized by the increase of Clark's Cavalry Battalion to a regiment in the spring of 1862. Apparently failed to complete its organization.

First Commander: H. E. Clark (Colonel)

75. MISSOURI CLARKSON'S-BUSTER'S INFANTRY BATTALION

See: MISSOURI CLARKSON'S-BUSTER'S CAVALRY BATTALION
First Commander: James J. Clarkson (Colonel)

76. MISSOURI COLEMAN'S CAVALRY REGIMENT, PARTISAN RANGERS

Organization: This regiment does not appear in the *Official Records.*
First Commander: Coleman (Colonel)

77. MISSOURI DAVIES' CAVALRY BATTALION

Organization: Organized in the summer of 1864. Field consolidation with the 7th Cavalry Regiment in the fall of 1864. Apparently permanently merged into 7th Cavalry Regiment in late 1864.
First Commander: J. F. Davies (Lieutenant Colonel)
Assignment: Marmaduke's-Clark's-Greene's Brigade, Marmaduke's Cavalry Division, Army of Missouri, Trans-Mississippi Department (August-December 1864)
Battles: Price's Missouri Raid (August-October 1864)
near California (October 9, 1864)
Boonville (October 11, 1864)
Glasgow (October 15, 1864)
Blue Mills (October 21, 1864)
Independence (October 22, 1864)
Big Blue (October 23, 1864)

78. MISSOURI DORSEY'S CAVALRY BATTALION

Organization: Organized by the increase of Dorsey's Cavalry Squadron to a battalion ca. June 1863. Apparently disbanded in the summer of 1863.
First Commander: Caleb Dorsey (Captain)
Assignment: Cabell's Cavalry Brigade, Steele's Division, District of Arkansas, Trans-Mississippi Department (July 1863)

79. MISSOURI DORSEY' CAVALRY SQUADRON

Organization: Organized early in 1864. Increased to a battalion and designated as Dorsey's Cavalry Battalion ca. June 1863.
First Commander: Caleb Dorsey (Captain)
Assignments: Sub-district of Northwestern Arkansas [Cabell], District of Arkansas, Trans-Mississippi Department (April 1863)

Cabell's Cavalry Brigade, Steele's Division, District of Arkansas, Trans-Mississippi Department (April-May 1863)

Battle: Fayetteville (April 18, 1863)

80. MISSOURI FREEMAN'S CAVALRY REGIMENT

Organization: Organized on January 26, 1864. Surrendered by Brigadier General M. Jeff. Thompson as part of the Army of the Northern Sub-district of Arkansas, District of Arkansas and West Louisiana, Trans-Mississippi Department, on May 11, 1865.

First Commander: Thomas R. Freeman (Colonel)

Field Officers: Joseph B. Love (Lieutenant Colonel)

Michael V. B. Shaver (Major)

Assignments: Shelby's Brigade, Marmaduke's Cavalry Division, District of Arkansas, Trans-Mississippi Department (May-June 1864)

Freeman's Brigade, Marmaduke's Cavalry Division, Army of Missouri, Trans-Mississippi Department (September-October 1864)

Freeman's Cavalry Brigade, Northern Sub-district of Arkansas, District of Arkansas, Trans-Mississippi Department (December1864-April 1865)

Freeman's Cavalry Brigade, Northern Sub-district of Arkansas, District of Arkansas and West Louisiana, Trans-Mississippi Department (April-May 1865)

Battle: Price's Missouri Raid (August-October 1864)

81. MISSOURI FRISTOE'S CAVALRY REGIMENT

Organization: Organized on July 5, 1864. Surrendered by Brigadier General M. Jeff. Thompson as part of the Army of the Northern Sub-district of Arkansas, District of Arkansas and West Louisiana, Trans-Mississippi Department, on May 11, 1865.

First Commander: Edward T. Fristoe (Colonel)

Field Officers: Matthew J. Norman (Major)

Jesse H. Tracey (Lieutenant Colonel)

Assignments: Freeman's Brigade, Marmaduke's Cavalry Division, Army of Missouri, Trans-Mississippi Department (September-October 1864)

Freeman's Cavalry Brigade, Northern Sub-district of Arkansas, District of Arkansas, Trans-Mississippi Department (September 1864-April 1865)

Freeman's Cavalry Brigade, Northern Sub-district of Arkansas, District of Arkansas and West Louisiana, Trans-Mississippi Department (April-May 1865)

Battle: Price's Missouri Raid (August-October 1864)

82. MISSOURI HUGHES' CAVALRY REGIMENT

Also Known As: Hughes' Infantry Battalion

Organization: Organized in early 1862. Apparently disbanded in the spring of 1862.

First Commander: John T. Hughes (Colonel)

Assignments: Slack's Brigade, Confederate Volunteers, Missouri State Guard, Trans-Mississippi District, Department #2 (March 1862)

Slack's Brigade, Confederate Volunteers, Missouri State Guard, Trans-Mississippi District, Department #2 (March 1862)

Battle: Pea Ridge (March 7-8, 1862)

Further Reading: Bevier, R. S., *History of the First and Second Missouri Confederate Brigades 1861-1865*. Anderson, Ephraim McD., *Memoirs: Historical and Personal; Including the Campaigns of the First Missouri Confederate Brigade*.

83. MISSOURI HUNTER'S (1864) CAVALRY REGIMENT

Also Known As: Hunter's Cavalry Battalion

Organization: Organized in early 1864. Apparently disbanded in late 1864.

First Commander: DeWitt C. Hunter (Colonel)

Assignments: Shelby's Brigade, Marmaduke's Cavalry Division, District of Arkansas, Trans-Mississippi Department (April-May 1864)

Jackman's Brigade, Marmaduke's Cavalry Division, Army of Missouri, Trans-Mississippi Department (September-December 1864)

Battles: Camden Expedition (March-May 1864)

Marks' Mills (April 25, 1864)

Ashley's and Jones' Stations, near Devall's Bluff (August 24, 1864)

Price's Missouri Raid (August-October 1864)

84. MISSOURI JACKMAN'S CAVALRY REGIMENT

Organization: Organized in the summer of 1864. Apparently disbanded in late 1864.

First Commander: Sidney D. Jackman (Colonel)

Field Officers: G. W. Newton (Major)

C. H. Nichols (Lieutenant Colonel)

Assignment: Jackman's Brigade, Marmaduke's Cavalry Division, Army of Missouri, Trans-Mississippi Department (August-December 1864)

Battles: Ashley's and Jones' Stations, near Devall's Bluff (August 24, 1864)

Price's Missouri Raid (August-October 1864)

85. MISSOURI KITCHEN'S CAVALRY BATTALION

Organization: Organized with eight companies in Greene County, Arkansas on April 9, 1863. Increased to a regiment and designated as the 7th Cavalry Regiment on July 9, 1863.

First Commander: Solomon G. Kitchen (Lieutenant Colonel)

Assignments: Unattached, Marmaduke's District of Arkansas, Trans-Mississippi Department (April 1863)

Burbridge's Brigade, Marmaduke's Cavalry Division, District of Arkansas, Trans-Mississippi Department (April 1863)

Unattached, Marmaduke's Cavalry Division, District of Arkansas, Trans-Mississippi Department (April-June 1863)

Marmaduke's Brigade, Marmaduke's Cavalry Division, District of Arkansas, Trans-Mississippi Department (June-July 1863)

Battle: Marmaduke's Expedition into Missouri (April 17-May 2, 1863)

86. MISSOURI LAWTHER'S TEMPORARY DISMOUNTED CAVALRY REGIMENT

Organization: This unit does not appear in the *Official Records*.

First Commander: Robert R. Lawther (Colonel)

87. MISSOURI MACDONALD'S CAVALRY REGIMENT

Organization: Organized in the fall of 1862. Apparently reduced to a battalion and designated as the 11th Cavalry Battalion in early 1863.

First Commander: Emmett MacDonald (Colonel)

Field Officers: George W. C. Bennett (Major)

Merritt L. Young (Lieutenant Colonel)

Assignments: Unattached, Marmaduke's Cavalry Division, 1st Corps, Trans-Mississippi Department (November-December 1862)

MacDonald's Brigade, Marmaduke's Cavalry Division, 1st Corps, Trans-Mississippi Department (December 1862)

Unattached, Marmaduke's Cavalry Division, District of Arkansas, Trans-Mississippi Department (December 1862-January 1863)

Battles: Cane Hill (November 28, 1862)

Prairie Grove (December 7, 1862)

Marmaduke's Expedition into Missouri (December 31, 1862-January 25, 1863)

Springfield (January 8, 1863)

Hartville (January 11, 1863)

88. MISSOURI PEERY'S CAVALRY REGIMENT

Organization: Failed to complete organization. This unit does not appear in the *Official Records*.

First Commander: William F. Peery (Colonel)

89. MISSOURI PERKINS' CAVALRY REGIMENT

Organization: Organized in the summer of 1864. NOTE: On December 15, 1864 this regiment was listed as being unarmed. Apparently disbanded in late 1864.

First Commander: Caleb Perkins (Colonel)

Assignment: Tyler's Cavalry Brigade, Army of Missouri, Trans-Mississippi Department (August-October 1864)

Battle: Price's Missouri Raid (August-October 1864)

90. MISSOURI PRESTON'S CAVALRY BATTALION

Organization: Apparently failed to complete its organization. This unit does not appear in the *Official Records*.

First Commander: William I. Preston (Major)

91. MISSOURI REVES' CAVALRY BATTALION

Organization: Organized in the spring of 1864. Increased to a regiment and designated as the 15th Cavalry Regiment in the summer of 1864.

First Commander: Timothy Reves (Major)

Assignment: McCray's Brigade, Sub-District of Northern Arkansas [Shelby], District of Arkansas, Trans-Mississippi Department (June 1864)

92. MISSOURI SCHNABLE'S CAVALRY BATTALION

Organization: Organized with six companies in the summer of 1864. Probably surrendered at Yellville, Arkansas in May or June 1865.

First Commander: John A. Schnable (Lieutenant Colonel)

Assignment: Jackman's Brigade, Shelby's Division, Army of Missouri, Trans-Mississippi Department (August-December 1864)

Battle: Price's Missouri Raid (August-October 1864)

93. MISSOURI SEARCY'S CAVALRY REGIMENT

Organization: Organized in the summer of 1864. Apparently dismounted and surrendered by General E. K. Smith, commanding Trans-Mississippi Department, on May 26, 1865.

First Commander: James J. Searcy (Colonel)

Assignment: Tyler's Cavalry Brigade, Army of Missouri, Trans-Mississippi Department (August-December 1864)

Battle: Price's Missouri Raid (August-October 1864)

94. MISSOURI SHANKS' CAVALRY BATTALION

Organization: Organized in early 1863. Apparently disbanded in late 1863.
First Commander: David Shanks (Major)
Assignment: Shelby's-Thompson's Brigade, Marmaduke's Cavalry Division, District of Arkansas, Trans-Mississippi Department (April-October 1863)
Battles: Marmaduke's Expedition into Missouri (April 17-May 2, 1863)
Patterson [skirmish] (April 20, 1863)
Jackson (April 26, 1863)
Shelby's Raid in Arkansas and Missouri (September 22-October 26, 1863)
Marshall (October 13, 1863)

95. MISSOURI SLAYBACK'S CAVALRY BATTALION

Organization: Organized in the summer of 1864. Apparently disbanded in December 1864.
First Commander: Alonzo W. Slayback (Colonel)
Field Officer: Caleb W. Dorsey (Lieutenant Colonel)
Assignment: Shelby's-Shanks'-Smith's-Thompson's Brigade, Shelby's Cavalry Division, Army of Missouri, Trans-Mississippi Department (August-December 1864)
Battle: Price's Missouri Raid (August-October 1864)

96. MISSOURI SNIDER'S CAVALRY BATTALION

Nickname: Northeast Cavalry Battalion
Organization: Apparently failed to complete its organization. This unit does not appear in the *Official Records.*
First Commander: Henry G. Snider (Major)

97. MISSOURI WILLIAMS' CAVALRY BATTALION

Organization: Organized in the summer of 1864. Apparently disbanded in early 1865.
First Commander: D. A. Williams (Lieutenant Colonel)
Assignment: Jackman's Brigade, Shelby's Cavalry Division, Army of Missouri, Trans-Mississippi Department (August-December 1864)
Battle: Price's Missouri Raid (August-October 1864)

98. MISSOURI WOODSON'S CAVALRY COMPANY

Organization: Organized in early 1864. Appears in Confederate records into February 1865 and Federal records into April 1865. Presumably included in the surrender of the Department of Northern Virginia by General Robert E. Lee at Appomattox Court House, Virginia on April 9, 1865.
First Commander: Charles H. Woodson (Captain)

Assignment: Northwest Virginia Brigade, Department of Northern Virginia (February-May 1864)
Battles: New Market (May 15, 1864)
New Creek (November 28, 1864)

INFANTRY

99. MISSOURI 1ST INFANTRY BATTALION

Organization: Organized in early 1862. Consolidated with Fagin's and MacFarlane's Infantry Battalions and designated as the 4th Infantry Regiment on April 30, 1862. This unit does not appear in the *Official Records*.

First Commander: Waldo P. Johnson (Major)

Assignments: Greene's Brigade, Confederate Volunteers, Missouri State Guard, Trans-Mississippi District, Department #2 (February-March 1862)

Greene's Brigade, Trans-Mississippi District, Department #2 (March-April 1862)

Battle: Pea Ridge (March 7-8, 1862)

Further Reading: Bevier, R. S., *History of the First and Second Missouri Confederate Brigades 1861-1865*. Anderson, Ephraim McD., *Memoirs: Historical and Personal; Including the Campaigns of the First Missouri Confederate Brigade*.

100. MISSOURI 1ST INFANTRY REGIMENT

Organization: Organized on June 11, 1861. Consolidated with the 4th Infantry Regiment and designated as the 1st and 4th Consolidated Infantry Regiment at Holly Springs, Mississippi on November 7, 1862.

First Commander: John S. Bowen (Colonel)

Field Officers: Martin Burke (Major, Lieutenant Colonel)

Charles C. Campbell (Major)

Robert J. Duffy (Major)

Hugh A. Garland (Colonel)

Bradford Keith (Major)

Lucius L. Rich (Lieutenant Colonel)

Amos C. Riley (Lieutenant Colonel)

Assignments: McCown's Brigade, 1st Geographical Division, Department #2 (September 1861)

Bowen's Brigade, 1st Geographical Division, Department #2 (October 1861)

Martin's Brigade, Bowen's Division, 1st Geographical Division, Department #2 (October-December 1861)

Bowen's Brigade, Central Army of Kentucky, Department #2 (January-February 1862)

Bowen's Brigade, Pillow's Division, Central Army of Kentucky, Department #2 (February-March 1862)

Bowen's-Helm's Brigade, Reserve Corps, Army of the Mississippi, Department #2 (March-June 1862)

Bowen's Brigade, District of the Mississippi, Department #2 (June-September 1862)

Bowen's Brigade, Lovell's Division, District of the Mississippi, Department #2 (September-October 1862)

Missouri Brigade, Bowen's Division, Price's Corps, Army of West Tennessee, Department of Mississippi and East Louisiana (October-November 1862)

Battles: Shiloh (April 6-7, 1862)

Corinth Campaign (April-June 1862)

Vicksburg Bombardments (May 18-July 27, 1862)

Corinth (October 3-4, 1862)

Further Reading: Bevier, R. S., *History of the First and Second Missouri Confederate Brigades 1861-1865*. Anderson, Ephraim McD., *Memoirs: Historical and Personal; Including the Campaigns of the First Missouri Confederate Brigade*.

101. MISSOURI 1ST AND 4TH CONSOLIDATED INFANTRY REGIMENT

Organization: Organized by the consolidation of the 1st and 4th Infantry Regiments at Holly Springs, Mississippi on November 7, 1862. Regiment surrendered at Vicksburg, Warren County, Mississippi on July 4, 1863. Paroled at Vicksburg, Warren County, Mississippi in July 1863. Declared exchanged on September 12, 1863. Surrendered by Lieutenant Richard Taylor, commanding the Department of Alabama, Mississippi, and East Louisiana, at Meridian, Mississippi on May 4, 1865.

First Commander: Archibald MacFarlane (Colonel)

Field Officers: Hugh A. Garland (Major, Lieutenant Colonel)

Amos C. Riley (Lieutenant Colonel, Colonel)

Assignments: Missouri Brigade, Bowen's Division, Price's Corps, Army of West Tennessee, Department of Mississippi and East Louisiana (November-December 1862)

Missouri Brigade, Bowen's Division, 2nd Corps, Army of North Mississippi, Department of Mississippi and East Louisiana (December 1862-January 1863)
Missouri Brigade, Price's Division, Army of the Department of Mississippi and East Louisiana (January-February 1863)
Missouri Brigade, Forney's-Bowen's Division, 2nd Military District, Department of Mississippi and East Louisiana (February-April 1863)
Missouri Brigade, Bowen's Division, Department of Mississippi and East Louisiana (April-July 1863)
Missouri Brigade, Department of Mississippi and East Louisiana (November 1863-January 1864)
Missouri Brigade, Department of the Gulf (January-February 1864)
Missouri Brigade, French's Division, Department of Alabama, Mississippi, and East Louisiana (February-May 1864)
Missouri Brigade, French's Division, Army of Mississippi (May-July 1864)
Missouri Brigade, French's Division, 3rd Corps, Army of Tennessee (July 1864-January 1865)
Missouri Brigade, French's Division, District of the Gulf, Department of Alabama, Mississippi, and East Louisiana (February-April 1865)
Missouri Brigade, French's Division, Department of Alabama, Mississippi, and East Louisiana (April 1865)
Battles: Grand Gulf (March 19, 1863)
Dunbar's Plantation, near Bayou Vidal (April 15, 1863)
Vicksburg Campaign (May-July 1863)
Champion's Hill (May 16, 1863)
Big Black River Bridge (May 17, 1863)
Vicksburg Siege (May-July 1863)
Meridian Campaign (February-March 1864)
Atlanta Campaign (May-September 1864)
New Hope Church (May 25-June 4, 1864)
Lattimer's Mills (June 20, 1864)
Kennesaw Mountain (June 27, 1864)
Smyrna Campground (July 4, 1864)
Chattahoochee River (July 5-17, 1864)
Atlanta (July 22, 1864)
Atlanta Siege (July-September 1864)
Jonesboro (August 31-September 1, 1864)
Lovejoy's Station (September 2-5, 1864)
Allatoona (October 5, 1864)
Franklin (November 30, 1864)
Mobile (March 17-April 12, 1865)

Fort Blakely (April 1-9, 1865)
Further Reading: Bevier, R. S., *History of the First and Second Missouri Confederate Brigades 1861-1865*. Anderson, Ephraim McD., *Memoirs: Historical and Personal; Including the Campaigns of the First Missouri Confederate Brigade.*

102. MISSOURI 1ST (BURBRIDGE'S) INFANTRY REGIMENT

See: MISSOURI 2ND INFANTRY REGIMENT

103. MISSOURI 2ND INFANTRY BATTALION

Organization: Organized with seven companies on January 28, 1862. Consolidated with three companies and designated as the 5th Infantry Regiment in May 1862.
First Commander: James McCown (Lieutenant Colonel)
Field Officer: Robert S. Bevier (Major)
Assignments: Slack's Brigade, Confederate Volunteers, Missouri State Guard, Trans-Mississippi District, Department #2 (January-March 1862)
Greene's Brigade, Trans-Mississippi District, Department #2 (March-April 1862)
Greene's Brigade, Army of the West, Department #2 (April-May 1862)
Battles: Pea Ridge (March 7-8, 1862)
Corinth Campaign (April-June 1862)
Further Reading: Bevier, R. S., *History of the First and Second Missouri Confederate Brigades 1861-1865*. Anderson, Ephraim McD., *Memoirs: Historical and Personal; Including the Campaigns of the First Missouri Confederate Brigade.*

104. MISSOURI 2ND INFANTRY REGIMENT

Also Known As: 1st Infantry Regiment
Organization: Organized as the 1st Infantry Regiment from the Missouri State Guard on January 16, 1862. Later designated as the 2nd Infantry Regiment. Regiment surrendered at Vicksburg, Warren County, Mississippi on July 4, 1863. Paroled at Vicksburg, Warren County, Mississippi in July 1863. Declared exchanged on September 12, 1863. Field consolidation with the 6th Infantry Regiment from September 1863 to April 1865. Surrendered by Lieutenant Richard Taylor, commanding the Department of Alabama, Mississippi, and East Louisiana, at Meridian, Mississippi on May 4, 1865.
First Commander: John Q. Burbridge (Colonel)
Field Officers: Thomas M. Carter (Major, Lieutenant Colonel)
William F. Carter (Major)
Francis M. Cockrell (Lieutenant Colonel, Colonel)

Robert D. A. Dwyer (Major)
Peter C. Flournoy (Colonel)
Edward B. Hull (Lieutenant Colonel)
Pembroke S. Senteny (Major, Lieutenant Colonel)

Assignments: Little's Brigade, Confederate Volunteers, Missouri State Guard, Trans-Mississippi District, Department #2 (January-April 1862)
Little's-Gates' Brigade, Price's-Little's Division, Army of the West, Department #2 (April-July 1862)
Gates' Brigade, Little's-Hébert's-Green's Division, Price's Corps, Army of West Tennessee, Department #2 (July-October 1862)
Green's Brigade, Bowen's Division, Army of West Tennessee, Department of Mississippi and East Louisiana (October-November 1862)
Missouri Brigade, Bowen's Division, Price's Corps, Army of West Tennessee, Department of Mississippi and East Louisiana (November-December 1862)
Missouri Brigade, Bowen's Division, 2nd Corps, Army of North Mississippi, Department of Mississippi and East Louisiana (December 1862-January 1863)
Missouri Brigade, Price's Division, Army of the Department of Mississippi and East Louisiana (January-February 1863)
Missouri Brigade, Forney's-Bowen's Division, 2nd Military District, Department of Mississippi and East Louisiana (February-April 1863)
Missouri Brigade, Bowen's Division, Department of Mississippi and East Louisiana (April-July 1863)
Missouri Brigade, Department of Mississippi and East Louisiana (November-December 1863)
Missouri Brigade, Department of the Gulf (January-February 1864)
Missouri Brigade, French's Division, Department of Alabama, Mississippi, and East Louisiana (February-May 1864)
Missouri Brigade, French's Division, Army of Mississippi (May-July 1864)
Missouri Brigade, French's Division, 3rd Corps, Army of Tennessee (July 1864-January 1865)
Missouri Brigade, French's Division, District of the Gulf, Department of Alabama, Mississippi, and East Louisiana (February-April 1865)
Missouri Brigade, French's Division, Department of Alabama, Mississippi, and East Louisiana (April 1865)

Battles: Pea Ridge (March 7-8, 1862)
Corinth Campaign (April-June 1862)
Iuka (September 19, 1862)
Corinth (October 3-4, 1862)
Grand Gulf (March 19, 1863)
Vicksburg Campaign (May-July 1863)

Champion's Hill (May 16, 1863)
Big Black River Bridge (May 17, 1863)
Vicksburg Siege (May-July 1863)
Meridian Campaign (February-March 1864)
Atlanta Campaign (May-September 1864)
New Hope Church (May 25-June 4, 1864)
Lattimer's Mills (June 20, 1864)
Kennesaw Mountain (June 27, 1864)
Smyrna Campground (July 4, 1864)
Chattahoochee River (July 5-17, 1864)
Atlanta (July 22, 1864)
Atlanta Siege (July-September 1864)
Jonesboro (August 31-September 1, 1864)
Lovejoy's Station (September 2-5, 1864)
Allatoona (October 5, 1864)
Franklin (November 30, 1864)
Mobile (March 17-April 12, 1865)
Fort Blakely (April 1-9, 1865)

Further Reading: Bevier, R. S., *History of the First and Second Missouri Confederate Brigades 1861-1865*. Anderson, Ephraim McD., *Memoirs: Historical and Personal; Including the Campaigns of the First Missouri Confederate Brigade.*

105. MISSOURI 2ND (HUNTER'S) INFANTRY REGIMENT

Organization: Organized on September 15, 1862. Designated as the 8th (Hunter's-Burns') Infantry Regiment on April 1, 1863.

First Commander: DeWitt C. Hunter (Colonel)

Field Officers: Simon P. Burns (Lieutenant Colonel)
Thomas H. Murray (Major)

Assignments: Parson's Brigade, Frost's Division, Trans-Mississippi Department (December 1862)
Steen's Brigade, Parson's Division, 1st Corps, Trans-Mississippi Department (December 1862-January 1863)
Parson's Brigade, Hindman's Division, District of Arkansas, Trans-Mississippi Department (January-February 1863)
Parson's Brigade, Price's Division, District of Arkansas, Trans-Mississippi Department (April 1862-April 1863)

Battles: Reed's Mountain (December 6, 1862)
Prairie Grove (December 7, 1862)

106. MISSOURI 2ND (RIVES') INFANTRY REGIMENT

See: MISSOURI 3RD INFANTRY REGIMENT

107. MISSOURI 3RD INFANTRY BATTALION

Also Known As: 5th Infantry Battalion

Organization: Organized with eight companies in early 1862. Consolidated with Hedgpeth's Infantry Battalion and designated as the 6th Infantry Regiment at Guntown, Mississippi in May 1862. This unit does not appear in the *Official Records.*

First Commander: Eugene Erwin (Lieutenant Colonel)

Field Officer: Joseph P. Vaughan (Major)

Assignment: Green's Brigade, Price's Division, Army of the West, Department #2 (May 1862)

Further Reading: Bevier, R. S., *History of the First and Second Missouri Confederate Brigades 1861-1865.* Anderson, Ephraim McD., *Memoirs: Historical and Personal; Including the Campaigns of the First Missouri Confederate Brigade.*

108. MISSOURI 3RD INFANTRY REGIMENT

Also Known As: 2nd Infantry Regiment

Organization: Organized as the 2nd Infantry Regiment on January 16, 1862. Later designated as the 3rd Infantry Regiment. Regiment surrendered at Vicksburg, Warren County, Mississippi on July 4, 1863. Paroled at Vicksburg, Warren County, Mississippi in July 1863. Declared exchanged on September 12, 1863. Field consolidation with the 5th Infantry Regiment from September 1863 to April 1865. Surrendered by Lieutenant Richard Taylor, commanding the Department of Alabama, Mississippi, and East Louisiana, at Meridian, Mississippi on May 4, 1865.

First Commander: Benjamin A. Rives (Colonel)

Field Officers: William R. Gause (Lieutenant Colonel, Colonel)

Finley L. Hubbell (Major, Lieutenant Colonel)

James K. McDowell (Major, Lieutenant Colonel)

James A. Pritchard (Lieutenant Colonel, Colonel)

Robert J. Williams (Major)

Assignments: Little's Brigade, Confederate Volunteers, Missouri State Guard, Trans-Mississippi District, Department #2 (January-April 1862)

Little's-Gates' Brigade, Price's-Little's Division, Army of the West, Department #2 (April-July 1862)

Gates' Brigade, Little's-Hébert's-Green's Division, Price's Corps, Army of West Tennessee, Department #2 (July-October 1862)

Green's Brigade, Bowen's Division, Army of West Tennessee, Department of Mississippi and East Louisiana (October-November 1862)
Missouri Brigade, Bowen's Division, Price's Corps, Army of West Tennessee, Department of Mississippi and East Louisiana (November-December 1862)
Missouri Brigade, Bowen's Division, 2nd Corps, Army of North Mississippi, Department of Mississippi and East Louisiana (December 1862-January 1863)
Missouri Brigade, Price's Division, Army of the Department of Mississippi and East Louisiana (January-February 1863)
Missouri Brigade, Forney's-Bowen's Division, 2nd Military District, Department of Mississippi and East Louisiana (February-April 1863)
Missouri Brigade, Bowen's Division, Department of Mississippi and East Louisiana (April-July 1863)
Missouri Brigade, Department of Mississippi and East Louisiana (November-December 1863)
Missouri Brigade, Department of the Gulf (January-February 1864)
Missouri Brigade, French's Division, Department of Alabama, Mississippi, and East Louisiana (February-May 1864)
Missouri Brigade, French's Division, Army of Mississippi (May-July 1864)
Missouri Brigade, French's Division, 3rd Corps, Army of Tennessee (July 1864-January 1865)
Missouri Brigade, French's Division, District of the Gulf, Department of Alabama, Mississippi, and East Louisiana (February-April 1865)
Missouri Brigade, French's Division, Department of Alabama, Mississippi, and East Louisiana (April 1865)
Battles: Pea Ridge (March 7-8, 1862)
Corinth Campaign (April-June 1862)
Iuka (September 19, 1862)
Corinth (October 3-4, 1862)
Grand Gulf (March 19, 1863)
Vicksburg Campaign (May-July 1863)
Champion's Hill (May 16, 1863)
Big Black River Bridge (May 17, 1863)
Vicksburg Siege (May-July 1863)
Meridian Campaign (February-March 1864)
Atlanta Campaign (May-September 1864)
New Hope Church (May 25-June 4, 1864)
Lattimer's Mills (June 20, 1864)
Kennesaw Mountain (June 27, 1864)
Smyrna Campground (July 4, 1864)
Chattahoochee River (July 5-17, 1864)

Atlanta (July 22, 1864)
Atlanta Siege (July-September 1864)
Jonesboro (August 31-September 1, 1864)
Lovejoy's Station (September 2-5, 1864)
Allatoona (October 5, 1864)
Franklin (November 30, 1864)
Mobile (March 17-April 12, 1865)
Fort Blakely (April 1-9, 1865)
Further Reading: Bevier, R. S., *History of the First and Second Missouri Confederate Brigades 1861-1865*. Anderson, Ephraim McD., *Memoirs: Historical and Personal; Including the Campaigns of the First Missouri Confederate Brigade.*

109. MISSOURI 4TH INFANTRY REGIMENT

Organization: Organized by the consolidation of the 1st, MacFarlane's, and Fagin's Infantry Battalions on April 30, 1862. Consolidated with the 4th Infantry Regiment and designated as the 1st and 4th Consolidated Infantry Regiment at Holly Springs, Mississippi on November 7, 1862.
First Commander: Archibald MacFarlane (Colonel)
Field Officers: Waldo P. Johnson (Lieutenant Colonel)
Stephen W. Wood (Major)
Assignments: MacFarlane's-Green's Brigade, Price's-Little's Division, Army of the West, Department #2 (May-July 1862)
Green's Brigade, Little's Division, Price's Corps, Army of West Tennessee, Department #2 (July-October 1862)
Missouri Brigade, Bowen's Division, Price's Corps, Army of West Tennessee, Department of Mississippi and East Louisiana (October-November 1862)
Battles: Corinth Campaign (April-June 1862)
Iuka (September 19, 1862)
Corinth (October 3-4, 1862)
Further Reading: Bevier, R. S., *History of the First and Second Missouri Confederate Brigades 1861-1865*. Anderson, Ephraim McD., *Memoirs: Historical and Personal; Including the Campaigns of the First Missouri Confederate Brigade.*

110. MISSOURI 5TH INFANTRY BATTALION

See: MISSOURI 3RD INFANTRY BATTALION

111. MISSOURI 5TH INFANTRY REGIMENT

Also Known As: 3rd Infantry Regiment

Organization: Organized by the addition of three companies to the 2nd Infantry Battalion in May 1862. Regiment surrendered at Vicksburg, Warren County, Mississippi on July 4, 1863. Paroled at Vicksburg, Warren County, Mississippi in July 1863. Declared exchanged on September 12, 1863. Field consolidation with the 3rd Infantry Regiment from September 1863 to April 1865. Surrendered by Lieutenant Richard Taylor, commanding the Department of Alabama, Mississippi, and East Louisiana, at Meridian, Mississippi on May 4, 1865.

First Commander: James McCown (Colonel)

Field Officers: Robert S. Bevier (Lieutenant Colonel)

Owen A. Waddell (Major)

Assignments: Little's-Gates' Brigade, Price's-Little's Division, Army of the West, Department #2 (May-July 1862)

Gates' Brigade, Little's-Hébert's-Green's Division, Price's Corps, Army of West Tennessee, Department #2 (July-October 1862)

Green's Brigade, Bowen's Division, Army of West Tennessee, Department of Mississippi and East Louisiana (October-November 1862)

Missouri Brigade, Bowen's Division, Price's Corps, Army of West Tennessee, Department of Mississippi and East Louisiana (November-December 1862)

Missouri Brigade, Bowen's Division, 2nd Corps, Army of North Mississippi, Department of Mississippi and East Louisiana (December 1862-January 1863)

Missouri Brigade, Price's Division, Army of the Department of Mississippi and East Louisiana (January-February 1863)

Missouri Brigade, Forney's-Bowen's Division, 2nd Military District, Department of Mississippi and East Louisiana (February-April 1863)

Missouri Brigade, Bowen's Division, Department of Mississippi and East Louisiana (April-July 1863)

Missouri Brigade, Department of Mississippi and East Louisiana (November-December 1863)

Missouri Brigade, Department of the Gulf (January-February 1864)

Missouri Brigade, French's Division, Department of Alabama, Mississippi, and East Louisiana (February-May 1864)

Missouri Brigade, French's Division, Army of Mississippi (May-July 1864)

Missouri Brigade, French's Division, 3rd Corps, Army of Tennessee (July 1864-January 1865)

Missouri Brigade, French's Division, District of the Gulf, Department of Alabama, Mississippi, and East Louisiana (February-April 1865)

Missouri Brigade, French's Division, Department of Alabama, Mississippi, and East Louisiana (April 1865)

Battles: Corinth Campaign (April-June 1862)

Iuka (September 19, 1862)
Corinth (October 3-4, 1862)
Grand Gulf (March 19, 1863)
Vicksburg Campaign (May-July 1863)
Champion's Hill (May 16, 1863)
Big Black River Bridge (May 17, 1863)
Vicksburg Siege (May-July 1863)
Meridian Campaign (February-March 1864)
Atlanta Campaign (May-September 1864)
New Hope Church (May 25-June 4, 1864)
Lattimer's Mills (June 20, 1864)
Kennesaw Mountain (June 27, 1864)
Smyrna Campground (July 4, 1864)
Chattahoochee River (July 5-17, 1864)
Atlanta (July 22, 1864)
Atlanta Siege (July-September 1864)
Jonesboro (August 31-September 1, 1864)
Lovejoy's Station (September 2-5, 1864)
Allatoona (October 5, 1864)
Franklin (November 30, 1864)
Mobile (March 17-April 12, 1865)
Fort Blakely (April 1-9, 1865)
Further Reading: Bevier, R. S., *History of the First and Second Missouri Confederate Brigades 1861-1865*. Anderson, Ephraim McD., *Memoirs: Historical and Personal; Including the Campaigns of the First Missouri Confederate Brigade.*

112. MISSOURI 6TH INFANTRY REGIMENT

Organization: Organized by the consolidation of the 3rd and Hedgpeth's Infantry Battalions at Guntown, Mississippi in May 1862. Regiment surrendered at Vicksburg, Warren County, Mississippi on July 4, 1863. Paroled at Vicksburg, Warren County, Mississippi in July 1863. Declared exchanged on September 12, 1863. Field consolidation with the 2nd Infantry Regiment from September 1863 to April 1865. Surrendered by Lieutenant Richard Taylor, commanding the Department of Alabama, Mississippi, and East Louisiana, at Meridian, Mississippi on May 4, 1865.
First Commander: Eugene Erwin (Colonel)
Field Officers: Stephen Cooper (Major, Lieutenant Colonel)
Jephta Duncan (Major)
Isaac N. Hedgpeth (Lieutenant Colonel, Colonel)
Joseph P. Vaughan (Major)

Assignments: Green's Brigade, Price's-Little's Division, Army of the West, Department #2 (May-July 1862)
Green's Brigade, Little's-Hébert's-Green's Division, Price's Corps, Army of West Tennessee, Department #2 (July-October 1862)
Green's Brigade, Bowen's Division, Army of West Tennessee, Department of Mississippi and East Louisiana (October-November 1862)
Missouri Brigade, Bowen's Division, Price's Corps, Army of West Tennessee, Department of Mississippi and East Louisiana (November-December 1862)
Missouri Brigade, Bowen's Division, 2nd Corps, Army of North Mississippi, Department of Mississippi and East Louisiana (December 1862-January 1863)
Missouri Brigade, Price's Division, Army of the Department of Mississippi and East Louisiana (January-February 1863)
Missouri Brigade, Forney's-Bowen's Division, 2nd Military District, Department of Mississippi and East Louisiana (February-April 1863)
Missouri Brigade, Bowen's Division, Department of Mississippi and East Louisiana (April-July 1863)
Missouri Brigade, Department of Mississippi and East Louisiana (November-December 1863)
Missouri Brigade, Department of the Gulf (January-February 1864)
Missouri Brigade, French's Division, Department of Alabama, Mississippi, and East Louisiana (February-May 1864)
Missouri Brigade, French's Division, Army of Mississippi (May-July 1864)
Missouri Brigade, French's Division, 3rd Corps, Army of Tennessee (July 1864-January 1865)
Missouri Brigade, French's Division, District of the Gulf, Department of Alabama, Mississippi, and East Louisiana (February-April 1865)
Missouri Brigade, French's Division, Department of Alabama, Mississippi, and East Louisiana (April 1865)
Battles: Corinth Campaign (April-June 1862)
Iuka (September 19, 1862)
Corinth (October 3-4, 1862)
Grand Gulf (March 19, 1863)
Vicksburg Campaign (May-July 1863)
Champion's Hill (May 16, 1863)
Big Black River Bridge (May 17, 1863)
Vicksburg Siege (May-July 1863)
Meridian Campaign (February-March 1864)
Atlanta Campaign (May-September 1864)
New Hope Church (May 25-June 4, 1864)
Lattimer's Mills (June 20, 1864)

Kennesaw Mountain (June 27, 1864)
Smyrna Campground (July 4, 1864)
Chattahoochee River (July 5-17, 1864)
Atlanta (July 22, 1864)
Atlanta Siege (July-September 1864)
Jonesboro (August 31-September 1, 1864)
Lovejoy's Station (September 2-5, 1864)
Allatoona (October 5, 1864)
Franklin (November 30, 1864)
Mobile (March 17-April 12, 1865)
Fort Blakely (April 1-9, 1865)
Further Reading: Bevier, R. S., *History of the First and Second Missouri Confederate Brigades 1861-1865*. Anderson, Ephraim McD., *Memoirs: Historical and Personal; Including the Campaigns of the First Missouri Confederate Brigade.*

113. MISSOURI 7TH INFANTRY BATTALION

Organization: Organized in late 1862. Increased to a regiment and designated as the 8th (Mitchell's) Infantry Regiment on January 23, 1863. This unit does not appear in the *Official Records.*
First Commander: Charles S. Mitchell (Lieutenant Colonel)
Field Officer: John W. Smizer (Major)
Assignment: Frost's Brigade, Hindman's Division, District of Arkansas, Trans-Mississippi Department (January 1863)
Battle: Prairie Grove (December 7, 1862)

114. MISSOURI 7TH INFANTRY REGIMENT

Organization: This unit does not appear in the *Official Records.*
First Commander: Cyrus Franklin (Colonel)
Field Officer: Elliott D. Majors (Major)

115. MISSOURI 7TH (JACKMAN'S-CALDWELL'S) INFANTRY REGIMENT

See: MISSOURI 16TH INFANTRY REGIMENT

116. MISSOURI 8TH INFANTRY BATTALION

Organization: Organized in 1862. Consolidated with Clarkson's-Buster's Cavalry Battalion and designated as the 9th (Clark's) Infantry Regiment on November 16, 1862.
First Commander: Richard H. Musser (Lieutenant Colonel)
Field Officer: Richard Gaines (Major)

117. MISSOURI 8TH (HUNTER'S-BURNS') INFANTRY REGIMENT

Organization: Organized by the redesignation of the 2nd (Hunter's) Infantry Regiment on April 1, 1863. Redesignated as the 11th Infantry Regiment in late 1863.

First Commander: DeWitt C. Hunter (Colonel)

Field Officers: Simon P. Burns (Lieutenant Colonel, Colonel)

Thomas H. Murray (Major, Lieutenant Colonel)

James Phillips (Major)

Assignment: Parson's Brigade, Price's Division, District of Arkansas, Trans-Mississippi Department (July-November 1863)

Battles: Helena (July 4, 1863)

Shelby's Raid in Arkansas and Missouri (September 22-October 26, 1863)

118. MISSOURI 8TH (MITCHELL'S) INFANTRY REGIMENT

Organization: Organized by the increase of the 7th Infantry Battalion to a regiment on January 23, 1863. Surrendered by General E. K. Smith, commanding Trans-Mississippi Department, on May 26, 1865.

First Commander: Charles S. Mitchell (Colonel)

Field Officers: John W. Hill (Major)

John W. Smizer (Lieutenant Colonel)

Assignments: Frost's Brigade, Hindman's Division, District of Arkansas, Trans-Mississippi Department (January 1863)

Clark's Brigade, Frost's Division, District of Arkansas, Trans-Mississippi Department (May-June 1863)

Drayton's Brigade, Price's Division, District of Arkansas, Trans-Mississippi Department (November 1863)

Parsons'-Burns' Brigade, Price's Division, District of Arkansas, Trans-Mississippi Department (January-March 1864)

Burns' Brigade, Parsons' Division, District of Arkansas, Trans-Mississippi Department (March-April 1864)

Burns' Brigade, Parsons' Division, Detachment District of Arkansas, District of West Louisiana, Trans-Mississippi Department (April 1864)

Burns' Brigade, Parsons' Division, District of Arkansas, Trans-Mississippi Department (April-September 1864)

1st Missouri Brigade, 1st Missouri Division, 2nd Corps, Trans-Mississippi Department (September 1864-April 1865)

Battles: Red River Campaign (March-May 1864)

Pleasant Hill (April 9, 1864)

Camden Expedition (March-May 1864)

Jenkins' Ferry (April 30, 1864)

119. MISSOURI 9TH INFANTRY BATTALION SHARPSHOOTERS

Organization: Organized in late 1862. Surrendered by General E. K. Smith, commanding Trans-Mississippi Department, on May 26, 1865.

First Commander: Lebbeus A. Pindall (Major)

Assignments: Parsons'-Burns' Brigade, Hindman's-Price's Division, District of Arkansas, Trans-Mississippi Department (January 1863-March 1864)

Burns' Brigade, Parsons' Division, District of Arkansas, Trans-Mississippi Department (March-April 1864)

Burns' Brigade, Parsons' Division, Detachment District of Arkansas, District of West Louisiana, Trans-Mississippi Department (April 1864)

Burns' Brigade, Parsons' Division, District of Arkansas, Trans-Mississippi Department (April-September 1864)

1st Missouri Brigade, 1st Missouri Division, 2nd Corps, Trans-Mississippi Department (September 1864-April 1865)

Battles: Helena (July 4, 1863)

Red River Campaign (March-May 1864)

Pleasant Hill (April 9, 1864)

Camden Expedition (March-May 1864)

Jenkins' Ferry (April 30, 1864)

120. MISSOURI 9TH (CLARK'S) INFANTRY REGIMENT

Organization: Organized by the consolidation of the 8th Infantry Battalion and Clarkson's-Buster's Cavalry Battalion on November 16, 1862. Surrendered by General E. K. Smith, commanding Trans-Mississippi Department, on May 26, 1865.

First Commander: John B. Clark, Jr. (Colonel)

Field Officers: Michael W. Buster (Lieutenant Colonel)

Richard Gaines (Major)

Harry H. Hughes (Major)

Richard H. Musser (Lieutenant Colonel)

Assignments: Frost's Brigade, Hindman's Division, District of Arkansas, Trans-Mississippi Department (December 1862-January 1863)

Clark's Brigade, Frost's Division, District of Arkansas, Trans-Mississippi Department (May-June 1863)

Drayton's Brigade, Price's Division, District of Arkansas, Trans-Mississippi Department (November 1863)

Parsons'-Burns' Brigade, Price's Division, District of Arkansas, Trans-Mississippi Department (January-March 1864)

Burns' Brigade, Parsons' Division, District of Arkansas, Trans-Mississippi Department (March-April 1864)

Burns' Brigade, Parsons' Division, Detachment District of Arkansas, District of West Louisiana, Trans-Mississippi Department (April 1864)
Burns' Brigade, Parsons' Division, District of Arkansas, Trans-Mississippi Department (April-September 1864)
1st Missouri Brigade, 1st Missouri Division, 2nd Corps, Trans-Mississippi Department (September 1864-April 1865)
Battles: Prairie Grove (December 7, 1862)
near Doniphan (March 21, 1863)
Red River Campaign (March-May 1864)
Pleasant Hill (April 9, 1864)
Camden Expedition (March-May 1864)
Jenkins' Ferry (April 30, 1864)
Further Reading: Mudd, Joseph Aloysius, *With Porter in North Missouri.*

121. MISSOURI 9TH (WHITE'S) INFANTRY REGIMENT

See: MISSOURI 12TH INFANTRY REGIMENT

122. MISSOURI 10TH INFANTRY REGIMENT

Also Known As: 12th (Steen's-Pickett's-Moore's) Infantry Regiment
Organization: Organized on November 10, 1862. Designated as the 10th Infantry Regiment on April 1, 1863. Surrendered by General E. K. Smith, commanding Trans-Mississippi Department, on May 26, 1865.
First Commander: Alexander E. Steen (Colonel)
Field Officers: Simon Harris (Major, Lieutenant Colonel)
Elijah Magoffin (Major)
William M. Moore (Lieutenant Colonel, Colonel)
Alexander C. Pickett (Colonel)
Assignments: Parsons' Brigade, Hindman's Division, Trans-Mississippi Department (January-February 1863)
Parsons' Brigade, Price's Division, District of Arkansas, Trans-Mississippi Department (July 1863-March 1864)
Burns' Brigade, Missouri (Parsons') Division, District of Arkansas, Trans-Mississippi Department (March-April 1864)
Burns' Brigade, Missouri (Parsons') Division, Detachment District of Arkansas, District of West Louisiana, Trans-Mississippi Department (April 1864)
Burns' Brigade, Missouri (Parsons') Division, District of Arkansas, Trans-Mississippi Department (April 1864)
2nd Missouri Brigade, 1st Missouri Division, 2nd Corps, Trans-Mississippi Department (September 1864-May 1865)
Battles: Helena (July 4, 1863)
Little Rock (September 10, 1863)

Red River Campaign (March-May 1864)
Pleasant Hill (April 9, 1864)
Camden Expedition (March-May 1864)
Jenkins' Ferry (April 30, 1864)

123. MISSOURI 11TH INFANTRY REGIMENT

Organization: Organized by the redesignation of the 8th (Burns') Infantry Regiment in late 1863. Surrendered by General E. K. Smith, commanding Trans-Mississippi Department, on May 26, 1865.
First Commander: Simon P. Burns (Colonel)
Field Officers: Thomas H. Murray (Lieutenant Colonel)
James Phillips (Major)
Assignments: Parsons'-Burns' Brigade, Price's-Drayton's Division, District of Arkansas, Trans-Mississippi Department (January-March 1864)
Burns' Brigade, Parsons' Division, District of Arkansas, Trans-Mississippi Department (March-April 1864)
Burns' Brigade, Parson's Division, Detachment District of Arkansas, District of West Louisiana, Trans-Mississippi Department (April 1864)
Burns' Brigade, Parson's Division, District of Arkansas, Trans-Mississippi Department (April-September 1864)
2nd (Missouri) Brigade, 1st Missouri Division, 2nd Corps, Trans-Mississippi Department (September 1864-April 1865)
Battles: Red River Campaign (March-May 1864)
Pleasant Hill (April 9, 1864)
Camden Expedition (March-May 1864)
Jenkins' Ferry (April 30, 1864)

124. MISSOURI 12TH INFANTRY REGIMENT

Also Known As: 3rd Infantry Regiment
9th Infantry Regiment
Organization: Organized as the 9th (White's) Infantry Regiment on October 22, 1862. Designated as the 12th Infantry Regiment on April 1, 1863. Surrendered by General E. K. Smith, commanding Trans-Mississippi Department, on May 26, 1865.
First Commander: James D. White (Colonel)
Field Officers: Richard C. Berryman (Major)
Benjamin Holmes (Major, Lieutenant Colonel)
Willis M. Ponder (Lieutenant Colonel, Colonel)
Thomas B. Sanford (Major)
Assignments: Steen's Brigade, Parsons' Division, District of Arkansas, Trans-Mississippi Department (January 1862-January 1863)

Parsons' Brigade, Hindman's-Price's-Drayton's Division, District of Arkansas, Trans-Mississippi Department (January 1863-March 1864)
Burns' Brigade, Parsons' Missouri Division, District of Arkansas, Trans-Mississippi Department (March-April 1864)
Burns' Brigade, Parsons' Missouri Division, Detachment District of Arkansas, District of West Louisiana, Trans-Mississippi Department (April 1864)
Burns' Brigade, Parsons' Missouri Division, District of Arkansas, Trans-Mississippi Department (April-September 1864)
1st Missouri Brigade, 1st Missouri Division, 2nd Corps, Trans-Mississippi Department (September 1864-April 1865)
Battles: Helena (July 4, 1863)
Red River Campaign (March-May 1864)
Pleasant Hill (April 9, 1864)
Camden Expedition (March-May 1864)
Jenkins' Ferry (April 30, 1864)

125. MISSOURI 12TH (STEEN'S-MOORE'S) INFANTRY REGIMENT

See: MISSOURI 10TH INFANTRY REGIMENT

126. MISSOURI 13TH INFANTRY REGIMENT

Organization: This unit does not appear in the *Official Records.*
First Commander: Benjamin A. Rives (Colonel)

127. MISSOURI 15TH INFANTRY REGIMENT

Organization: This unit does not appear in the *Official Records.*
First Commander: Timothy Rines (Colonel)

128. MISSOURI 16TH INFANTRY REGIMENT

Also Known As: 7th (Jackman's) Infantry Regiment
Organization: Organized as the 7th Infantry Regiment on August 31, 1862. Designated as the 16th Infantry Regiment on April 1, 1863. Surrendered by General E. K. Smith, commanding Trans-Mississippi Department, on May 26, 1865.
First Commander: Sidney D. Jackman (Colonel)
Field Officers: Josiah H. Caldwell (Lieutenant Colonel, Colonel)
Pleasant W. H. Cumming (Major, Lieutenant Colonel)
Jesse P. Herrell (Major, Lieutenant Colonel)
Levin M. Lewis (Lieutenant Colonel, Colonel)
Assignments: Parsons' Brigade, Hindman's-Price's-Drayton's Division, District of Arkansas, Trans-Mississippi Department (January 1863-March 1864)

Burns' Brigade, Parsons' Missouri Division, District of Arkansas, Trans-Mississippi Department (March-April 1864)

Burns' Brigade, Parsons' Division, Detachment District of Arkansas, District of West Louisiana, Trans-Mississippi Department (April 1864)

Burns' Brigade, Parsons' Missouri Division, District of Arkansas, Trans-Mississippi Department (April-September 1864)

1st Missouri Brigade, 1st Missouri Division, 2nd Corps, Trans-Mississippi Department (September 1864-April 1865)

Battles: Helena (July 4, 1863)

Red River Campaign (March-May 1864)

Pleasant Hill (April 9, 1864)

Camden Expedition (March-May 1864)

Jenkins' Ferry (April 30, 1864)

129. MISSOURI BUSTER'S INFANTRY BATTALION

See: MISSOURI CLARKSON'S-BUSTER'S INFANTRY BATTALION

130. MISSOURI CLARKSON'S-BUSTER'S INFANTRY BATTALION

Also Known As: Clarkson's-Buster's Cavalry Battalion

Nickname: Indian Battalion

Organization: Organized in the summer of 1862. Consolidated with the 8th Infantry Battalion and designated as the 9th (Clark's) Infantry Regiment on November 16, 1862.

First Commander: James J. Clarkson (Colonel)

Field Officers: Michael W. Buster (Major, Lieutenant Colonel)

J. Quin Morton (Major)

Assignment: Cooper's Brigade, District of Arkansas, Trans-Mississippi Department (August-October 1862)

Battles: Newtonia (September 30, 1862)

Granby (October 4, 1862)

131. MISSOURI FAGIN'S INFANTRY BATALLION

Organization: Organized in early 1862. Consolidated with the 1st and MacFarlane's Infantry Battalions and designated as the 4th Infantry Regiment on April 30, 1862.

First Commander: Fagin

Further Reading: Bevier, R. S., *History of the First and Second Missouri Confederate Brigades 1861-1865.*

132. MISSOURI FRAZIER'S INFANTRY BATTALION

Organization: Organized in early 1862. Apparently disbanded in the spring of 1862.
First Commander: W. L. H. Frazier (Major)

133. MISSOURI HEDGPETH'S INFANTRY BATTALION

Organization: Organized with two companies in early 1862. Consolidated with the 3rd Infantry Battalion and designated as the 6th Infantry Regiment at Guntown, Mississippi in May 1862.
First Commander: Isaac N. Hedgpeth (Major)
Further Reading: Bevier, R. S., *History of the First and Second Missouri Confederate Brigades 1861-1865*. Anderson, Ephraim McD., *Memoirs: Historical and Personal; Including the Campaigns of the First Missouri Confederate Brigade*.

134. MISSOURI HUGHES' INFANTRY BATTALION

Organization: Organized in early 1862. It was apparently disbanded in the spring of 1862.
First Commander: John T. Hughes (Colonel)
Assignment: Slack's Brigade, Confederate Volunteers, Missouri State Guard, Trans-Mississippi District, Department #2 (March 1862)
Battle: Pea Ridge (March 7-8, 1862)
Further Reading: Bevier, R. S., *History of the First and Second Missouri Confederate Brigades 1861-1865*. Anderson, Ephraim McD., *Memoirs: Historical and Personal; Including the Campaigns of the First Missouri Confederate Brigade*.

135. MISSOURI MACFARLANE'S INFANTRY BATTALION

Organization: Organized in early 1862. Consolidated with the 1st and Fagin's Infantry Battalions and designated as the 4th Infantry Regiment on April 30, 1862.
First Commander: Archibald MacFarlane (Major)
Further Reading: Bevier, R. S., *History of the First and Second Missouri Confederate Brigades 1861-1865*. Anderson, Ephraim McD., *Memoirs: Historical and Personal; Including the Campaigns of the First Missouri Confederate Brigade*.

136. MISSOURI ROSSER'S INFANTRY BATTALION

Organization: Organized in early 1862. Apparently disbanded in the spring of 1862.
First Commander: Thomas H. Rosser (Colonel)

Assignment: Slack's Brigade, Confederate Volunteers, Missouri State Guard, Trans-Mississippi District, Department #2 (March 1862)
Battles: Pea Ridge (March 7-8, 1862)
Corinth Campaign (April-June 1862)
Further Reading: Bevier, R. S., *History of the First and Second Missouri Confederate Brigades 1861-1865*. Anderson, Ephraim McD., *Memoirs: Historical and Personal; Including the Campaigns of the First Missouri Confederate Brigade.*

137. MISSOURI STEARNS' INFANTRY BATTALION

Organization: Organized in early 1862. Apparently disbanded in early 1862.
First Commander: Stearns (Lieutenant Colonel)
Field Officer: Alexander C. Pickett (Major)

STATE GUARD

138. Missouri Bowman's Artillery Battery, 1st Division, Missouri State Guard

Organization: Organized in 1861. Serving on board the River Defense Fleet in May and June 1862. Apparently disbanded in the summer of 1862.
First Commander: Benjamin L. Bowman (Captain)
Assignment: 1st Division, Missouri State Guard (May-June 1862)

139. Missouri Harris' Artillery Battery, 1st Division, Missouri State Guard

Organization: Organized in 1861. Serving on board the River Defense Fleet in May and June 1862. Apparently disbanded in the summer of 1862.
First Commander: S. S. Harris (Captain)
Assignment: 1st Division, Missouri State Guard (May-June 1862)

140. Missouri MacDonald's Artillery Battery, 1st Division, Missouri State Guard

Organization: Organized in 1861. Serving on board the River Defense Fleet in May and June 1862. Apparently disbanded in the summer of 1862.
First Commander: Robert MacDonald (Captain)
Assignment: 1st Division, Missouri State Guard (May-June 1862)

141. Missouri 1st Cavalry Battalion, 1st Division, Missouri State Guard

Organization: Organized in 1861. Apparently disbanded in early 1862.
First Commander: James D. White (Lieutenant Colonel)
Field Officer: William H. Couzens (Major)
Further Reading: Bevier, R. S., *History of the First and Second Missouri Confederate Brigades 1861-1865*.

142. MISSOURI 1ST CAVALRY REGIMENT, 1ST DIVISION, MISSOURI STATE GUARD

Organization: Organized in 1861. Apparently disbanded in early 1861.
First Commander: Andrew F. Jones (Colonel)
Field Officers: Columbus C. Kalfus (Major)
Edward A. Lewis (Lieutenant Colonel)
Further Reading: Bevier, R. S., *History of the First and Second Missouri Confederate Brigades 1861-1865.*

143. MISSOURI 2ND CAVALRY BATTALION, 1ST DIVISION, MISSOURI STATE GUARD

Organization: Organized in 1861. Apparently disbanded in early 1862.
First Commander: Jason H. Hunter (Major)
Further Reading: Bevier, R. S., *History of the First and Second Missouri Confederate Brigades 1861-1865.*

144. MISSOURI 2ND CAVALRY REGIMENT, 1ST DIVISION, MISSOURI STATE GUARD

Organization: Organized in 1861. Apparently disbanded in early 1862.
First Commander: William L. Jeffers (Colonel)
Field Officers: Henry H. Bedford (Major)
Solomon G. Kitchen (Major, Lieutenant Colonel)
John J. Smith (Colonel)
Battles: Big River Bridge and Blackwell Station (October 15, 1861)
Fredericktown (October 21, 1861)
Further Reading: Bevier, R. S., *History of the First and Second Missouri Confederate Brigades 1861-1865.*

145. MISSOURI 1ST INFANTRY BATTALION 1ST DIVISION, MISSOURI STATE GUARD

Organization: Organized in 1861. Apparently disbanded in early 1862.
First Commander: Thomas Brown (Major, Lieutenant Colonel)
Field Officer: B. F. Herr (Major)
Further Reading: Bevier, R. S., *History of the First and Second Missouri Confederate Brigades 1861-1865.*

146. MISSOURI 1ST INFANTRY REGIMENT, 1ST DIVISION, MISSOURI STATE GUARD

Organization: Organized in 1861. Apparently disbanded in early 1862.
First Commander: James A. Walker (Colonel)
Field Officers: C. E. Birthright (Major)

David Y. Panky (Lieutenant Colonel)
Further Reading: Bevier, R. S., *History of the First and Second Missouri Confederate Brigades 1861-1865*.

147. MISSOURI 2ND INFANTRY BATTALION, 1ST DIVISION, MISSOURI STATE GUARD

Organization: Organized in 1861. Apparently disbanded in early 1862.
First Commander: D. L. Jennings (Major)
Further Reading: Bevier, R. S., *History of the First and Second Missouri Confederate Brigades 1861-1865*.

148. MISSOURI 2ND INFANTRY REGIMENT, 1ST DIVISION, MISSOURI STATE GUARD

Organization: Organized in 1861. Apparently disbanded in early 1862.
First Commander: William G. Pheelan (Colonel)
Field Officers: Benjamin Farmer (Major, Lieutenant Colonel)
Thomas Powers (Major)
William Tippen (Colonel)
Further Reading: Bevier, R. S., *History of the First and Second Missouri Confederate Brigades 1861-1865*.

149. MISSOURI 3RD INFANTRY BATTALION, 1ST DIVISION, MISSOURI STATE GUARD

Organization: Organized in 1861. Apparently disbanded in early 1862.
First Commander: W. F. Rapley (Major)
Further Reading: Bevier, R. S., *History of the First and Second Missouri Confederate Brigades 1861-1865*.

150. MISSOURI 3RD INFANTRY REGIMENT, 1ST DIVISION, MISSOURI STATE GUARD

Organization: Organized in 1861. Apparently disbanded in early 1862.
First Commander: Jonas Eaker (Lieutenant Colonel)
Field Officers: Isaac N. Hedgpeth (Lieutenant Colonel)
Aden Lowe (Colonel)
Willis M. Ponder (Major)
M. Jeff Thompson (Lieutenant Colonel)
Assignment: 1st Division, Missouri State Guard (October 1861-January 1862)
Battles: Big River Bridge and Blackwell Station (October 15, 1861)
Fredericktown (October 21, 1861)

Further Reading: Bevier, R. S., *History of the First and Second Missouri Confederate Brigades 1861-1865.*

151. MISSOURI 4TH INFANTRY REGIMENT, 1ST DIVISION, MISSOURI STATE GUARD

Organization: Organized in 1861. Apparently disbanded in early 1862.
First Commander: Jason H. Hunter (Colonel)
Field Officers: William C. Grimsley (Major)
James Parrott (Lieutenant Colonel)
Alexander Waugh (Major, Colonel)
Assignment: 1st Division, Missouri Sate Guard (August 1861-January 2, 1862)
Battle: Charleston (August 19, 1861)
Further Reading: Bevier, R. S., *History of the First and Second Missouri Confederate Brigades 1861-1865.*

152. MISSOURI KNEISLEY'S ARTILLERY BATTERY, 2ND DIVISION, MISSOURI STATE GUARD

Organization: Organized in the summer of 1861. Transferred to Confederate service ca. March 1862.
First Commander: J. W. Kneisley (Captain)
Assignments: 2nd Division, Missouri State Guard (September 1861-January 1862)
2nd Division, Missouri State Guard, Trans-Mississippi District, Department #2 (January-March 1862)
Battles: Siege of Lexington (September 13-20, 1861)
Pea Ridge (March 7-8, 1862)

153. MISSOURI BRUCE'S CAVALRY REGIMENT, 2ND DIVISION, MISSOURI STATE GUARD

Organization: Organized in the summer of 1861. Apparently disbanded in the spring of 1862.
First Commander: Thomas Bruce (Colonel)
Field Officers: G. B. Milton (Major)
W. C. Splaun (Lieutenant Colonel)
Assignments: 2nd Division, Missouri State Guard (September 1861-January 1862)
2nd Division, Missouri State Guard, Trans-Mississippi District, Department #2 (January-March 1862)
Battle: Siege of Lexington (September 13-20, 1861)

Further Reading: Bevier, R. S., *History of the First and Second Missouri Confederate Brigades 1861-1865*.

154. MISSOURI BURBRIDGE'S CAVALRY REGIMENT, 2ND DIVISION, MISSOURI STATE GUARD

Organization: Organized in the summer of 1861. Apparently disbanded in the spring of 1862.

First Commander: John Q. Burbridge (Colonel)

Field Officers: Robert D. A. Dwyer (Major)

Edward B. Hull (Lieutenant Colonel)

Assignment: 2nd Division, Missouri State Guard (September 1861-January 1862)

Battle: Siege of Lexington (September 13-20, 1861)

Further Reading: Bevier, R. S., *History of the First and Second Missouri Confederate Brigades 1861-1865*.

155. MISSOURI FRANKLIN'S CAVALRY REGIMENT, 2ND DIVISION, MISSOURI STATE GUARD

Organization: Organized ca. September 1861. Apparently disbanded in the spring of 1862.

First Commander: B. H. Franklin (Colonel)

Assignments: 2nd Division, Missouri State Guard (September 1861-January 1862)

2nd Division, Missouri State Guard, Trans-Mississippi District, Department #2 (January-March 1862)

Battle: Siege of Lexington (September 13-20, 1861)

Further Reading: Bevier, R. S., *History of the First and Second Missouri Confederate Brigades 1861-1865*.

156. MISSOURI GREEN'S CAVALRY REGIMENT, 2ND DIVISION, MISSOURI STATE GUARD

Organization: Organized in the summer of 1861. Apparently disbanded in the spring of 1862.

First Commander: Martin E. Green (Colonel)

Field Officer: Joseph C. Porter (Lieutenant Colonel)

Assignments: 2nd Division, Missouri State Guard (September 1861-January 1862)

2nd Division, Missouri State Guard, Trans-Mississippi District, Department #2 (January-March 1862)

Battle: Siege of Lexington (September 13-20, 1861)

Further Reading: Bevier, R. S., *History of the First and Second Missouri Confederate Brigades 1861-1865.*

157. MISSOURI HAWKINS' CAVALRY BATTALION, 2ND DIVISION, MISSOURI STATE GUARD

Organization: Organized in the fall of 1861. Apparently disbanded in the spring of 1862.

First Commander: B. W. Hawkins (Lieutenant Colonel)

Field Officer: John L. Owen (Major)

Assignments: 2nd Division, Missouri State Guard (November 1861-January 1862)

2nd Division, Missouri State Guard, Trans-Mississippi District, Department #2 (January-March 1862)

Further Reading: Bevier, R. S., *History of the First and Second Missouri Confederate Brigades 1861-1865.*

158. MISSOURI RAWLINGS' INFANTRY BATTALION, 2ND DIVISION, MISSOURI STATE GUARD

Organization: Organized in the fall of 1861. Apparently disbanded in the spring of 1862.

First Commander: S. A. Rawlings (Lieutenant Colonel)

Field Officer: C. Adams (Major)

Assignments: 2nd Division, Missouri State Guard (November 1861-January 1862)

2nd Division, Missouri State Guard, Trans-Mississippi District, Department #2 (January-March 1862)

Further Reading: Bevier, R. S., *History of the First and Second Missouri Confederate Brigades 1861-1865.*

159. MISSOURI ROBINSON'S INFANTRY BATTALION, 2ND DIVISION, MISSOURI STATE GUARD

Organization: Organized in the fall of 1861. Apparently disbanded in the spring of 1862.

First Commander: J. W. Robinson (Major)

Assignments: 2nd Division, Missouri State Guard (November 1861-January 1862)

2nd Division, Missouri State Guard, Trans-Mississippi District, Department #2 (January-March 1862)

Further Reading: Bevier, R. S., *History of the First and Second Missouri Confederate Brigades 1861-1865.*

160. MISSOURI MAJOR'S CAVALRY REGIMENT, 3RD DIVISION, MISSOURI STATE GUARD

Organization: Organized in 1861. Apparently disbanded in the spring of 1862.

First Commander: James P. Major (Colonel)

Field Officer: A. H. Chalmers (Major)

Assignments: 3rd Division, Missouri State Guard (November 1861-January 1862)

3rd Division, Missouri State Guard, Trans-Mississippi District, Department #2 (January-March 1862)

161. MISSOURI 1ST INFANTRY BATTALION, 3RD DIVISION, MISSOURI STATE GUARD

Organization: Organized in the summer of 1861. Increased to a regiment and designated as the 5th Infantry Regiment, 3rd Division, Missouri State Guard in the fall of 1861.

First Commander: Robert S. Bevier (Major)

Assignment: 3rd Division, Missouri State Guard (September 1861)

Battle: Siege of Lexington (September 13-20, 1861)

162. MISSOURI 1ST INFANTRY REGIMENT, 3RD DIVISION, MISSOURI STATE GUARD

Organization: Organized in the summer of 1861. Disbanded in the spring of 1862.

First Commander: John Q. Burbridge (Colonel)

Field Officers: Thomas Boyce (Major)

John B. Clark, Jr. (Major, Colonel)

S. Farrington (Lieutenant Colonel)

Edwin Price (Lieutenant Colonel)

Assignments: 3rd Division, Missouri State Guard (August 1861-January 1862)

3rd Division, Missouri State Guard, Trans-Mississippi District, Department #2 (January-March 1862)

Battles: Wilson's Creek (August 10, 1861)

Siege of Lexington (September 13-20, 1861)

Pea Ridge (March 7-8, 1862)

Further Reading: Bevier, R. S., *History of the First and Second Missouri Confederate Brigades 1861-1865*.

163. MISSOURI 2ND INFANTRY BATTALION, 3RD DIVISION, MISSOURI STATE GUARD

Organization: Organized in the summer of 1861. Increased to a regiment and designated as the 4th Infantry Regiment, 3rd Division, Missouri State Guard in the fall of 1861.

First Commander: M. G. Singleton (Lieutenant Colonel)

Field Officer: L. Peacher (Major)

Assignment: 3rd Division, Missouri State Guard (September 1861)

Battle: Siege of Lexington (September 13-20, 1861)

164. MISSOURI 2ND INFANTRY REGIMENT, 3RD DIVISION, MISSOURI STATE GUARD

Organization: Organized in the summer of 1861. Disbanded in the spring of 1862.

First Commander: Congreve Jackson (Colonel)

Field Officers: Joseph Vaughn (Major)

John R. White (Lieutenant Colonel)

Assignments: 3rd Division, Missouri State Guard (September 1861-January 1862)

3rd Division, Missouri State Guard, Trans-Mississippi District, Department #2 (January-March 1862)

Battles: Siege of Lexington (September 13-20, 1861)

Pea Ridge (March 7-8, 1862)

Further Reading: Bevier, R. S., *History of the First and Second Missouri Confederate Brigades 1861-1865.*

165. MISSOURI 3RD INFANTRY REGIMENT, 3RD DIVISION, MISSOURI STATE GUARD

Organization: Organized in 1861. Disbanded in the spring of 1862.

First Commander: Edwin Price (Colonel)

Field Officers: Robert Randolph Hutchinson (Major)

W. S. Hyde (Lieutenant Colonel)

Assignments: 3rd Division, Missouri State Guard (November 1861-January 1862)

3rd Division, Missouri State Guard, Trans-Mississippi District, Department #2 (January-March 1862)

Battle: Pea Ridge (March 7-8, 1862)

Further Reading: Bevier, R. S., *History of the First and Second Missouri Confederate Brigades 1861-1865.*

166. MISSOURI 4TH INFANTRY REGIMENT, 3RD DIVISION, MISSOURI STATE GUARD

Organization: Organized by the increase of the 2nd Infantry Battalion, 3rd Division, Missouri State Guard to a regiment in the fall of 1861. Field consolidation with the 5th Infantry Regiment, 3rd Division, Missouri State Guard in March 1862. Disbanded in the spring of 1862.

First Commander: Marion McKinney (Colonel)

Field Officers: L. Peacher (Major, Lieutenant Colonel)

M. G. Singleton (Lieutenant Colonel)

Assignments: 3rd Division, Missouri State Guard (November 1861-January 1862)

3rd Division, Missouri State Guard, Trans-Mississippi District, Department #2 (January-March 1862)

Battle: Pea Ridge (March 7-8, 1862)

Further Reading: Bevier, R. S., *History of the First and Second Missouri Confederate Brigades 1861-1865*.

167. MISSOURI 5TH INFANTRY REGIMENT, 3RD DIVISION, MISSOURI STATE GUARD

Organization: Organized by the increase of the 1st Infantry Battalion, 3rd Division, Missouri State Guard to a regiment in the fall of 1861. Field consolidation with the 4th Infantry Regiment, 3rd Division, Missouri State Guard in March 1862. Disbanded in the spring of 1862.

First Commander: Robert S. Bevier (Colonel)

Field Officers: James Lovern (Major)

X. J. Pindall (Lieutenant Colonel)

Assignments: 3rd Division, Missouri State Guard (November 1861-January 1862)

3rd Division, Missouri State Guard, Trans-Mississippi District, Department #2 (January-March 1862)

Battle: Pea Ridge (March 7-8, 1862)

Further Reading: Bevier, R. S., *History of the First and Second Missouri Confederate Brigades 1861-1865*.

168. MISSOURI 6TH INFANTRY REGIMENT, 3RD DIVISION, MISSOURI STATE GUARD

Organization: Organized in the fall of 1861. Disbanded in the spring of 1862.

First Commander: J. A. Poindexter (Colonel)

Assignments: 3rd Division, Missouri State Guard (November 1861-January 1862)

3rd Division, Missouri State Guard, Trans-Mississippi District, Department #2 (January-March 1862)

Battles: Siege of Lexington [as independent companies] (September 13-20, 1861)

Pea Ridge (March 7-8, 1862)

Further Reading: Bevier, R. S., *History of the First and Second Missouri Confederate Brigades 1861-1865.*

169. MISSOURI CLARK'S ARTILLERY BATTERY, 4TH DIVISION, MISSOURI STATE GUARD

Organization: Organized in the summer of 1861. Transferred to Confederate service and became the 2nd Artillery Battery in early 1862.

First Commander: Chruchill Clark (Captain)

Assignment: 4th Division, Missouri State Guard (September 1861-January 1862)

Battle: Siege of Lexington (September 13-20, 1861)

Further Reading: Bevier, R. S., *History of the First and Second Missouri Confederate Brigades 1861-1865.*

170. MISSOURI 1ST CAVALRY, 4TH DIVISION, MISSOURI STATE GUARD

Organization: Organized in the summer of 1861. Disbanded in the spring of 1862.

First Commander: Benjamin A. Rives (Colonel)

Field Officers: A. J. Austin (Lieutenant Colonel)

Lewis Bohannan (Lieutenant Colonel)

John B. Corner (Major)

Assignments: 4th Division, Missouri State Guard (August 1861-January 1862)

4th Division, Missouri State Guard, Trans-Mississippi District, Department #2 (January-March 1862)

Battles: Wilson's Creek (August 10, 1861)

Siege of Lexington (September 13-20, 1861)

Further Reading: Bevier, R. S., *History of the First and Second Missouri Confederate Brigades 1861-1865.*

171. MISSOURI EXTRA CAVALRY BATTALION, 4TH DIVISION, MISSOURI STATE GUARD

Organization: Organized in the summer of 1861. Disbanded in the spring of 1862.

First Commander: Richard B. Chiles (Lieutenant Colonel)

Field Officer: John Patton (Major)

Assignments: 4th Division, Missouri State Guard (September 1861-January 1862)

4th Division, Missouri State Guard, Trans-Mississippi District, Department #2 (January-March 1862)

Battles: Liberty (September 17, 1862)

Blue Mills Landing (September 17, 1862)

Further Reading: Bevier, R. S., *History of the First and Second Missouri Confederate Brigades 1861-1865*.

172. MISSOURI 1ST INFANTRY REGIMENT, 4TH DIVISION, MISSOURI STATE GUARD

Organization: Organized in the summer of 1861. Disbanded in the spring of 1862.

First Commander: John T. Hughes (Colonel)

Field Officers: William Mirick (Major)

James A. Pritchard (Lieutenant Colonel)

Assignments: 4th Division, Missouri State Guard (August 1861-January 1862)

4th Division, Missouri State Guard, Trans-Mississippi District, Department #2 (January-March 1862)

Battles: Wilson's Creek (August 10, 1861)

Siege of Lexington (September 13-20, 1861)

Further Reading: Bevier, R. S., *History of the First and Second Missouri Confederate Brigades 1861-1865*.

173. MISSOURI 2ND INFANTRY REGIMENT, 4TH DIVISION, MISSOURI STATE GUARD

Organization: Organized in the summer of 1861. Disbanded in early 1862.

First Commander: Thomas Patton (Colonel)

Field Officers: William R. Gause (Major)

Robert A. Hewitt (Lieutenant Colonel)

Assignment: 4th Division, Missouri State Guard (September 1861-January 1862)

Battle: Blue Mills Landing (September 17, 1862)

Further Reading: Bevier, R. S., *History of the First and Second Missouri Confederate Brigades 1861-1865*.

174. MISSOURI EXTRA INFANTRY BATTALION, 4TH DIVISION, MISSOURI STATE GUARD

Organization: Organized in the summer of 1861. Attached to the 1st Infantry Regiment. Disbanded in the spring of 1862.

First Commander: C. B. Housand (Major)

Assignments: 4th Division, Missouri State Guard (September 1861-January 1862)

4th Division, Missouri State Guard, Trans-Mississippi District, Department #2 (January-March 1862)

Battle: Siege of Lexington (September 13-20, 1861)

Further Reading: Bevier, R. S., *History of the First and Second Missouri Confederate Brigades 1861-1865.*

175. MISSOURI THORNTON'S INFANTRY BATTALION, 4TH DIVISION, MISSOURI STATE GUARD

Organization: Organized in the summer of 1861. Disbanded in the spring of 1862.

First Commander: J. C. Thornton (Major)

Assignment: 4th Division, Missouri State Guard (August 1861)

Battle: Wilson's Creek (August 10, 1861)

Further Reading: Bevier, R. S., *History of the First and Second Missouri Confederate Brigades 1861-1865.*

176. MISSOURI 1ST ARTILLERY BATTALION, 5TH DIVISION, MISSOURI STATE GUARD

Organization: Organized in 1861. Disbanded in early 1862.

First Commander: John Landis (Major)

Assignment: 5th Division, Missouri State Guard (November-December 1861)

Further Reading: Bevier, R. S., *History of the First and Second Missouri Confederate Brigades 1861-1865.*

177. MISSOURI KELLY'S ARTILLERY BATTERY, 5TH DIVISION, MISSOURI STATE GUARD

Organization: Organized in the summer of 1861. It was armed with three guns on September 13-20, 1861 and with five guns on March 6-8, 1862. Transferred to Confederate service as Kelly's Missouri Artillery Battery in the spring of 1862.

First Commander: E. V. Kelly (Captain)

Assignments: 5th Division, Missouri State Guard (September 1861-January 1862)

5th Division, Missouri State Guard, Trans-Mississippi District, Department #2 (January-March 1862)
Battles: Siege of Lexington (September 13-20, 1861)
Pea Ridge (March 7-8, 1862)

178. MISSOURI 1ST CAVALRY REGIMENT, 5TH DIVISION, MISSOURI STATE GUARD

Organization: Organized in the fall of 1861. Six companies came from the 1st Infantry Battalion, 5th Division, Missouri State Guard. Disbanded in the spring of 1862.
First Commander: James T. Cearnal (Colonel)
Field Officers: Ney Bostick (Major)
Elijah Gates (Lieutenant Colonel)
Assignments: 5th Division, Missouri State Guard (November 1861-January 1862)
5th Division, Missouri State Guard, Trans-Mississippi District, Department #2 (January-March 1862)
Battle: Pea Ridge (March 7-8, 1862)
Further Reading: Bevier, R. S., *History of the First and Second Missouri Confederate Brigades 1861-1865*.

179. MISSOURI 1ST INFANTRY BATTALION, 5TH DIVISION, MISSOURI STATE GUARD

Organization: Organized with six cavalry companies and three infantry companies in the summer of 1861. The cavalry companies were transferred to the 1ts Cavalry Regiment, 5th Division, Missouri State Guard in the fall of 1861. Disbanded in the spring of 1862.
First Commander: John R. Boyd (Lieutenant Colonel)
Field Officer: John J. Hash (Major)
Assignments: 5th Division, Missouri State Guard (September 1861-January 1862)
5th Division, Missouri State Guard, Trans-Mississippi District, Department #2 (January-March 1862)
Battles: Siege of Lexington (September 13-20, 1861)
Pea Ridge (March 7-8, 1862)
Further Reading: Bevier, R. S., *History of the First and Second Missouri Confederate Brigades 1861-1865*.

180. MISSOURI 1ST (PLATTE COUNTY) INFANTRY BATTALION, 5TH DIVISION, MISSOURI STATE GUARD

Organization: Organized in the summer of 1861. Increased to a regiment and designated as the 2nd Infantry Regiment, 5th Division, Missouri State Guard in the fall of 1861.

First Commander: James H. Winston (Major)
Assignment: 5th Division, Missouri State Guard (September 1861)
Battle: Siege of Lexington (September 13-20, 1861)

181. MISSOURI 1ST INFANTRY REGIMENT, 5TH DIVISION, MISSOURI STATE GUARD

Organization: Organized in the summer of 1861. Disbanded in the spring of 1862.
First Commander: J. P. Saunders (Colonel)
Field Officers: W. H. Cundiff (Lieutenant Colonel)
D. Todd Samuels (Major)
Assignments: 5th Division, Missouri State Guard (September 1861-January 1862)
5th Division, Missouri State Guard, Trans-Mississippi District, Department #2 (January-March 1862)
Battles: Pea Ridge (March 7-8, 1862)
Blue Mills Landing (September 17, 1862)
Further Reading: Bevier, R. S., *History of the First and Second Missouri Confederate Brigades 1861-1865.*

182. MISSOURI 2ND INFANTRY REGIMENT, 5TH DIVISION, MISSOURI STATE GUARD

Organization: Organized by the increase of the 1st Platte County Infantry Battalion, 5th Division, Missouri State Guard in the fall of 1861. Disbanded in the spring of 1862.
First Commander: John H. Winston (Colonel)
Field Officers: W. P. Chiles (Lieutenant Colonel)
J. Murphy (Major)
Assignments: 5th Division, Missouri State Guard (November 1861-January 1862)
5th Division, Missouri State Guard, Trans-Mississippi District, Department #2 (January-March 1862)
Battle: Pea Ridge (March 7-8, 1862)
Further Reading: Bevier, R. S., *History of the First and Second Missouri Confederate Brigades 1861-1865.*

183. MISSOURI 3RD INFANTRY REGIMENT, 5TH DIVISION, MISSOURI STATE GUARD

Organization: Organized by the increase of the Clay County Infantry Battalion to a regiment in the fall of 1861. Disbanded in the spring of 1862.
First Commander: Levin M. Lewis (Colonel)

Field Officers: Gideon W. Thompson (Major)
John C. C. Thornton (Lieutenant Colonel)

Assignments: 5th Division, Missouri State Guard (November 1861-January 1862)
5th Division, Missouri State Guard, Trans-Mississippi District, Department #2 (January-March 1862)

Battle: Pea Ridge (March 7-8, 1862)

Further Reading: Bevier, R. S., *History of the First and Second Missouri Confederate Brigades 1861-1865.*

184. MISSOURI 5TH [MOUNTED] INFANTRY REGIMENT, 5TH DIVISION, MISSOURI STATE GUARD

Organization: Organized in 1861. Mounted in the fall of 1861. Disbanded in the spring of 1862.

First Commander: Alonzo W. Slayback (Colonel)

Assignments: 5th Division, Missouri State Guard (November 1861-January 1862)
5th Division, Missouri State Guard, Trans-Mississippi District, Department #2 (January-March 1862)

Battle: Pea Ridge (March 7-8, 1862)

Further Reading: Bevier, R. S., *History of the First and Second Missouri Confederate Brigades 1861-1865.*

185. MISSOURI CLAY COUNTY INFANTRY BATTALION, 5TH DIVISION, MISSOURI STATE GUARD

Organization: Organized in the summer of 1861. Increased to a regiment and designated as the 3rd Infantry Regiment, 5th Division, Missouri State Guard in the fall of 1861.

First Commander: John C. C. Thornton (Major)

Assignment: 5th Division, Missouri State Guard (September 1861)

Battle: Siege of Lexington (September 13-20, 1861)

186. MISSOURI GORHAM'S ARTILLERY BATTERY, 6TH DIVISION, MISSOURI STATE GUARD

Organization: Organized in 1861. It was armed with four guns on March 7-8, 1862. Transferred to Confederate service in March 1862, as Gorham's Battery, which eventually became the 3rd Missouri Field Artillery Battery [q.v.].

First Commander: James C. Gorham (Captain)

Assignment: 6th Division, Missouri State Guard, Trans-Mississippi District, Department #2 (February-March 1862)

Battle: Pea Ridge (March 7-8, 1862)

187. MISSOURI GUIBOR'S ARTILLERY BATTERY, 6TH DIVISION, MISSOURI STATE GUARD

Organization: Organized in the summer of 1861. It was armed with four guns on August 10, 1861. Transferred on to Confederate service, as Guibor's Missouri Artillery Battery in the spring of 1862.

First Commander: Henry Guibor (Captain)

Assignments: 6th Division, Missouri State Guard (July 1861-January 1862)
6th Division, Missouri State Guard, Trans-Mississippi District, Department #2 (January-March 1862)

Battles: Wilson's Creek (August 10, 1861)
Siege of Lexington (September 13-20, 1861)
Pea Ridge (March 7-8, 1862)

188. MISSOURI 1ST CAVALRY REGIMENT, 6TH DIVISION, MISSOURI STATE GUARD

Organization: Organized in the summer of 1861. Disbanded in the spring of 1862.

First Commander: Benjamin Brown (Colonel)

Assignment: 6th Division, Missouri State Guard (August 1861)

Battle: Wilson's Creek (August 10, 1861)

Further Reading: Bevier, R. S., *History of the First and Second Missouri Confederate Brigades 1861-1865.*

189. MISSOURI MCCULLOCH'S CAVALRY REGIMENT, 6TH DIVISION, MISSOURI STATE GUARD

Organization: Organized in the summer of 1861. Disbanded in the spring of 1862.

First Commander: Robert McCulloch (Colonel)

Assignments: 6th Division, Missouri State Guard (September 1861-January 1862)
6th Division, Missouri State Guard, Trans-Mississippi District, Department #2 (January-March 1862)

Battles: Siege of Lexington (September 13-20, 1861)
Pea Ridge (March 7-8, 1862)

190. MISSOURI 1ST INFANTRY REGIMENT, 6TH DIVISION, MISSOURI STATE GUARD

Organization: Organized in the summer of 1861. Disbanded in the spring of 1862.

First Commander: Joseph Kelly (Colonel)

Assignments: 6th Division, Missouri State Guard (August 1861-January 1862)

6th Division, Missouri State Guard, Trans-Mississippi District, Department #2 (January-March 1862)

Battles: Wilson's Creek (August 10, 1861)

Siege of Lexington (September 13-20, 1861)

Pea Ridge (March 7-8, 1862)

Further Reading: Bevier, R. S., *History of the First and Second Missouri Confederate Brigades 1861-1865*.

191. MISSOURI ALEXANDER'S INFANTRY REGIMENT, 6TH DIVISION, MISSOURI STATE GUARD

Organization: Organized in the summer of 1861. Disbanded in the spring of 1862.

First Commander: Charles B. Alexander (Colonel)

Assignments: 6th Division, Missouri State Guard (September 1861-January 1862)

6th Division, Missouri State Guard, Trans-Mississippi District, Department #2 (January-March 1862)

Battles: Siege of Lexington (September 13-20, 1861)

Pea Ridge (March 7-8, 1862)

192. MISSOURI DILLS' INFANTRY BATTALION, 6TH DIVISION, MISSOURI STATE GUARD

Organization: Organized in the fall of 1861. Disbanded in early 1862.

First Commander: Dills (Major, Colonel)

Assignment: 6th Division, Missouri State Guard (September 1861)

Battle: Siege of Lexington (September 13-20, 1861)

Further Reading: Bevier, R. S., *History of the First and Second Missouri Confederate Brigades 1861-1865*.

193. MISSOURI CAMPBELL'S CAVALRY COMPANY, 7TH DIVISION, MISSOURI STATE GUARD

Organization: Organized in the summer of 1861. Disbanded in early 1862.

First Commander: A. J. Campbell (Captain)

Assignment: 7th Division, Missouri State Guard (August 1861)

Battle: Wilson's Creek (August 10, 1861)

194. MISSOURI FOSTER'S INFANTRY REGIMENT, 7TH DIVISION, MISSOURI STATE GUARD

Organization: Organized in the summer of 1861. Disbanded in the spring of 1862.

First Commander: J. A. Foster (Colonel)

Assignments: 7th Division, Missouri State Guard (August 1861-January 1862)

7th Division, Missouri State Guard, Trans-Mississippi District, Department #2 (January-March 1862)

Battles: Wilson's Creek (August 10, 1861)

Pea Ridge (March 7-8, 1862)

195. MISSOURI WINGO'S INFANTRY REGIMENT, 7TH DIVISION, MISSOURI STATE GUARD

Organization: Organized in the summer of 1861. Disbanded in the spring of 1862.

First Commander: Edmond T. Wingo (Colonel)

Assignments: 7th Division, Missouri State Guard (August 1861-January 1862)

7th Division, Missouri State Guard, Trans-Mississippi District, Department #2 (January-March 1862)

Battles: Wilson's Creek (August 10, 1861)

Siege of Lexington (September 13-20, 1861)

Pea Ridge (March 7-8, 1862)

196. MISSOURI BLEDSOE'S ARTILLERY BATTERY, 8TH DIVISION, MISSOURI STATE GUARD

Organization: Organized on June 11, 1861. It was armed with one 12-lb. and two 6-lb. Smoothbores from August 10 to September 20, 1861. Transferred to Confederate service and designated as Bledsoe's Missouri Artillery Battery on April 21, 1862.

First Commander: Hiram M. Bledsoe (Captain)

Captain: Emmett MacDonald

Assignments: 1st Brigade, 8th Division, Missouri State Guard (June 1861-January 1862)

8th Division, Missouri State Guard, Trans-Mississippi District, Department #2 (January-March 1862)

Frost's Artillery Brigade, Price's Division, Trans-Mississippi District, Department #2 (March-April 1862)

Frost's Artillery Brigade, Price's Division, Army of the West, Trans-Mississippi Department (April 1862)

Battles: Dug Springs (August 2, 1861)
Wilson's Creek (August 10, 1861)
Siege of Lexington (September 13-20, 1861)
Pea Ridge (March 7-8, 1862)
Further Reading: Bevier, R. S., *History of the First and Second Missouri Confederate Brigades 1861-1865.*

197. MISSOURI 1ST CAVALRY REGIMENT, 8TH DIVISION, MISSOURI STATE GUARD

Organization: Organized in July 1861. Disbanded in the spring of 1862.
First Commander: Richard H. Weightman (Colonel)
Field Officers: Elijah Chiles (Lieutenant Colonel)
Howard Chisum (Major)
John S. Hamilton (Major)
Upton Hays (Lieutenant Colonel)
John W. Martin (Colonel)
Assignments: 8th Division, Missouri State Guard (August 1861-January 1862)
8th Division, Missouri State Guard, Trans-Mississippi District, Department #2 (January-March 1862)
Battles: Dug Springs (August 2, 1861)
Siege of Lexington (September 13-20, 1861)
Pea Ridge (March 7-8, 1862)
Further Reading: Bevier, R. S., *History of the First and Second Missouri Confederate Brigades 1861-1865.*

198. MISSOURI 2ND CAVALRY REGIMENT, 8TH DIVISION, MISSOURI STATE GUARD

Organization: Organized in July 1861. Disbanded in the spring of 1862.
First Commander: James McCown (Lieutenant Colonel)
Field Officers: R. K. Murrell (Lieutenant Colonel)
A. Sayers (Major)
Moses W. Smith (Major)
Royal G. Stokely (Major)
Assignments: 2nd Brigade, 8th Division, Missouri State Guard (August 1861-January 1862)
8th Division, Missouri State Guard, Trans-Mississippi District, Department #2 (January-March 1862)
Battles: Dug Springs (August 2, 1861)
Wilson's Creek [1st Battalion] (August 10, 1861)
Siege of Lexington (September 13-20, 1861)

Pea Ridge (March 7-8, 1862)

Further Reading: Bevier, R. S., *History of the First and Second Missouri Confederate Brigades 1861-1865.*

199. MISSOURI 3RD CAVALRY REGIMENT, 8TH DIVISION, MISSOURI STATE GUARD

Organization: Organized in July 1861. Disbanded in the spring of 1862.

First Commander: Robert L. Y. Petron (Colonel)

Field Officers: Nathan L. Taylor (Major)

Martin White (Lieutenant Colonel)

Assignments: 2nd Brigade, 8th Division, Missouri State Guard (August 1861-January 1862)

8th Division, Missouri State Guard, Trans-Mississippi District, Department #2 (January-March 1862)

Battles: Dug Springs (August 2, 1861)

Wilson's Creek [Companies A, B, & H] (August 10, 1861)

Siege of Lexington (September 13-20, 1861)

Pea Ridge (March 7-8, 1862)

Further Reading: Bevier, R. S., *History of the First and Second Missouri Confederate Brigades 1861-1865.*

200. MISSOURI 4TH CAVALRY REGIMENT, 8TH DIVISION, MISSOURI STATE GUARD

Organization: Organized in July 1861. Disbanded in the spring of 1862.

First Commander: James Cawthorn (Colonel)

Field Officers: B. F. Walker (Lieutenant Colonel, Colonel)

Henry K. Hartley (Lieutenant Colonel)

Thomas J. Hartley (Major)

James Musgrove (Major)

Assignments: 2nd Brigade, 8th Division, Missouri State Guard (July 1861-January 1862)

8th Division, Missouri State Guard, Trans-Mississippi District, Department #2 (January-March 1862)

Battles: Dug Springs (August 2, 1861)

Wilson's Creek [battalion] (August 10, 1861)

Siege of Lexington (September 13-20, 1861)

Pea Ridge (March 7-8, 1862)

Further Reading: Bevier, R. S., *History of the First and Second Missouri Confederate Brigades 1861-1865.*

201. MISSOURI 5TH CAVALRY REGIMENT, 8TH DIVISION, MISSOURI STATE GUARD

Organization: Organized in July 1861. Disbanded in the spring of 1862.
First Commander: Jesse L. Cravens (Colonel)
Field Officers: William C. Langston (Major)
Thomas H. Slover (Lieutenant Colonel)
Assignments: 8th Division, Missouri State Guard (July 1861-January 1862)
8th Division, Missouri State Guard, Trans-Mississippi District, Department #2 (January-March 1862)
Battles: Dug Springs (August 2, 1861)
Siege of Lexington (September 13-20, 1861)
Pea Ridge (March 7-8, 1862)
Further Reading: Bevier, R. S., *History of the First and Second Missouri Confederate Brigades 1861-1865*.

202. MISSOURI 6TH CAVALRY REGIMENT, 8TH DIVISION, MISSOURI STATE GUARD

Organization: Organized in the fall of 1861. Disbanded in the spring of 1862.
First Commander: John T. Coffee (Colonel)
Field Officers: E. G. Bogart (Lieutenant Colonel)
John W. Payne (Lieutenant Colonel)
Moses W. Smith (Major)
Assignments: 8th Division, Missouri State Guard (November 1861-January 1862)
8th Division, Missouri State Guard, Trans-Mississippi District, Department #2 (January-May 1862)
Battles: Dug Springs (August 2, 1861)
Siege of Lexington (September 13-20, 1861)
Pea Ridge (March 7-8, 1862)
Neosho [skirmish] (April 26, 1862)
near Neosho [skirmish] (May 31, 1862)
Further Reading: Bevier, R. S., *History of the First and Second Missouri Confederate Brigades 1861-1865*.

203. MISSOURI 7TH CAVALRY REGIMENT, 8TH DIVISION, MISSOURI STATE GUARD

Organization: Organized in July 1861. Disbanded in the spring of 1862.
First Commander: DeWitt C. Hunter (Colonel)
Field Officers: George W. Bolton (Major)
Richard A. Boughan (Lieutenant Colonel)
Assignments: 8th Division, Missouri State Guard (July 1861-January 1862)

8th Division, Missouri State Guard, Trans-Mississippi District, Department #2 (January-March 1862)
Battles: Dug Springs (August 2, 1861)
Siege of Lexington (September 13-20, 1861)
Pea Ridge (March 7-8, 1862)
Further Reading: Bevier, R. S., *History of the First and Second Missouri Confederate Brigades 1861-1865.*

204. MISSOURI 8TH CAVALRY REGIMENT, 8TH DIVISION, MISSOURI STATE GUARD

Organization: Organized in July 1861. Disbanded in the spring of 1862.
First Commander: T. E. Owen (Lieutenant Colonel)
Field Officer: R. K. Murrell (Major)
Assignments: 8th Division, Missouri State Guard (July 1861-January 1862)
8th Division, Missouri State Guard, Trans-Mississippi District, Department #2 (January-March 1862)
Battles: Dug Springs (August 2, 1861)
Siege of Lexington (September 13-20, 1861)
Pea Ridge (March 7-8, 1862)
Further Reading: Bevier, R. S., *History of the First and Second Missouri Confederate Brigades 1861-1865.*

205. MISSOURI 9TH CAVALRY REGIMENT, 8TH DIVISION, MISSOURI STATE GUARD

Organization: Organized in July 1861. Disbanded in the spring of 1862.
First Commander: Thomas B. Cummings (Lieutenant Colonel)
Field Officer: J. Alexander Smith (Major)
Assignments: 8th Division, Missouri State Guard (July 1861-January 1862)
8th Division, Missouri State Guard, Trans-Mississippi District, Department #2 (January-March 1862)
Battles: Dug Springs (August 2, 1861)
Siege of Lexington (September 13-20, 1861)
Pea Ridge (March 7-8, 1862)
Further Reading: Bevier, R. S., *History of the First and Second Missouri Confederate Brigades 1861-1865.*

206. MISSOURI 10TH CAVALRY REGIMENT, 8TH DIVISION, MISSOURI STATE GUARD

Organization: Organized in July 1861. Disbanded in the spring of 1862.
First Commander: William H. Erwin (Colonel)
Field Officers: Robert Cunningham (Lieutenant Colonel)

David P. Fleming (Major)
Assignments: 8th Division, Missouri State Guard (July 1861-January 1862)
8th Division, Missouri State Guard, Trans-Mississippi District, Department #2 (January-March 1862)
Battles: Dug Springs (August 2, 1861)
Siege of Lexington (September 13-20, 1861)
Pea Ridge (March 7-8, 1862)
Further Reading: Bevier, R. S., *History of the First and Second Missouri Confederate Brigades 1861-1865*.

207. MISSOURI 11TH CAVALRY REGIMENT, 8TH DIVISION, MISSOURI STATE GUARD

Organization: Organized in July 1861. Disbanded in the spring of 1862.
First Commander: Sanford J. Talbot (Colonel)
Field Officers: Andrew J. Piercey (Lieutenant Colonel)
William Warner (Major)
Assignments: 8th Division, Missouri State Guard (July 1861-January 1862)
8th Division, Missouri State Guard, Trans-Mississippi District, Department #2 (January-March 1862)
Battles: Dug Springs (August 2, 1861)
Siege of Lexington (September 13-20, 1861)
Pea Ridge (March 7-8, 1862)
Further Reading: Bevier, R. S., *History of the First and Second Missouri Confederate Brigades 1861-1865*.

208. MISSOURI 12TH CAVALRY REGIMENT, 8TH DIVISION, MISSOURI STATE GUARD

Organization: Organized in late 1861. Disbanded in the spring of 1862.
Field Officer: Richard J. Robertson (Major)
Assignments: 8th Division, Missouri State Guard (December 1861-January 1862)
8th Division, Missouri State Guard, Trans-Mississippi District, Department #2 (January-March 1862)
Battle: Pea Ridge (March 7-8, 1862)
Further Reading: Bevier, R. S., *History of the First and Second Missouri Confederate Brigades 1861-1865*.

209. MISSOURI 13TH CAVALRY REGIMENT, 8TH DIVISION, MISSOURI STATE GUARD

Organization: Organized in late 1861. Disbanded in the spring of 1862.
Field Officer: Robert W. Crawford (Lieutenant Colonel)

Assignments: 8th Division, Missouri State Guard (December 1861-January 1862)
8th Division, Missouri State Guard, Trans-Mississippi District, Department #2 (January-March 1862)
Battle: Pea Ridge (March 7-8, 1862)
Further Reading: Bevier, R. S., *History of the First and Second Missouri Confederate Brigades 1861-1865.*

210. MISSOURI 14TH CAVALRY REGIMENT, 8TH DIVISION, MISSOURI STATE GUARD

Organization: Organized in late 1861. Disbanded in the spring of 1862.
Field Officer: H. W. King (Major)
Assignments: 8th Division, Missouri State Guard (December 1861-January 1862)
8th Division, Missouri State Guard, Trans-Mississippi District, Department #2 (January-March 1862)
Battle: Pea Ridge (March 7-8, 1862)
Further Reading: Bevier, R. S., *History of the First and Second Missouri Confederate Brigades 1861-1865.*

211. MISSOURI 1ST INFANTRY REGIMENT, 8TH DIVISION, MISSOURI STATE GUARD

Organization: Organized in July 1861. Disbanded in the spring of 1862.
First Commander: Thomas H. Rosser (Lieutenant Colonel, Colonel)
Field Officers: Eugene Erwin (Major)
Edmond B. Holloway (Colonel)
William Martin (Lieutenant Colonel)
Assignments: 1st Brigade, 8th Division, Missouri State Guard (August 1861-January 1862)
8th Division, Missouri State Guard, Trans-Mississippi District, Department #2 (January-March 1862)
Battles: Dug Springs (August 2, 1861)
Wilson's Creek [detachment] (August 10, 1861)
Siege of Lexington (September 13-20, 1861)
Pea Ridge (March 7-8, 1862)
Further Reading: Bevier, R. S., *History of the First and Second Missouri Confederate Brigades 1861-1865.*

212. MISSOURI 2ND INFANTRY REGIMENT, 8TH DIVISION, MISSOURI STATE GUARD

Organization: Organized in July 1861. Disbanded in the spring of 1862.

First Commander: John R. Graves (Colonel)
Field Officers: Ezra M. Brashear (Major)
Lawrence W. Counselman (Lieutenant Colonel)
Benjamin Elliott (Colonel)
Cave J. Kirtley (Lieutenant Colonel)
Samuel F. Taylor (Major)
Assignments: 1st Brigade, 8th Division, Missouri State Guard (August 1861-January 1862)
8th Division, Missouri State Guard, Trans-Mississippi District, Department #2 (January-March 1862)
Battles: Dug Springs (August 2, 1861)
Wilson's Creek (August 10, 1861)
Siege of Lexington (September 13-20, 1861)
Pea Ridge (March 7-8, 1862)
Further Reading: Bevier, R. S., *History of the First and Second Missouri Confederate Brigades 1861-1865*.

213. MISSOURI 3RD INFANTRY REGIMENT, 8TH DIVISION, MISSOURI STATE GUARD

Organization: Organized in July 1861. Disbanded in the spring of 1862.
First Commander: Edgar V. Hurst (Colonel)
Field Officers: Ferdinand Ruth (Major)
John C. Tracy (Lieutenant Colonel)
Assignments: 1st Brigade, 8th Division, Missouri State Guard (August 1861-January 1862)
8th Division, Missouri State Guard, Trans-Mississippi District, Department #2 (January-March 1862)
Battles: Dug Springs (August 2, 1861)
Wilson's Creek (August 10, 1861)
Siege of Lexington (September 13-20, 1861)
Pea Ridge (March 7-8, 1862)
Further Reading: Bevier, R. S., *History of the First and Second Missouri Confederate Brigades 1861-1865*.

214. MISSOURI 4TH INFANTRY REGIMENT, 8TH DIVISION, MISSOURI STATE GUARD

Organization: Organized in July 1861. Disbanded in the spring of 1862.
First Commander: Stephen F. Hale (Colonel)
Field Officers: Elbert S. Feaster (Major)
Thomas H. Murray (Major)
Walter S. O'Kane (Lieutenant Colonel, Colonel)

Assignments: 1st Brigade, 8th Division, Missouri State Guard (July 1861-January 1862)

8th Division, Missouri State Guard, Trans-Mississippi District, Department #2 (January-March 1862)

Battles: Dug Springs (August 2, 1861)

Wilson's Creek [battalion] (August 10, 1861)

Siege of Lexington (September 13-20, 1861)

Pea Ridge (March 7-8, 1862)

Further Reading: Bevier, R. S., *History of the First and Second Missouri Confederate Brigades 1861-1865.*

215. MISSOURI 5TH INFANTRY BATTALION, 8TH DIVISION, MISSOURI STATE GUARD

Organization: Organized in 1861. Disbanded in the spring of 1862.

First Commander: John W. Priest (Lieutenant Colonel)

Assignments: 8th Division, Missouri State Guard (December 1861-January 1862)

8th Division, Missouri State Guard, Trans-Mississippi District, Department #2 (January-March 1862)

Battle: Pea Ridge (March 7-8, 1862)

Further Reading: Bevier, R. S., *History of the First and Second Missouri Confederate Brigades 1861-1865.*

216. MISSOURI 5TH INFANTRY REGIMENT, 8TH DIVISION, MISSOURI STATE GUARD

Organization: Organized in July 1861. Disbanded in the spring of 1862.

First Commander: James J. Clarkson (Colonel)

Field Officers: Robert W. Crawford (Lieutenant Colonel)

Alexander C. Lemmon (Major)

Assignments: 1st Brigade, 8th Division, Missouri State Guard (July 1861-January 1862)

8th Division, Missouri State Guard, Trans-Mississippi District, Department #2 (January-March 1862)

Battles: Dug Springs (August 2, 1861)

Wilson's Creek (August 10, 1861)

Siege of Lexington (September 13-20, 1861)

Pea Ridge (March 7-8, 1862)

Further Reading: Bevier, R. S., *History of the First and Second Missouri Confederate Brigades 1861-1865.*

217. MISSOURI 6TH INFANTRY REGIMENT, 8TH DIVISION, MISSOURI STATE GUARD

Organization: Organized in 1861. Disbanded in the spring of 1862.

Field Officers: Hiram M. Bledsoe (Lieutenant Colonel)

John P. Bowman (Major)

Daniel Veitch (Major)

Assignments: 8th Division, Missouri State Guard (December 1861-January 1862)

8th Division, Missouri State Guard, Trans-Mississippi District, Department #2 (January-March 1862)

Battle: Pea Ridge (March 7-8, 1862)

Further Reading: Bevier, R. S., *History of the First and Second Missouri Confederate Brigades 1861-1865*.

THE CONFEDERATE UNITS

CONFEDERATE UNITS

These are the units that were organized directly by the Confederate government by the incorporation of the companies from various states. In some cases they were subsequently broken up, with the companies attached to regiments from their parent states.

It should be noted that there is an extra sub-chapter in this chapter for the Engineer units.

Note: The index for the Confederate units begins on page 229.

ARTILLERY

1. CONFEDERATE 1ST ARTILLERY BATTERY

Also Known As: Louisiana 1st Artillery Battery Regulars

Organization: Organized for five years in the Confederate Regular Army from the Infantry School of Practice, New Orleans' Barracks, New Orleans, Louisiana on October 29, 1861. It was armed with two 3" Rifles and four 6-lb. Smoothbores on April 11-23, 1863. Surrendered by General E. K. Smith, commanding Trans-Mississippi Department, on May 26, 1865.

First Commander: Edward Higgins (Captain)

Captains: Oliver J. Semmes

John T. Mason Barnes

Assignments: Department #1 (October 1861-April 1862)

Port Hudson, Department #1 (April-June 1862)

Port Hudson, Department of Southern Mississippi and East Louisiana (June-July 1862)

1st Sub-district, District of the Mississippi, Department #2 (July-August 1862)

Allen's Brigade, Ruggles' Division, Breckinridge's Command, District of the Mississippi, Department #2 (August 1862)

1st Sub-district, District of the Mississippi, Department #2 (August-September 1862)

Artillery, District of West Louisiana, Trans-Mississippi Department (September 1862-May 1863)

Artillery, Sub-district of Southwestern Louisiana, District of West Louisiana, Trans-Mississippi Department (May-December 1863)

Artillery, District of West Louisiana, Trans-Mississippi Department (December 1863-September 1864)

3rd (Faries') Mounted Artillery Battalion, 2nd (Polignac's) Division, 1st Corps, Trans-Mississippi Department (September-November 1864)

4th (Squiers') Artillery Battalion, 1st (Forney's) Texas Division, 1st Corps, Trans-Mississippi Department (November 1864-May 1865)

Battles: New Orleans (April 18-25, 1862)

Baton Rouge (August 5, 1862)
Koch's Plantation, near Donaldsonville (September 24, 1862)
Georgia Landing, near Labadieville (October 27, 1862)
Berwick Bay (November 1-6, 1862)
Fort Bisland (April 12-13, 1863)
Jeanerette [section] (April 14, 1863)
Donaldsonville (June 28, 1863)
Mississippi River, near Donaldsonville [section] (July 3-4, 1863)
Stirling's Plantation (September 29, 1863)
Bayou Teche [detachment] (October 3, 1863)
Bayou Bourbeau [section] (November 3, 1863)
Red River Campaign (March-May 1864)
Mansfield [not engaged] (April 8, 1864)
Pleasant Hill [not engaged] (April 9, 1864)
Cloutierville (April 22-24, 1864)
Mansura (May 16, 1864)
Yellow Bayou (May 18, 1864)

2. CONFEDERATE 1ST (FITZGERALD'S) ARTILLERY REGIMENT

Organization: Failed to complete organization.

3. CONFEDERATE ROBERTSON'S-DENT'S ARTILLERY BATTERY

See: ALABAMA [& FLORIDA] ROBERTSON'S-DENT'S ARTILLERY BATTERY

4. CONFEDERATE WHITE'S HORSE ARTILLERY BATTERY

Also Known As: White's (Tenn.) Horse Artillery Battery

Organization: Organized on July 1, 1862. One section was armed with two 6-lb. Smoothbores on November 25, 1862. Surrendered by General Joseph E. Johnston at Durham Station, Orange County, North Carolina on April 26, 1865.

First Commander: Benjamin F. White, Jr. (Captain)

Assignments: Wharton's Cavalry Brigade, Left Wing, Army of the Mississippi, Department #2 (November 1862)

Wharton's Cavalry Brigade, 1st Corps, Army of the Mississippi, Department #2 (November 1862)

Wharton's Cavalry Brigade, 1st Corps, Army of Tennessee (November-December 1862)

Wharton's Brigade, Wharton's Cavalry Division, Army of Tennessee (December 1862-March 1863)

Artillery, Wharton's Division, Wheeler's Cavalry Corps, Army of Tennessee (March-December 1863)

Artillery, Morgan's Division, Martin's Cavalry Corps, Department of East Tennessee (December 1863-February 1864)
Robertson's-Hamilton's Artillery Battalion, Wheeler's Cavalry Corps, Army of Tennessee (April-November 1864)
Horse Artillery Battalion, Wheeler's Cavalry Corps, Department of South Carolina, Georgia, and Florida (November 1864-February 1865)
Horse Artillery Battalion, Wheeler's Cavalry Corps, Hampton's Cavalry Command (February-April 1865)
Horse Artillery Battalion, Wheeler's Cavalry Corps, Hampton's Cavalry Command, Army of Tennessee (April 1865)
Battles: Murfreesboro (December 31, 1862-January 3, 1863)
Wheeler's Louisville & Nashville and Nashville & Chattanooga Railroad Raid (April 7-11, 1863)
Chickamauga (September 19-20, 1863)
Chattanooga Siege (September-November 1863)
Chattanooga (November 23-25, 1863)
Knoxville Siege (November-December 1863)
Atlanta Campaign (May-September 1864)
Atlanta Siege (July-September 1864)
Savannah Campaign (November-December 1864)
Carolinas Campaign (February-April 1865)

CAVALRY

5. Confederate 1st Trans-Mississippi Cavalry Battalion

Also Known As: 1st Arkansas and Louisiana Cavalry Battalion

Organization: Organized with four companies on March 18, 1864. Company E was organized on June 1, 1864. Surrendered by General E. K. Smith, commanding Trans-Mississippi Department, on May 26, 1865.

First Commander: Thompson J. Bird (Major)

Assignment: Headquarters, Trans-Mississippi Department (March 1864-May 1865)

6. Confederate 1st Cavalry Regiment

Also Known As: 6th Cavalry Regiment
12th Cavalry Regiment
16th Cavalry Regiment

Organization: Organized by the increasing of the 1st (King's) Kentucky Cavalry Battalion to a regiment by the addition of four companies on April 1, 1862. Reorganized on January 28, 1863. Companies D and A, 4th (Murray's) Tennessee Cavalry Regiment became 2nd Companies C and D, respectively. Company B, 2nd Alabama and Mississippi Cavalry Battalion became Company L and later 2nd Company G in this regiment. Companies H and 1st K became L and K, 4th (Roddey's) Alabama Cavalry Regiment, respectively. Surrendered at Gainesville, Alabama on May 4, 1865.

First Commander: Thomas Claiborne (Colonel)

Field Officers: Henry C. Bate (Major)
John T. Cox (Colonel)
Henry C. King (Major, Colonel)
James A. Pell (Lieutenant Colonel)
Charles S. Robertson (Lieutenant Colonel)
Moses J. Wicks (Major)

Assignments: Wheeler's Cavalry Brigade, Left Wing, Army of the Mississippi, Department #2 (September-November 1862)
Wheeler's Cavalry Brigade, 2nd Corps, Army of the Mississippi, Department #2 (November 1862)
Wharton's Cavalry Brigade, 2nd Corps, Army of Tennessee (November-December 1862)
Wharton's Brigade, Wheeler's Cavalry Division, Army of Tennessee (December 1862-March 1863)
Russell's Brigade, Martin's Division, Wheeler's Cavalry Corps, Army of Tennessee (March-September 1863)
Wade's-Anderson's Brigade, Kelly's Division, Wheeler's Cavalry Corps, Army of Tennessee (October 1863-September 1864)
Armistead's Cavalry Brigade, District of the Gulf, Department of Alabama, Mississippi, and East Louisiana (March-April 1865)
Armistead's Cavalry Brigade, Maury's Command, Department of Alabama, Mississippi, and East Louisiana (April 1865)
Battles: near Lockridge's Mill [skirmish] (May 5, 1862)
Perryville (October 8, 1862)
Murfreesboro (December 31, 1862-January 3, 1863)
Guy's Gap (June 25, 27, 1863)
Tullahoma Campaign (June-July 1863)
Trenton (June 15, 1863)
Shelbyville (June 27, 1863)
Lafayette [skirmish] (September 13-14, 1863)
Chickamauga (September 19-20, 1863)
Chattanooga Siege (September-November 1863)
Atlanta Campaign (May-September 1864)
McAfee's Crossroads (June 11, 1864)
Noonday Creek (June 21, 1864)
Atlanta Siege (July-September 1864)
Mobile (March 17-April 12, 1865)

7. CONFEDERATE 1ST CAVALRY REGIMENT REGULARS

Organization: Only one company was organized for this regiment. Company A, under Captain Edward Ingraham, was organized on April 25, 1861 from men enlisting for three or five year terms in the fledgling Confederate Regular Army. The company served as escort to Major General Earl Van Dorn and Brigadier General Frank C. Armstrong. Surrendered by Lieutenant General Richard Taylor, commanding the Department of Alabama, Mississippi, and East Louisiana, at Citronelle, Alabama on May 4, 1865.
First Commander: Earl Van Dorn (Colonel)

Field Officer: Edmund Kirby Smith (Colonel)
Battle: near Campbellton (July 28, 1864)

8. CONFEDERATE 3RD CAVALRY REGIMENT

Also Known As: 11th Alabama Cavalry Battalion
11th Cavalry Regiment
13th Cavalry Regiment
Organization: Organization begun in May 1862. Completed organization on August 20, 1862. Companies A, B, and C had previously served in the 2nd (Smith's) Tennessee Cavalry Regiment. Surrendered by General Joseph E. Johnston at Durham Station, Orange County, North Carolina on April 26, 1865.
First Commander: James R. Howard (Colonel)
Field Officers: Francis N. Corns (Major, Lieutenant Colonel)
William N. Estes (Lieutenant Colonel, Colonel)
John McCaskill (Lieutenant Colonel)
P. H. Rice (Colonel)
G. C. Sandusky (Major)
James G. Yeiser (Major)
Assignments: Unattached, Department of East Tennessee (May-August 1862)
Pegram's Cavalry Brigade, Department of East Tennessee (October-November 1862)
Wharton's Cavalry Brigade, 1st Corps, Army of Tennessee (November-December 1862)
Wharton's Brigade, Wheeler's Cavalry Division, Army of Tennessee (December 1862-March 1863)
Harrison's Brigade, Wharton's Division, Wheeler's Cavalry Corps, Army of Tennessee (March-September 1863)
Wade's-Hume's-Allen's-Anderson's Brigade, Kelly's Division, Wheeler's Cavalry Corps, Army of Tennessee (October 1863-November 1864)
Anderson's Brigade, Kelly's-Anderson's Division, Wheeler's Cavalry Corps, Department of South Carolina, Georgia, and Florida (November 1864-February 1865)
Anderson's Brigade, Allen's Division, Wheeler's Cavalry Corps, Hampton's Cavalry Command (February-April 1865)
Anderson's Brigade, Allen's Division, Wheeler's Cavalry Corps, Hampton's Cavalry Command, Army of Tennessee (April 1865)
Battles: near Readyville (June 7, 1862)
Bridgeport and Battle Creek (August 27, 1862)
near Tompkinsville [skirmish] (November 19, 1862)

Murfreesboro (December 31, 1862-January 3, 1863)
Fort Donelson (February 3, 1863)
near Triune (March 21, 1863)
Tullahoma Campaign (June-July 1863)
Triune (June 11, 1863)
Hoover's Gap (June 24-26, 1863)
Chickamauga (September 19-20, 1863)
Chattanooga Siege (September-November 1863)
Philadelphia (October 20, 1863)
Chattanooga (November 23-25, 1863)
Bridgeport (April 12, 1864)
Atlanta Campaign (May-September 1864)
McAfee's Crossroads (June 11, 1864)
Trenton (June 15, 1864)
Noonday Creek (June 21, 1864)
Atlanta Siege (July-September 1864)
Savannah Campaign (November-December 1864)
Carolinas Campaign (February-April 1865)
Bentonville (March 19-21, 1865)

9. CONFEDERATE 6TH CAVALRY BATTALION

Organization: Organized with six companies by the change of designation of the 3rd (Jessee's) Kentucky Cavalry Battalion on September 29, 1863. Company G was assigned on October 16, 1864. Companies E and F became McFarlane's Virginia Cavalry Squadron. Disbanded by Brigadier General John Echols, commanding Department of Southwestern Virginia and East Tennessee, at Christianburg, Virginia on April 12, 1865.

First Commander: George M. Jessee (Major, Lieutenant Colonel)

Field Officer: Allen F. McAfee (Major)

Assignments: Hodge's Brigade, Armstrong's Division, Wheeler's Cavalry Corps, Army of Tennessee (September-November 1863)

Hodge's Brigade, Armstrong's Division, Martin's Cavalry Corps, Department of East Tennessee (November 1863-January 1864)

Hodge's Brigade, Jones' Division, Ransom's Cavalry Corps, Department of East Tennessee (March-April 1864)

Giltner's Cavalry Brigade, Department of Western Virginia and East Tennessee (April-November 1864)

Cosby's Cavalry Brigade, Department of Western Virginia and East Tennessee (February-April 1865)

10. CONFEDERATE 6TH CAVALRY REGIMENT

See: CONFEDERATE 1ST CAVALRY REGIMENT

11. CONFEDERATE 7TH CAVALRY BATTALION

Organization: Organized with nine companies behind enemy lines in Kentucky and western Virginia under authority of the Secretary of War granted on May 22, 1863. Disbanded by Brigadier General John Echols, commanding Department of Southwestern Virginia and East Tennessee, at Christianburg, Virginia on April 12, 1865.

First Commander: Clarence J. Prentice (Lieutenant Colonel)

Field Officer: W. G. Repass (Major)

Assignments: Hodge's Brigade, Jones' Division, Ransom's Cavalry Corps, Department of East Tennessee (March-April 1864)

Giltner's Cavalry Brigade, Department of Western Virginia and East Tennessee (April 1864-April 1865)

12. CONFEDERATE 7TH CAVALRY REGIMENT

Also Known As: 7th Partisan Rangers Regiment

Organization: Organized on September 16, 1862. Disbanded with the seven Georgia companies being transferred to the 10th Georgia Cavalry Regiment and the five North Carolina companies being transferred to the 16th North Carolina Cavalry Battalion on November 30, 1864, per S.O. #161, Adjutant and Inspector General's Office, dated July 11, 1864.

First Commander: William C. Claiborne (Colonel)

Field Officers: Thomas D. Claiborne (Major, Lieutenant Colonel)

Jesse H. Sikes (Major)

Valentine H. Taliaferro (Lieutenant Colonel, Colonel)

Assignments: Cavalry, Department of North Carolina (May-July 1863)

District of North Carolina, Department of North Carolina (July 1863-May 1864)

District of the Cape Fear, Department of North Carolina [Companies D, E, and I] (July-September 1863)

District of the Cape Fear [Companies D, E, and I] (September 1863-January 1864)

District of the Cape Fear [Companies D and E] (January-April 1864)

District of the Cape Fear, Department of North Carolina [Companies D and E] (April-May 1864)

Dearing's Cavalry Brigade, District of North Carolina, Department of North Carolina (May 1864)

Dearing's Cavalry Brigade, 2nd Military District, Department of North Carolina and Southern Virginia (May-September 1864)

1862. Surrendered by General Joseph E. Johnston at Durham Station, nge County, North Carolina on April 26, 1865.

st Commander: Richard H. Brewer (Colonel)

d Officers: Jefferson Falkner (Lieutenant Colonel)

ph H. Field (Colonel)

n S. Prather (Major, Lieutenant Colonel)

liam B. Wade (Colonel)

n T. Wright (Major)

ignments: Wheeler's Cavalry Brigade, 1st Corps, Army of Tennessee November 1862)

eeler's Brigade, Wheeler's Cavalry Division, Army of Tennessee (December 1862-March 1863)

gan's-Morgan's Brigade, Martin's Division, Wheeler's Cavalry Corps, Army f Tennessee (March-September 1863)

de's-Hume's-Allen's-Anderson's Brigade, Kelly's Division, Wheeler's Cavalry Corps, Army of Tennessee (October 1863-November 1864)

derson's Brigade, Kelly's-Allen's Division, Wheeler's Cavalry Corps, Department of South Carolina, Georgia, and Florida (November 1864-February 865)

derson's Brigade, Allen's Division, Wheeler's Cavalry Corps, Hampton's Cavalry Corps (February-April 1865)

derson's Brigade, Allen's Division, Wheeler's Cavalry Corps, Hampton's Cavalry Command, Army of Tennessee (April 1865)

tles: Clear Creek, near Baldwyn [skirmish] (June 14, 1862)

lly Springs to Bolivar and Jackson, expedition from [detachment] (July 5-August 1, 1862)

rfreesboro (December 31, 1862-January 3, 1863)

ldleton, Unionville, and Rover (January 31, 1863)

er (February 19, 1863)

lahoma Campaign (June-July 1863)

lbyville (June 27, 1863)

ckamauga (September 19-20, 1863)

attanooga Siege (September-November 1863)

attanooga (November 23-25, 1863)

anta Campaign (May-September 1864)

anta Siege (July-September 1864)

wn's Mill (July 30, 1864)

tville (October 2, 1864)

annah Campaign (November-December 1864)

olinas Campaign (February-April 1865)

ntonville (March 19-21, 1865)

District of the Cape Fear, Department of North Carolina an [Companies D and E] (May-September 1864)

Dearing's Brigade, Cavalry Corps, Army of Northern Virgir vember 1864)

Battles: Joyner's Ford, Blackwater River [detachment 1862)

Petersburg (June 9, 1864)

Petersburg Siege (June 1864-April 1865)

Peebles' Farm (September 29-October 2, 1864)

Harman Road (October 2, 1864)

Jones' Farm (September 30, 1864)

13. CONFEDERATE 8TH (DEARING'S) CAVALRY

Organization: Organized with nine companies per instru tary of War on January 13, 1864. Companies A, B, and C the assignment of Companies A, B, and C, respectively, 1 Cavalry Battalion. Companies D and E were organized Company L, 62nd Georgia Cavalry Regiment. Compa organized by the assignment of Companies 2nd I and Cavalry Regiment. Company H was apprently a new orga I was formerly the Petersburg Virginia Horse Artillery disbanded ca. April 29, 1864. Companies A, B, and C, res tions as Companies A, B, and C, respectively, 12th Nort Regiment. Companies D and E eventually [on June 8, 18 nies I and K, respectively, 24th Virginia Cavalry Regimen G resumed their designations as Companies 2nd I and Cavalry Regiment. Company H became 2nd Compan Cavalry Regiment. Company I [the Petersburg (Va.) Hor again became an independent unit.

First Commander: James Dearing (Colonel)

Assignment: Cavalry, Department of North Carolina (Ja

Battles: Plymouth Siege (April 17-20, 1864)

Petersburg (June 9, 1864)

14. CONFEDERATE 8TH (WADE'S) CAVALRY R

Also Known As: 2nd Mississippi and Alabama Cavalry F

Organization: Organized by the consolidation of the 1st Cavalry Battalion (three companies) and the 2nd (Brewe Alabama Cavalry Battalion (six companies) in May 186 formerly Company K, 2nd Mississippi Infantry Battalion.

15. CONFEDERATE 10TH CAVALRY REGIMENT

Organization: Organized by the consolidation of the 19th Georgia Cavalry Battalion (five companies) and the 5th [Cavalry] Battalion, Hilliard's Alabama Legion (five companies) on December 27, 1862. Surrendered by General Joseph E. Johnston at Durham Station, Orange County, North Carolina on April 26, 1865.

First Commander: Charles T. Goode (Colonel)

Field Officers: John B. Rudolph (Major)
Miles M. Slaughter (Lieutenant Colonel)
William I. Vason (Lieutenant Colonel, Colonel)

Assignments: Department of East Tennessee (December 1862-March 1863)
Scott's Cavalry Brigade, Department of East Tennessee (April-July 1863)
Scott's Cavalry Brigade, Army of East Tennessee, Department of Tennessee (July-September 1863)
Scott's Brigade, Pegram's Division, Forrest's Cavalry Corps, Army of Tennessee (September-October 1863)
Wade's-Hume's-Allen's-Anderson's Brigade, Kelly's Division, Wheeler's Cavalry Corps, Army of Tennessee (October 1863-November 1864)
Anderson's Brigade, Kelly's-Allen's Division, Wheeler's Cavalry Corps, Department of South Carolina, Georgia, and Florida (November 1864-February 1865)
Anderson's Brigade, Allen's Division, Wheeler's Cavalry Corps, Hampton's Cavalry Command (February-April 1865)
Anderson's Brigade, Allen's Division, Wheeler's Cavalry Corps, Hampton's Cavalry Command, Army of Tennessee (April 1865)

Battles: Scott's Raid in Eastern Kentucky (July 25-August 6, 1863)
Monticello (June 9, 1863)
Chickamauga (September 19-20, 1863)
Chattanooga Siege (September-November 1863)
Chattanooga (November 23-25, 1863)
Atlanta Campaign (May-September 1864)
Resaca (May 14-15, 1864)
New Hope Church (May 25-June 5, 1864)
Atlanta Siege (July-September 1864)
Savannah Campaign (November-December 1864)
Carolinas Campaign (February-April 1865)
Bentonville (March 19-21, 1865)

16. CONFEDERATE 11TH CAVALRY REGIMENT

See: CONFEDERATE 3RD CAVALRY REGIMENT

17. CONFEDERATE 12TH CAVALRY REGIMENT

See: CONFEDERATE 1ST CAVALRY REGIMENT

18. CONFEDERATE 13TH CAVALRY REGIMENT

See: CONFEDERATE 3RD CAVALRY REGIMENT

19. CONFEDERATE 14TH CAVALRY REGIMENT

Organization: Organized by the consolidation of Garland's Mississippi Cavalry Battalion (three companies), the Cavalry Battalion, Miles' Louisiana Legion (three companies), Rhodes' Mississippi Partisan Rangers Company, and Mullen's Louisiana Scouts and Sharpshooters Company on September 14, 1863. However, Company A, Cavalry Battalion, Miles' Louisiana Legion refused to recognize its assignment to this regiment as Company E and maintained its independence. Company I was organized on November 25, 1863. Company K was organized on January 22, 1864. Regiment disbanded in early 1865. The four Louisiana companies [i.e. Companies D, E, G, and H] became Companies A, I, C, and E, respectively, Ogden's Louisiana Cavalry Regiment. The six Mississippi companies [i.e. Companies A, B, C, F, I, and K] were consolidated into two companies and assigned as Companies C and H, 3rd, 14th (Confederate), and 28th Mississippi Cavalry Regiment Consolidated.

First Commander: F. Dumonteil (Colonel)

Field Officers: John B. Cage (Major, Lieutenant Colonel)

William H. Garland (Lieutenant Colonel)

Pinckney C. Harrington (Major, Lieutenant Colonel)

Assignments: Logan's Cavalry Command, Department of Mississippi and East Louisiana (September 1863)

Griffith's-Adams' Brigade, Jackson's Division, Lee's Cavalry Corps, Department of Mississippi and East Louisiana (November 1863-January 1864)

Adams' Brigade, Jackson's Division, Lee's Cavalry Corps, Department of Alabama, Mississippi, and East Louisiana (January-March 1864)

District of Southwest Mississippiand East Louisiana, Department of Alabama, Mississippi, and East Louisiana [Company H] (February 1864)

Scott's Brigade, Lee's Cavalry Corps, Department of Alabama, Mississippi, and East Louisiana [Company H] (April 1864)

District of Southwest Mississippi and East Louisiana, Department of Alabama, Mississippi, and East Louisiana [Companies A, D, and G] (May 1864)

Scott's Brigade, Adams' Cavalry Division, Department of Alabama, Mississippi, and East Louisiana [Companies D and H] (June 1864)

Mabry's Brigade, Adams' Cavalry Division, Department of Alabama, Mississippi, and East Louisiana (June-August 1864)

Mabry's Brigade, District North of Homochitto [Adams' Command], Department of Alabama, Mississippi, and East Louisiana (August-October 1864)

Mabry's Brigade, Northern Sub-district of Mississippi, District of Mississippi and East Louisiana, Department of Alabama, Mississippi, and East Louisiana (October-December 1864)

Battles: Meridian Campaign (February-March 1864)

A.J. Smith's 1st Mississippi Invasion (July 5-21, 1864)

Tupelo (July 14, 1864)

20. CONFEDERATE 15TH CAVALRY REGIMENT

Also Known As: 1st Alabama & Florida Cavalry Regiment

Organization: Organized by the consolidation of the 3rd Florida Cavalry Battalion (four companies), Murphy's Alabama Cavalry Battalion (three companies), and three independent companies at Mobile, Alabama on September 24, 1863. Surrendered by Lieutenant Richard Taylor, commanding the Department of Alabama, Mississippi, and East Louisiana, at Citronelle, Alabama on May 4, 1865.

First Commander: Henry Maury (Colonel)

Field Officers: Thomas J. Myers (Lieutenant Colonel)

Robert H. Partridge (Major)

Assignments: Department of the Gulf (September-October 1863)

Quarles' Brigade, Department of the Gulf (November 1863)

Clanton's Brigade, Department of the Gulf (December 1863-December 1862)

Jenifer's Cavalry Brigade, Department of the Gulf (December 1863-March 1864)

Reynolds' Brigade, Department of the Gulf (March-April 1864)

Reynolds' Brigade, District of the Gulf, Department of Alabama, Mississippi, and East Louisiana (April-May 1864)

Patton's Brigade, District of the Gulf, Department of Alabama, Mississippi, and East Louisiana (June-August 1864)

Liddell's Brigade, District of the Gulf, Department of Alabama, Mississippi, and East Louisiana (September-October 1864)

Cavalry, Liddell's Division, District of the Gulf, Department of Alabama, Mississippi, and East Louisiana (October-November 1864)

McCulloch's Cavalry Brigade, District of the Gulf, Department of Alabama, Mississippi, and East Louisiana (November 1864)

Cavalry, Liddell's Division, District of the Gulf, Department of Alabama, Mississippi, and East Louisiana (November-December 1864)

H. Maury's Command, District of the Gulf, Department of Alabama, Mississippi, and East Louisiana (March-April 1865)

H. Maury's Command, D. H. Maury's Command, Department of Alabama, Mississippi, and East Louisiana (April 1865)

Battles: Tunica Landing (November 8, 1863)

Bayou Sara (November 9, 1863)

Yellow River [Company I] (June 25, 1864)

Mobile (March 17-April 12, 1865)

21. CONFEDERATE 16TH CAVALRY REGIMENT

See: CONFEDERATE 1ST CAVALRY REGIMENT

22. CONFEDERATE 20TH CAVALRY REGIMENT

Also Known As: Lay's Mississippi Cavalry Regiment

Organization: Organized with mixed companies from Arkansas, Louisiana, and Mississippi ca. April 23, 1864. Disbanded due to the failure of the War Department to recognize its organization in December 1864.

First Commander: Benjamin D. Lay (Colonel)

Field Officer: Lawrence W. O'Bannon (Major)

Assignments: Scott's Brigade, Adams' Cavalry Division, Department of Alabama, Mississippi, and East Louisiana (June-August 1864)

Scott's Brigade, District South of Homochitto, Department of Alabama, Mississippi, and East Louisiana (August-October 1864)

Sub-district of Southwest Mississippi and East Louisiana, District of Mississippi and East Louisiana, Department of Alabama, Mississippi, and East Louisiana (October-December 1864)

23. CONFEDERATE ADAMS', CAVALRY REGIMENT

See: MISSISSIPPI W. ADAMS'-WOOD'S CAVALRY REGIMENT

24. CONFEDERATE BAXTER'S CAVALRY BATTALION

Organization: Organized with four companies on January 20, 1863. This unit appears as a Mississippi unit in the *Official Records*. Broken up in June 1863.

First Commander: George Baxter (Major)

Assignment: General Headquarters, Van Dorn's Cavalry Corps, Department of Mississippi and East Louisiana (January-May 1863)

25. CONFEDERATE GILLUM'S CAVALRY REGIMENT, MOUNTED RIFLEMEN

Organization: Failed to complete its organization.

26. CONFEDERATE MEAD'S CAVALRY REGIMENT

Also Known As: Mead's Partisan Rangers Regiment

Organization: Organized behind enemy lines in Northern Alabama and Tennessee during 1864 under authority of January 18, 1864. Several companies failed to complete their organization. Disbanded with the five Alabama companies being transferred to the 25th Alabama Cavalry Battalion and the six Tennessee companies being transferred to the 27th Tennessee Cavalry Battalion on March 3, 1865.

First Commander: Lemuel H. Mead (Colonel)

27. CONFEDERATE POWERS' CAVALRY REGIMENT

Also Known As: Powers' Mississippi and Louisiana Cavalry Regiment

Organization: Organized with seven Louisiana and three Mississippi companies from December 1863 to May 1864. Disbanded with six Louisiana companies being transferred to the 18th Louisiana Cavalry Battalion and the three Mississippi companies being transferred to the 23rd Mississippi Cavalry Battalion on November 21, 1864, per S.O. #276, Adjutant and Inspector General's Office.

First Commander: Frank P. Powers (Colonel)

Field Officer: John C. McKowen (Lieutenant Colonel)

Assignments: District of South Mississippi and East Louisiana, Department of Alabama, Mississippi, and East Louisiana (February-May 1864)

Scott's Brigade, W. Adams' Cavalry Division, Department of Alabama, Mississippi, and East Louisiana (May-August 1864)

Scott's Cavalry Brigade, District South of Homochitto, Department of Alabama, Mississippi, and East Louisiana (August-September 1864)

[Sub-]District of Southwest Mississippi and East Louisiana, Department of Alabama, Mississippi, and East Louisiana (September-November 1864)

Battles: near Port Hudson (April 7, 1864)

Jackson [skirmishes] (July 5-7, 1864)

Bayou Sara [skirmish] (October 4, 1864)

Jackson (October 5, 1864)

28. CONFEDERATE POWERS' [NEW] CAVALRY REGIMENT

See: MISSISSIPPI POWERS' [NEW] CAVALRY REGIMENT

29. CONFEDERATE WOOD'S CAVALRY REGIMENT

See: MISSISSIPPI W. ADAMS'-WOOD'S CAVALRY REGIMENT

ENGINEERS

30. CONFEDERATE 1ST ENGINEERS BATTALION

Organization: Organized on April 1, 1864. Increased to a regiment and designated as the 4th Engineers Regiment ca. April 1865.

First Commander: Hugh T. Douglas (Lieutenant Colonel)

Field Officer: R. P. Rowley (Major)

Assignments: Unattached, Trans-Mississippi Department (April 1864-April 1865)

Defenses of Galveston, District of Texas, New Mexico, and Arizona, Trans-Mississippi Department [Company E] (March-April 1865)

Further Reading: Nichols, James L., *Confederate Engineers.*

31. CONFEDERATE 1ST ENGINEERS REGIMENT

Organization: Organized from January 19 to April 1, 1864. Surrendered at Appomattox Court House, Virginia on April 9, 1865.

First Commander: Thomas M. R. Talcott (Lieutenant Colonel, Colonel)

Field Officers: William W. Blackford (Major, Lieutenant Colonel)

Peyton Randolph (Major)

Assignments: Department of Richmond [Company D] (February-July 1864)

Department of Henrico (March-April 1864)

Engineers, Army of Northern Virginia (April 1864-April 1865)

Battles: Petersburg Siege (June 1864-April 1865)

Appomattox Court House (April 9, 1865)

Further Reading: Nichols, James L., *Confederate Engineers.*

32. CONFEDERATE 2ND ENGINEERS REGIMENT

Organization: Organization never completed. The companies were from Alabama, Georgia, and North Carolina. Companies C, G, H, and K surrendered at Appomattox Court House, Virginia on April 9, 1865.

First Commander: D. Wintter (Major)

Assignments: District of the Cape Fear [Company A] (October 1863-April 1864)

Military District of Georgia, Department of South Carolina, Georgia, and Florida [Company D] (October 1863-October 1864)

District of the Cape Fear, Department of North Carolina [Company A] (April-June 1864)

District of the Cape Fear, Department of North Carolina and Southern Virginia [Company A] (June 1864-February 1865)

Engineers, Army of Northern Virginia [Companies C, G, H, and K] (September 1864-April 1865)

McLaws' Division, Department of South Carolina, Georgia, and Florida [Company D] (October-November 1864)

Battles: Petersburg Siege [Companies C, G, H, and K] (June 1864-April 1865)

Appomattox Court House [Companies C, G, H, and K] (April 9, 1865)

Further Reading: Nichols, James L., *Confederate Engineers.*

33. CONFEDERATE 3RD ENGINEERS REGIMENT

Organization: Organized begun in 1863 but never completed. The eight companies included ones from Tennessee and Virginia. Companies A and E were disbanded by Brigadier General John Echols, commanding Department of Southwestern Virginia and East Tennessee, at Christianburg, Virginia on April 12, 1865. The balance of the regiment surrendered by General Joseph E. Johnston at Durham Station, Orange County, North Carolina on April 26, 1865.

First Commander: Stephen W. Presstman (Major, Lieutenant Colonel)

Field Officer: John W. Green (Major)

Assignments: Unattached, Department of Western Virginia and East Tennessee [Company E] (October 1863-April 1865)

Engineers, Army of Tennessee (December 1863-April 1865)

Unattached, Department of Western Virginia and East Tennessee [Company A] (February-April 1865)

Battles: Atlanta Campaign (May-September 1864)

Atlanta Siege (July-September 1864)

Carolinas Campaign (February-April 1865)

Further Reading: Nichols, James L., *Confederate Engineers.*

34. CONFEDERATE 4TH ENGINEERS REGIMENT

Organization: Organized with eight companies by increasing of the 1st Engineers Battalion to a regiment ca. April 1865. Surrendered by General E.K. Smith, commanding Trans-Mississippi Department, on May 26, 1865.

First Commander: Hugh T. Douglas (Colonel)

Assignment: Unattached, Trans-Mississippi Department (April-May 1865)

Further Reading: Nichols, James L., *Confederate Engineers.*

INFANTRY

35. CONFEDERATE 1ST INFANTRY BATTALION

Organization: Organized with five companies composed principally of re-enlistees from the 2nd Alabama and 1st Confederate Infantry Regiments on April 7, 1862. Eventually increased to nine companies. Reorganized on July 15, 1862. Surrendered at Appomattox Court House, Virginia on April 9, 1865.

First Commander: Lawrence W. O'Bannon (Lieutenant Colonel)

Field Officers: George H. Forney (Major, Lieutenant Colonel)
James C. Gordon (Major, Lieutenant Colonel)
Francis B. McClung (Major, Lieutenant Colonel)

Assignments: Fort Pillow, Department #2 (April-June 1862)
Grenada, Mississippi, Army of Mississippi (June-July 1862)
3rd Sub-district, District of the Mississippi, Department #2 (July-August 1862)
Rust's Brigade, 3rd Military District, Department of Mississippi and East Louisiana (March-April 1863)
Tilghman's-Adams' Brigade, Loring's Division, Department of Mississippi and East Louisiana (April-May 1863)
Adams' Brigade, Loring's Division, Department of the West (May-July 1863)
Adams' Brigade, Loring's Division, Department of Mississippi and East Louisiana (July 1863-January 1864)
Adams' Brigade, Loring's Division, Department of Alabama, Mississippi, and East Louisiana (January-March 1864)
Davis' Brigade, Heth's Division, 3rd Corps, Army of Northern Virginia (March 1864-April 1865)

Battles: Corinth (October 3-4, 1862)
Grand Gulf (April 29, 1863)
Vicksburg Campaign (May-July 1863)
Champion's Hill (May 16, 1863)
Meridian Campaign (February-March 1864)
Fort Pillow (April 12, 1864)
The Wilderness (May 5-6, 1864)

Spotsylvania Court House (May 8-21, 1864)
North Anna (May 23-26, 1864)
Cold Harbor (June 1-3, 1864)
Petersburg Siege (June 1864-April 1865)
Weldon Railroad (August 18-19, 1864)
Appomattox Court House (April 9, 1865)

36. CONFEDERATE 1ST FOREIGN INFANTRY BATTALION

Organization: Organized at Richmond, Virginia from foreign prisoners of war, under authority granted on September 28, 1864, with three companies on October 16, 1864. Companies D, E, F, G & H were organized at Salisbury, North Carolina on November 7, 1864. Company I organized at Salisbury, North Carolina on December 1, 1864. Increased to a regiment and designated as Tucker's Infantry Regiment on February 28, 1865.
First Commander: Julius G. Tucker (Lieutenant Colonel)

37. CONFEDERATE 1ST INFANTRY REGIMENT

Organization: Organized by the change of designation of the 36th (Villepigue's) Georgia Infantry Regiment on January 31, 1862. Field consolidation with the 66th Georgia Infantry Regiment from September 1864 to April 9, 1865. Consolidated with the 25th, 29th, 30th, and 66th Georgia Infantry Regiments and 1st Georgia Sharpshooters Battalion and designated as the 1st Georgia Sharpshooters Battalion on April 9, 1865.
First Commander: John B. Villepigue (Colonel)
Field Officers: Jacob Aderhold (Lieutenant Colonel)
Elijah M. Dodson (Major)
William S. Lovell (Major)
George A. Smith (Lieutenant Colonel, Colonel)
Assignments: Army of Pensacola (January-March 1862)
Department of Alabama and West Florida (March-June 1862)
District of the Gulf, Department #2 (July 1862-April 1863)
Powell's-Shoup's-Higgins' Brigade, Department of the Gulf [1st Battalion] (April 1863-January 1864)
Cumming's Brigade, Department of the Gulf [2nd Battalion] (April-May 1863)
Jackson's Independent Brigade, Army of Tennessee [2nd Battalion] (July-August 1863)
Jackson's Brigade, Cheatham's Division, 1st Corps, Army of Tennessee [2nd Battalion] (September 1863-February 1864)
Jackson's Brigade, Walker's Division, 1st Corps, Army of Tennessee [2nd Battalion] (February-May 1864)

Jackson's Brigade, Walker's Division, 1st Corps, Army of Tennessee [1st Battalion] (April-May 1864)
Stevens' Brigade, Walker's Division, 1st Corps, Army of Tennessee (May-July 1864)
Stevens'-Jackson's Brigade, Bate's Division, 1st Corps, Army of Tennessee (July-December 1864)
Jackson's Brigade, Clayton's Division, 2nd Corps, Army of Tennessee (March-April 1865)
Battles: Chickamauga [2nd Battalion] (September 19-20, 1863)
Chattanooga Siege [2nd Battalion] (September-November 1863)
Chattanooga [2nd Battalion] (November 23-25, 1863)
Atlanta Campaign (May-September 1864)
Peach Tree Creek (July 20, 1864)
Atlanta (July 22, 1864)
Atlanta Siege (July-September 1864)
Jonesborough (August 31-September 1, 1864)
Franklin (November 30, 1864)
Nashville (December 15-16, 1864)
Carolinas Campaign (February-April 1865)
Bentonville (March 19-21, 1865)

38. CONFEDERATE 1ST FOREIGN LEGION INFANTRY REGIMENT

See: CONFEDERATE TUCKER'S INFANTRY REGIMENT

39. CONFEDERATE 2ND INFANTRY BATTALION

Organization: Organized in the spring of 1862. No record after September 1862. This unit is not listed at the National Archives.
First Commander: James C. Malone, Jr. (Major)
Assignment: Bowen's Brigade, District of the Mississippi, Department #2 (June-August 1862)
Battle: Vicksburg Bombardments (May 18-July 27, 1862)

40. CONFEDERATE 2ND FOREIGN INFANTRY BATTALION

See: CONFEDERATE 8TH INFANTRY BATTALION

41. CONFEDERATE 2ND FOREIGN LEGION INFANTRY BATTALION

See: CONFEDERATE 8TH INFANTRY BATTALION

42. CONFEDERATE 2ND INFANTRY REGIMENT

Organization: Organized by the change of designation of the 25th Mississippi Infantry Regiment on January 31, 1862. Disbanded on May 8, 1862. Companies A, H, and I became Companies B, D, and A, respectively, of the 1st Mississippi Sharpshooters Battalion. Companies B and D became Companies D and A, respectively, of the 55th Alabama Infantry Regiment. Company C became Company K, 7th Infantry Regiment. Company E became Company E, 2nd South Carolina Artillery Regiment. Companies F and K were consolidated and became 2nd Company C, 1st Missouri Infantry Regiment. Company G became 2nd Company I, 9th Arkansas Infantry Regiment.

First Commander: John D. Martin (Colonel)

Field Officers: Edward F. McGehee (Lieutenant Colonel)

Thomas H. Mangham (Major)

Assignment: Bowen's Brigade, Reserve Corps, Army of the Mississippi, Department #2 (March-May 1862)

Battle: Shiloh (April 6-7, 1862)

43. CONFEDERATE 3RD INFANTRY REGIMENT

Organization: Organized by the change of designation of the 18th (Marmaduke's) Arkansas Infantry Regiment on January 31, 1862. Reorganized with eight companies on April 23, 1862. Field consolidation with the 5th Infantry Regiment in 1863 and 1864. Consolidated with the 1st, 2nd, 5th, 6th, 7th, 8th, 13th, 15th, & 24th Arkansas Infantry Regiments and designated as Company K, 1st Arkansas Infantry Regiment Consolidated at Smithfield, North Carolina on April 9, 1865.

First Commander: John S. Marmaduke (Colonel)

Field Officers: John F. Cameron (Major, Lieutenant Colonel)

James Cole (Lieutenant Colonel)

James B. Johnson (Lieutenant Colonel)

Henry V. Keep (Major, Lieutenant Colonel)

Assignments: Hindman's Brigade, Hardee's Division, Central Army of Kentucky, Department #2 (January-March 1862)

Hindman's Brigade, 3rd Corps, Army of the Mississippi, Department #2 (March-April 1862)

Marmaduke's Brigade, 3rd Corps, Army of the Mississippi, Department #2 (April-July 1862)

Wood's Brigade, Buckner's Division, Left Wing, Army of the Mississippi, Department #2 (August-November 1862)

Wood's Brigade, Buckner's Division, 2nd Corps, Army of the Mississippi, Department #2 (November 1862)

Wood's Brigade, Buckner's-Cleburne's Division, 2nd Corps, Army of Tennessee (November 1862-January 1863)
Polk's Brigade, Cleburne's Division, 2nd Corps, Army of Tennessee (July-November 1863)
Polk's Brigade, Cleburne's Division, 1st Corps, Army of Tennessee (November 1863-January 1864)
Govan's Brigade, Cleburne's Division, 1st Corps, Army of Tennessee (April 1864-April 1865)
Battles: Shiloh (April 6-7, 1862)
Corinth Campaign (April-June 1862)
Perryville (October 8, 1862)
Murfreesboro (December 31, 1862-January 3, 1863)
Chickamauga (September 19-20, 1863)
Chattanooga Siege (September-November 1863)
Chattanooga (November 23-25, 1863)
Ringgold Gap (November 26, 1863)
Taylor's Ridge (November 27, 1863)
Atlanta Campaign (May-September 1864)
New Hope Church (May 25-June 5, 1864)
Kennesaw Mountain (June 27, 1864)
Atlanta (July 22, 1864)
Atlanta Siege (July-September 1864)
Jonesborough (August 31-September 1, 1864)
Franklin (November 30, 1864)
Nashville (December 15-16, 1864)
Carolinas Campaign (February-April 1865)
Bentonville (March 19-21, 1865)

44. CONFEDERATE 4TH INFANTRY BATTALION

See: CONFEDERATE GUARD RESPONSE INFANTRY BATTALION
Also Known As: Confederate Guards Response Battalion
Organization: Organized with companies in early 1862. Merged into Crescent Louisiana Infantry Regiment.
First Commander: Franklin H. Clack (Lieutenant Colonel)

45. CONFEDERATE 4TH INFANTRY REGIMENT

Also Known As: 1st Alabama, Tennessee, and Mississippi Infantry Regiment
1st Mississippi Valley Infantry Regiment
Organization: Organized with a mixture of companies from Alabama, Tennessee, and Mississippi at Fort Pillow, Tennessee on December 27, 1861. Surrendered at Island #10 on April 8, 1862. Exchanged at Vicksburg, Warren

County, Mississippi in September 1862. Reorganized at Vicksburg, Warren County, Mississippi on September 27, 1862. Disbanded on October 9, 1862. Companies A, G, H, and K became 2nd Companies I, A, C, and D, respectively, of the 42nd Tennessee Infantry Regiment. Companies B, C, D, E, F, and I became Companies C, G, E, D, F, and I, respectively, of the 54th Alabama Infantry Regiment.

First Commander: Alpheus Baker (Colonel)

Field Officers: Joseph Barbiere (Major)

John A. Minter (Lieutenant Colonel)

Thaddeus S. H. Shackelford (Major)

Assignments: Fort Pillow, 1st Geographical Division, Department #2 (December 1861-February 1862)

Unattached, McCown's Command, 1st Geographical Division, Department #2 (February-April 1862)

Unattached, District of the Mississippi, Department #2 (September-October 1862)

Unattached, Department of Mississippi and East Louisiana (October 1862)

Battle: Island #10 (April 6-7, 1862)

46. CONFEDERATE 5TH INFANTRY REGIMENT

Also Known As: 9th Infantry Regiment

5th Tennessee (Confederate) Infantry Regiment

Organization: Organized with eight companies by the consolidation of the 2nd (Walker's) and 21st Tennessee Infantry Regiments on July 21, 1862. Field consolidation with the 3rd Infantry Regiment in 1863 and 1864. Became Company I, 3rd Tennessee Infantry Regiment Consolidated at Smithfield, North Carolina on April 9, 1865.

First Commander: James A. Smith (Colonel)

Field Officers: James C. Cole (Lieutenant Colonel)

Richard J. Person (Major)

Assignments: B. R. Johnson's Brigade, Buckner's Division, Left Wing, Army of the Mississippi, Department #2 (October 1862)

Cleburne's Brigade, Buckner's Division, Left Wing, Army of the Mississippi, Department #2 (October-November 1862)

Cleburne's-Polk's Brigade, Buckner's-Cleburne's Division, 2nd Corps, Army of Tennessee (November 1862-November 1863)

Polk's Brigade, Cleburne's Division, 1st Corps, Army of Tennessee (November 1863-July 1864)

Smith's-Granbury's Brigade, Cleburne's Division, 1st Corps, Army of Tennessee (July 1864-April 1865)

Battles: Perryville (October 8, 1862)

Murfreesboro (December 31, 1862-January 3, 1863)
Chickamauga (September 19-20, 1863)
Chattanooga Siege (September-November 1863)
Chattanooga (November 23-25, 1863)
Ringgold Gap (November 26, 1863)
Taylor's Ridge (November 27, 1863)
Atlanta Campaign (May-September 1864)
New Hope Church (May 25-June 5, 1864)
Kennesaw Mountain (June 27, 1864)
Atlanta (July 22, 1864)
Atlanta Siege (July-September 1864)
Jonesborough (August 31-September 1, 1864)
Franklin (November 30, 1864)
Nashville (December 15-16, 1864)
Carolinas Campaign (February-April 1865)

47. CONFEDERATE 5TH (WALKER'S) INFANTRY REGIMENT

See: TENNESSEE 40TH INFANTRY REGIMENT

48. CONFEDERATE 8TH INFANTRY BATTALION

Also Known As: 2nd Foreign Battalion
2nd Foreign Infantry Battalion

Organization: Organized with six companies from foreign-born prisoners of war at Salisbury, North Carolina on February 13, 1865 under authority granted by the War Department on September 18, 1864. Officially designated as the 8th Infantry Battalion on March 28, 1865. Surrendered at Salisbury, North Carolina on April 12, 1865.

First Commander: Garnett Andrews (Major, Lieutenant Colonel)

Field Officer: R. T. Fouch **(Major)**

Assignment: District of Western North Carolina, Department of East Tennessee (February-April 1865)

Battle: Salisbury (April 12, 1865)

49. CONFEDERATE 9TH INFANTRY REGIMENT

See: CONFEDERATE 5TH INFANTRY REGIMENT

50. CONFEDERATE 5TH COMPANY, CS RETRIBUTORS INFANTRY COMPANY

Organization: Organized behind enemy lines in Canada, mostly from escaped prisoners of war, for special service on June 16, 1864. Company arrested in Canada on October 19, 1864.

First Commander: Bennett H. Young (Lieutenant)
Assignment: Unattached, Canada (June-October 1864)
Battle: St. Albans (October 19, 1864)

51. CONFEDERATE BRADFORD'S INFANTRY BATTALION

Organization: Organized with two companies in August 1864. Surrendered by Lieutenant General Richard Taylor, commanding the Department of Alabama, Mississippi, and East Louisiana, at Citronelle, Alabama on May 4, 1865.
First Commander: J. D. Bradford (Major)

52. CONFEDERATE BROOKS' INFANTRY BATTALION

Organization: Organized with six companies from prisoners of war in late 1864. Mustered into Confederate service on November 17, 1864. Disbanded and returned to prison for conspiring to desert in late December 1864.
First Commander: John H. Brooks (Major)
Assignments: Cumming's Brigade, McLaws' Division, Department of South Carolina, Georgia, and Florida (November-December 1864)
Harrison's Brigade, Smith's Division, Department of South Carolina, Georgia, and Florida (December 1864)
Mercer's Brigade, Wright's Division, Department of South Carolina, Georgia, and Florida (December 1864)
Battle: Savannah Campaign (November-December 1864)

53. CONFEDERATE BRUSH INFANTRY BATTALION

Organization: Organized with five companies composed of deserters, militia, and conscripts for duty on the frontier against Indians for pardon on November 6, 1863. No officers are listed.

54. CONFEDERATE TUCKER'S INFANTRY REGIMENT

Also Known As: 1st Foreign Legion
Organization: Organized by the addition of Company K [composed of foreign-born prisoners of war from camps at Richmond, Virginia; Salisbury, North Carolina; and Florence, South Carolina] to the 1st Foreign Infantry Battalion on February 28, 1865. Served as pioneers in April 1865. Surrendered by General Joseph E. Johnston at Durham Station, Orange County, North Carolina on April 26, 1865.
First Commander: Julius G. Tucker (Colonel)
Assignment: Unattached, Army of Tennessee (April 1865)
Battle: Carolinas Campaign (February-April 1865)

THE INDIAN UNITS

INDIAN UNITS

In the summer and fall of 1861, Confederate Indian commisioner Albert Pike signed treaties of alliance with tribes in the Indian Territory (now Oklahoma). The Indian units are broken down by tribe and not by the branch of service since they mostly served mounted. The records on these units are understandably sketchy. These units tended to disband at will and large numbers later joined the Union Army's Indian Home Guard regiments.

Note: The index for the Indian units begins on page 233.

CAVALRY

1. CHEROKEE 1ST CAVALRY BATTALION, PARTISAN RANGERS

Also Known As: 1st (Bryan's) Cherokee Cavalry Battalion
Organization: Organized with five companies on September 3, 1862. Increased to a regiment and designated as the 2nd Cherokee Mounted Volunteers on February 3, 1863.
First Commander: J. M. Bryan (Major)
Assignments: Cooper's Brigade, District of Arkansas, Trans-Mississippi Department (September 1862)
Cooper's Brigade, Roane's Division, 1st Corps, Trans-Mississippi Department (December 1862)
Battles: Newtonia (September 30, 1862)
Granby (October 4, 1862)
Operations in Cherokee County (December 4-12, 1862)

2. CHEROKEE 1ST (BRYAN'S) CAVALRY BATTALION

See: CHEROKEE 1ST CAVALRY BATTALION, PARTISAN RANGERS

3. CHEROKEE 1ST (MEYER'S) CAVALRY BATTALION

Organization: This battalion is not listed at the National Archives and does not appear in the *Official Records.*
First Commander: Benjamin W. Meyer (Major)

4. CHEROKEE 1ST CAVALRY REGIMENT

See: CHEROKEE 1ST CAVALRY REGIMENT, MOUNTED RIFLES

5. CHEROKEE 1ST CAVALRY REGIMENT, MOUNTED RIFLES

Also Known As: 1st Cherokee Cavalry Regiment
2nd Cherokee Cavalry Regiment Mounted Rifles
Drew's Cherokee Cavalry Regiment Mounted Rifles

Organization: Enrolled for twelve months on October 4, 1861. Mustered in on October 25, 1861. Mustered into Confederate service on November 5, 1861 to date from October 25, 1861. Dispersed with many of the men joining the Union 3rd Indian Home Guard in June 1862.
First Commander: John Drew (Colonel)
Field Officers: Thomas Pegg (Major)
William P. Ross (Lieutenant Colonel)
Assignments: Indian Territory (October-November 1861)
Department of the Indian Territory (November 1861-January 1862)
Indian (Pike's) Brigade, Trans-Mississippi District, Department #2 (January-March 1862)
Department of the Indian Territory (May-June 1862)
Battles: Chusto-Talasah (December 9, 1861)
Pea Ridge (March 6-8, 1862)
Honey Springs (July 17, 1863)
Fort Gibson (September 16, 1864)
Cabin Creek (September 19, 1864)
Further Reading: Gaines, W. Craig, *The Confederate Cherokees.*

6. CHEROKEE 1ST CAVALRY SQUADRON, MOUNTED VOLUNTEERS

Organization: Organized as a temporary field organization of two or three companies for two years service on December 12, 1862.
First Commander: Charles H. Holt (Captain)

7. CHEROKEE 2ND CAVALRY REGIMENT, MOUNTED RIFLES

See: CHEROKEE 2ND CAVALRY REGIMENT, MOUNTED VOLUNTEERS
First Commander: Stand Watie (Colonel)

8. CHEROKEE 2ND (DREW'S) CAVALRY REGIMENT, MOUNTED RIFLES

See: CHEROKEE 1ST CAVALRY REGIMENT, MOUNTED RIFLES

9. CHEROKEE 2ND CAVALRY REGIMENT, MOUNTED RIFLES

Also Known As: 1st Cherokee Mounted Rifles
1st Cherokee Mounted Volunteers
Organization: Organized for twelve months on July 12, 1861. Reorganized for two years on July 12, 1862. Five companies transferred to the 2nd Cherokee Mounted Volunteers on February 3, 1863. Surrendered by General E. K. Smith, commanding Trans-Mississippi Department, at Doaksville, Indian Territory, on June 23, 1865.

First Commander: Stand Watie (Colonel)
Field Officers: James M. Bell (Lieutenant Colonel, Colonel)
Elias C. Boudinot (Major)
Erastus J. Howland (Major)
Thomas F. Taylor (Lieutenant Colonel)
Joseph F. Thompson (Major, Lieutenant Colonel)
Clem. N. Vann (Lieutenant Colonel)
Assignments: Indian Territory (July-November 1861)
Department of the Indian Territory (November 1861-January 1862)
Indian (Pike's) Brigade, Trans-Mississippi District, Department #2 (January-March 1862)
Department of the Indian Territory (May 1862)
Cooper's Brigade, District of Arkansas, Trans-Mississippi Department (September 1862)
Cooper's Brigade, Roane's Division, 1st Corps, Trans-Mississippi Department (October 1862-January 1863)
Cooper's Brigade, Steele's Division, District of Arkansas, Trans-Mississippi Department (April 1863)
1st Indian (Watie's) Brigade, Indian (Cooper's) Cavalry Division, Trans-Mississippi Department (September 1864-May 1865)
Battles: Wilson's Creek (August 10, 1861)
near Grand River (December 27, 1861)
Pea Ridge (March 6-8, 1862)
Neosho [skirmish] (April 26, 1862)
Neosho [skirmish] (May 31, 1862)
Old Fort Wayne (October 22, 1862)
Operations in Cherokee County (December 4-12, 1862)
near Honey Springs (July 17, 1863)
Cabin Creek (September 19, 1864)

10. CHEROKEE 2ND CAVALRY REGIMENT, MOUNTED VOLUNTEERS

Also Known As: 2nd Cherokee Cavalry Regiment, Mounted Rifles
Organization: Organized by the increase of the 1st Cherokee Partisan Rangers Battalion by the assignment of five companies from the 2nd Cherokee Cavalry Regiment, Mounted Rifles on February 3, 1863. Surrendered by General E. K. Smith, commanding Trans-Mississippi Department, on May 26, 1865.
First Commander: William P. Adair (Colonel)
Field Officers: James M. Bell (Lieutenant Colonel)
O. H. P. Brewer (Lieutenant Colonel)
Porter Hammock (Major)

J. R. Harden (Major)
John Vann (Major)
Assignments: Cooper's Brigade, Steele's Division, District of Arkansas, Trans-Mississippi Department (April 1863-July 1864)
Watie's Brigade, Cooper's Division, District of the Indian Territory, Trans-Mississippi Department (July-September 1864)
Watie's Brigade, Cooper's Indian Cavalry Division, Trans-Mississippi Department (September 1864-May 1865)
Battle: near Honey Springs (July 17, 1863)

11. CHEROKEE DREW'S CAVALRY REGIMENT, MOUNTED RIFLES

See: CHEROKEE 1ST CAVALRY REGIMENT, MOUNTED RIFLES

12. CHEROKEE FRYE'S-SCALES' CAVALRY BATTALION

Organization: Apparently organized in 1864. Surrendered by General E. K. Smith, commanding Trans-Mississippi Department, at Doaksville, Indian Territory, on June 23, 1865.
First Commander: Moses C. Frye (Major)
Field Officer: Joseph A. Scales (Major)
Assignment: 1st (Watie's) Indian Brigade, Indian (Cooper's) Cavalry Division, Trans-Mississippi Department (September 1864-May 1865)

13. CHICKASAW 1ST CAVALRY BATTALION

Organization: Organized in early 1862. Surrendered by General E. K. Smith, commanding Trans-Mississippi Department, on May 26, 1865.
First Commander: Joseph D. Harris (Lieutenant Colonel)
Field Officer: Lemuel M. Reynolds (Major, Lieutenant Colonel)
Assignments: Department of the Indian Territory (May-June 1862)
Cooper's Brigade, District of Arkansas, Trans-Mississippi Department (September 1862)
Cooper's Brigade, Roane's Division, 1st Corps, Trans-Mississippi Department (December 1862)
Cooper's Brigade, Steele's Division, District of Arkansas, Trans-Mississippi Department (April 1863-April 1864)
Choctaw (Walker's) Brigade, Maxey's Cavalry Division, District of Arkansas, Trans-Mississippi Department (April-May 1864)
Walker's Brigade, Cooper's Division, District of the Indian Territory, Trans-Mississippi Department (September 1864)
2nd (Walker's) Indian Brigade, Indian (Cooper's) Cavalry Division, Trans-Mississippi Department (September 1864-May 1865)
Battle: Arkansas Campaign (April 1864)

14. CHICKASAW 1ST CAVALRY REGIMENT

Also Known As: 1st Chickasaw Infantry Regiment

Organization: Organized for three years or the war, under authority granted on May 25, 1863, on October 23, 1863, to date from September 25, 1863. Surrendered by General E. K. Smith, commanding Trans-Mississippi Department, on May 26, 1865.

First Commander: William L. Hunter (Colonel)

Field Officers: Abram B. Hays (Major)

Samuel H. Martin (Lieutenant Colonel)

Assignment: District of the Indian Territory, Trans-Mississippi Department (October 1863-May 1865)

15. CHICKASAW SHECO'S CAVALRY BATTALION

Organization: This battalion is not listed at the National Archives and does not appear in the *Official Records*.

First Commander: Martin Sheco (Lieutenant Colonel)

Field Officer: Jonathan Nail (Major)

16. CHICKASAW 1ST INFANTRY REGIMENT

See: CHICKASAW 1ST CAVALRY REGIMENT

17. CHICKASAW AND CHOCTAW 1ST CAVALRY BATTALION, MOUNTED RIFLES

See: CHICKASAW AND CHOCTAW 1ST CAVALRY REGIMENT, MOUNTED RIFLES

18. CHICKASAW AND CHOCTAW 1ST CAVALRY REGIMENT, MOUNTED RIFLES

Also Known As: 1st Chickasaw and Choctaw Cavalry Battalion, Mounted Rifles

2nd Chickasaw and Choctaw Cavalry Regiment, Mounted Rifles

Organization: Organized during the summer of 1861. Surrendered by General E. K. Smith, commanding Trans-Mississippi Department, on May 26, 1865.

First Commander: Douglas H. Cooper (Colonel)

Field Officers: Willis J. Jones (Major)

Mitchell Le Flore (Major)

Sampson Loering (Major)

James Riley (Lieutenant Colonel)

Tandy Walker (Major, Lieutenant Colonel)

Assignments: Indian Territory (August-November 1861)

Department of the Indian Territory (November 1861-January 1862)

Trans-Mississippi District, Department #2 (January-March 1862)

Department of the Indian Territory (March-June 1862)
Cooper's Brigade, District of Arkansas, Trans-Mississippi Department (September 1862)
Cooper's Brigade, Roane's Division, 1st Corps, Trans-Mississippi Department (December 1862)
Cooper's Brigade, Steele's Division, District of Arkansas, Trans-Mississippi Department (April 1863-April 1864)
Choctaw (Walker's) Brigade, Maxey's Cavalry Division, District of Arkansas, Trans-Mississippi Department (April-May 1864)
District of the Indian Territory, Trans-Mississippi Department (July-August 1864)
Walker's Brigade, Cooper's Division, District of the Indian Territory, Trans-Mississippi Department (September 1864)
2nd (Walker's) Indian Cavalry Brigade, Indian (Cooper's) Cavalry Division, Trans-Mississippi Department (September 1864-May 1865)
Battles: Round Mountain [six companies] (November 19, 1861)
Chusto-Talasah (December 9, 1861)
Neosho [skirmish] (April 26, 1862)
Newtonia (September 30, 1862)
near Honey Springs (July 17, 1863)
Poison Springs (April 18, 1864)
Massard's Prairie, near Fort Smith [detachment] (July 27, 1864)

19. CHICKASAW AND CHOCTAW 2ND CAVALRY REGIMENT, MOUNTED RIFLES

See: CHICKASAW AND CHOCTAW 1ST CAVALRY REGIMENT, MOUNTED RIFLES

20. CHICKASAW AND CHOCTAW 1ST CAVALRY BATTALION, MOUNTED RIFLES

See: CHICKASAW AND CHOCTAW 1ST CAVALRY REGIMENT, MOUNTED RIFLES

21. CHICKASAW AND CHOCTAW 1ST CAVALRY REGIMENT, MOUNTED RIFLES

Also Known As: 1st Chickasaw and Choctaw Cavalry Battalion, Mounted Rifles
2nd Chickasaw and Choctaw Cavalry Regiment, Mounted Rifles
Organization: Organized during the summer of 1861. Surrendered by General E. K. Smith, commanding Trans-Mississippi Department, on May 26, 1865.
First Commander: Douglas H. Cooper (Colonel)
Field Officers: Willis J. Jones (Major)
Mitchell Le Flore (Major)

Sampson Loering (Major)
James Riley (Lieutenant Colonel)
Tandy Walker (Major, Lieutenant Colonel)
Assignments: Indian Territory (August-November 1861)
Department of the Indian Territory (November 1861-January 1862)
Trans-Mississippi District, Department #2 (January-March 1862)
Department of the Indian Territory (March-June 1862)
Cooper's Brigade, District of Arkansas, Trans-Mississippi Department (September 1862)
Cooper's Brigade, Roane's Division, 1st Corps, Trans-Mississippi Department (December 1862)
Cooper's Brigade, Steele's Division, District of Arkansas, Trans-Mississippi Department (April 1863-April 1864)
Choctaw (Walker's) Brigade, Maxey's Cavalry Division, District of Arkansas, Trans-Mississippi Department (April-May 1864)
District of the Indian Territory, Trans-Mississippi Department (July-August 1864)
Walker's Brigade, Cooper's Division, District of the Indian Territory, Trans-Mississippi Department (September 1864)
2nd (Walker's) Indian Cavalry Brigade, Indian (Cooper's) Cavalry Division, Trans-Mississippi Department (September 1864-May 1865)
Battles: Round Mountain [six companies] (November 19, 1861)
Chusto-Talasah (December 9, 1861)
Neosho [skirmish] (April 26, 1862)
Newtonia (September 30, 1862)
near Honey Springs (July 17, 1863)
Poison Springs (April 18, 1864)
Massard's Prairie, near Fort Smith [detachment] (July 27, 1864)

22. CHICKASAW AND CHOCTAW 2ND CAVALRY REGIMENT, MOUNTED RIFLES

See: CHICKASAW AND CHOCTAW 1ST CAVALRY REGIMENT, MOUNTED RIFLES

23. CHOCTAW 1ST (FOLSOM'S) CAVALRY BATTALION

Organization: Organized in early 1862. Increased to a regiment and designated as the 1st Choctaw War Regiment.
First Commander: Simpson Folsom (Major, Lieutenant Colonel)
Field Officer: Franceway Battice (Major)
Assignments: Department of the Indian Territory (April-June 1862)
Cooper's Brigade, District of Arkansas, Trans-Mississippi Department (September-October 1862)

Cooper's Brigade, Roane's Division, 1st Corps, Trans-Mississippi Department (October-December 1862)

Battles: Newtonia (September 30, 1862)

Operations in Cherokee County (December 4-12, 1862)

24. CHOCTAW 1ST (MCCURTAIN'S) CAVALRY BATTALION

Organization: Apparently organized in 1864. Increased to a regiment and designated as the 3rd Choctaw Cavalry Regiment in early 1865.

First Commander: Jackson McCurtain (Lieutenant Colonel)

Field Officer: John Page (Major)

Assignment: 2nd (Walker's) Indian Brigade, Indian (Cooper's) Cavalry Division, Trans-Mississippi Department (September 1864-January 1865)

25. CHOCTAW 1ST CAVALRY REGIMENT

See: CHOCTAW 1ST CAVALRY REGIMENT, MOUNTED RIFLES

26. CHOCTAW 1ST CAVALRY REGIMENT

See: CHOCTAW 1ST WAR CAVALRY REGIMENT

27. CHOCTAW 1ST CAVALRY REGIMENT, MOUNTED RIFLES

Also Known As: 1st Cavalry Regiment

Organization: Organized in early 1862. No record after May 1862.

First Commander: Sampson Folsom (Colonel)

Field Officer: David F. Hawkins (Lieutenant Colonel)

Assignment: Department of the Indian Territory (April-May 1862)

28. CHOCTAW 1ST WAR CAVALRY REGIMENT

Also Known As: 1st Cavalry Regiment

2nd Cavalry Regiment

Organization: Organized by the increase of the 1st (S. N. Folsom's) Cavalry Battalion to a regiment. Surrendered by General E. K. Smith, commanding Trans-Mississippi Department, on May 26, 1865.

First Commander: Simpson Folsom (Colonel)

Field Officer: Franceway Battice (Lieutenant Colonel)

Assignments: Choctaw (Walker's) Brigade, Maxey's Cavalry Division, District of Arkansas, Trans-Mississippi Department (March-May 1864)

District of the Indian Territory (July-August 1864)

Walker's Brigade, Cooper's Division, District of the Indian Territory, Trans-Mississippi Department (September 1864)

2nd (Walker's) Brigade, Indian (Cooper's) Cavalry Division, Trans-Mississippi Department (September 1864-May 1865)

Battles: Camden Expedition (March-May 1864)
Poison Springs (April 18, 1864)
Massard's Prairie, near Fort Smith [detachment] (July 27, 1864)

29. CHOCTAW 2ND CAVALRY REGIMENT

See: CHOCTAW 1ST WAR CAVALRY REGIMENT

30. CHOCTAW 3RD CAVALRY REGIMENT

Organization: Organized by the increase of the 1st (McCurtain's) Cavalry Battalion to a regiment in early 1865. Surrendered by General E. K. Smith, commanding Trans-Mississippi Department, on May 26, 1865.
First Commander: Jackson McCurtain (Colonel)
Field Officers: Tom Lewis (Lieutenant Colonel)
John Page (Major)
Assignment: 2nd (Walker's) Brigade, Indian (Cooper's) Cavalry Division, Trans-Mississippi Department (April-May 1865)

31. CHOCTAW DENEALE'S CAVALRY BATTALION

Organization: Organized with five companies on January 14, 1862 under authority granted on December 14, 1861. Disbanded ca. May 5, 1862. However the National Archives indicates that this was temporary and the unit was reorganized as a regiment but it gives no details.
First Commander: George E. Deneale (Lieutenant Colonel)
Assignments: Trans-Mississippi District, Department #2 (January-March 1862)
Department of the Indian Territory (March-May 1862)

32. CHOCTAW DENEALE'S CAVALRY REGIMENT

See: CHOCTAW DENEALE'S CAVALRY BATTALION

33. CREEK 1ST CAVALRY BATTALION

Organization: Organized in 1861 and served jointly with the 1st Seminole Cavalry Battalion. Increased to a regiment and designated as the 2nd Creek Cavalry Regiment in late 1862.
First Commander: Chilly McIntosh (Lieutenant Colonel)
Assignments: Department of the Indian Territory (December 1861-January 1862)
Trans-Mississippi District, Department #2 (January-March 1862)
Department of the Indian Territory (March-June 1862)
Cooper's Brigade, District of Arkansas, Trans-Mississippi Department (September 1862)

34. CREEK 1ST CAVALRY REGIMENT

Also Known As: 1st Mounted Rifles
1st Mounted Volunteers

Organization: Organized for twelve months on August 19, 1861. Reenlisted for two years on August 17, 1862. Surrendered by General E. K. Smith, commanding Trans-Mississippi Department, on May 26, 1865.

First Commander: Daniel N. McIntosh (Colonel)

Field Officers: Samuel Chekote (Lieutenant Colonel)
Jacob Derrysaw (Major)
James McHenry (Major)
William R. McIntosh (Lieutenant Colonel)

Assignments: Indian Territory (August-November 1861)
Department of the Indian Territory (November 1861-January 1862)
Indian (Pike's) Brigade, Trans-Mississippi District, Department #2 (January-March 1862)
Department of the Indian Territory (March-June 1862)
Cooper's Brigade, District of Arkansas, Trans-Mississippi Department (September 1862)
Cooper's Brigade, Roane's Division, 1st Corps, Trans-Mississippi Department (December 1862)
Cooper's Brigade, Steele's Division, District of Arkansas, Trans-Mississippi Department (April 1863-July 1864)
Watie's Brigade, Cooper's Division, District of the Indian Territory, Trans-Mississippi Department (July-September 1864)
1st (Watie's) Indian Brigade, Indian (Cooper's) Cavalry Division, Trans-Mississippi Department (September 1864-May 1865)

Battles: Chusto-Talasah (December 9, 1861)
Pea Ridge (March 6-8, 1862)
near Honey Springs (July 17, 1863)
Cabin Creek (September 19, 1864)

35. CREEK 1ST CAVALRY REGIMENT, MOUNTED RIFLES

See: CREEK 1ST CAVALRY REGIMENT

36. CREEK 1ST CAVALRY REGIMENT, MOUNTED VOLUNTEERS

See: CREEK 1ST CAVALRY REGIMENT

37. CREEK 2ND CAVALRY REGIMENT

Also Known As: 2nd Creek Mounted Rifles
2nd Creek Mounted Volunteers

Organization: Organized by the increase of the 1st Creek Cavalry Battalion to a regiment in 1862. Surrendered by General E. K. Smith, commanding Trans-Mississippi Department, on May 26, 1865.
First Commander: Chilly McIntosh (Colonel)
Field Officers: Timothy Barnett (Major, Colonel)
Pink Hawkins (Lieutenant Colonel)
Assignments: Cooper's Brigade, Roane's Division, 1st Corps, Trans-Mississippi Department (December 1862)
Cooper's Brigade, Steele's Division, District of Arkansas, Trans-Mississippi Department (April 1863-July 1864)
Watie's Brigade, Cooper's Division, District of the Indian Territory, Trans-Mississippi Department (July-September 1864)
1st (Watie's) Indian Cavalry Brigade, Indian (Cooper's) Cavalry Division, Trans-Mississippi Department (September 1864-May 1865)
Battles: Old Fort Wayne (October 22, 1862)
near Honey Springs (July 17, 1863)
Fort Gibson (September 16, 1864)
Cabin Creek (September 19, 1864)

38. CREEK 2ND CAVALRY REGIMENT, MOUNTED RIFLES

See: CREEK 2ND MOUNTED VOLUNTEERS

39. CREEK 2ND CAVALRY REGIMENT, MOUNTED VOLUNTEERS

See: CREEK 2ND MOUNTED VOLUNTEERS

40. CREEK KENARD'S CAVALRY BATTALION

Organization: Organized with two companies apparently in 1864. Surrendered by General E. K. Smith, commanding Trans-Mississippi Department, on May 26, 1865.
First Commander: R. Kenard (Captain)
Assignment: 1st (Watie's) Indian Cavalry Brigade, Indian (Cooper's) Cavalry Division, Trans-Mississippi Department (September 1864-May 1865)

41. OSAGE BROKE ARM'S CAVALRY BATTALION

Organization: Organized with three companies in early 1863. Surrendered by Brigadier General Stand Watie, commanding Trans-Mississippi Department at Doaksville, Indian Territory, on June 23, 1865.
First Commander: Broke Arm (Major)
Assignments: Cooper's Brigade, Steele's Division, District of Arkansas, Trans-Mississippi Department (April 1863-July 1864)

Watie's Brigade, Cooper's Division, District of the Indian Territory, Trans-Mississippi Department (July-September 1864)
1st (Watie's) Indian Brigade, Indian (Cooper's) Cavalry Division, Trans-Mississippi Department (September 1864-May 1865)

42. SEMINOLE 1ST CAVALRY BATTALION

Organization: Organized with six companies on September 21, 1861. Reorganized on July 1, 1864. The National Archives indicates that this battalion was increased to a regiment and designated as the 1st Seminole Cavalry Regiment but gives no date. Surrendered by Brigadier General Stand Watie, commanding Trans-Mississippi Department, at Doaksville, Indian Territory. Although the Trans-Mississippi Region was surrendered by Lieutenant General Simon B. Buckner without Kirby-Smith's knowledge May 26, 1865, Smith accepted the terms in Galveston, Texas on June 2, 1865.
First Commander: John Jumper (Major, Lieutenant Colonel, Colonel)
Field Officer: George Cloud (Major)
Assignments: Indian Territory (September-November 1861)
Department of the Indian Territory (November 1861-January 1862)
Indian (Pike's) Brigade, Trans-Mississippi District, Department #2 (January-March 1862)
Department of the Indian Territory (March-June 1862)
Cooper's Brigade, District of Arkansas, Trans-Mississippi Department (September 1862)
Cooper's Brigade, Roane's Division, 1st Corps, Trans-Mississippi Department (December 1862)
Cooper's Brigade, Steele's Division, District of Arkansas, Trans-Mississippi Department (April 1863-July 1864)
Watie's Brigade, Cooper's Division, District of the Indian Territory, Trans-Mississippi Department (July-September 1864)
1st (Watie's) Indian Brigade, Indian (Cooper's) Cavalry Division, Trans-Mississippi Department (September 1864-May 1865)
Battle: Cabin Creek (September 19, 1864)

43. SEMINOLE 1ST CAVALRY REGIMENT

See: SEMINOLE 1ST CAVALRY BATTALION

44. INDIAN WASHINGTON'S CAVALRY SQUADRON

Also Known As: Reserve Squadron
Organization: Apparently organized in 1864 with two companies. Surrendered by General E. K. Smith, commanding Trans-Mississippi Department, at Doaksville, Indian Territory, on June 23, 1865.

First Commander: George Washington (Captain)
Assignment: 2nd (Walker's) Indian Brigade, Indian (Cooper's) Cavalry Division, Trans-Mississippi Department (September 1864-May 1865)

BIBLIOGRAPHY

Abel, Annie Heloise, *The American Indian as Slaveholder and Secessionist*. Lincoln: University of Nebraska Press, 1992.

Amman, William. *Personnel of the Civil War*. 2 volumes. New York: Thomas Yoseloff, 1961. Provides valuable information on local unit designations, general officers' assignments and organizational data on geographical commands.

Bedinger, Singleton B. *Missouri's Confederates*, 1861–1965. Tailor, Tex., Merchants Press, 1967.

Bergeron, Arthur W. *Guide to Louisiana Confederate Military Units, 1861–1865*. Baton Rouge: Louisiana State University Press, 1989.

Boatner, Mark Mayo III. *The Civil War Dictionary*. New York: David McKay Company, 1959. Provides thumbnail sketches of leaders, battles, campaigns, events and units.

Bowman, John S. *The Civil War Almanac*. New York: Facts On File, 1982. Basically a chronology, it is valuable for its 130 biographical sketches, many of them military personalities.

Briton, Wile. *The Union Indian Brigade in the Civil War*. Kansas City, Mo.: F. Hudson Publishing, 1922.

Chute, Joseph H. *Units of the Confederate States Army*. Midlothian, Va.: Darwinist Books, 1987.

Cleft, Garret Glean. *Civil War Engagements, Skirmishes, etc. in Kentucky, 1861–1865: A Finding List Designed for Use by Researchers, Speakers, and Students during the Civil War Centennial, 1961–1965*. Frankfort, Ky.: Kentucky Historical Society, 1959.

Confederate States of America. War Dept. *Army regulations: Adopted for the Use of the Army of the Confederate States, in Accordance with Late Acts of Congress. Revised from the Army Regulations of the Old U.S. Army, 1857; Retaining All That is Essential for Officers of the Line; to Which is Added, An Act for the Establishment and Organization of the Army of the Confederate States of America*. New Orleans: Bloomfield & Steel, 1861.

Counter, Ells Menton. *The Civil War and Readjustment in Kentucky*. Chapel Hill, N.C.: University of North Carolina Press, 1926.

Cross Reference of Local Florida Confederate Units and Their Regimental Designations. Kingsburg, Calif.: Pacific Specialties, 1971.

Dyer, Robert. *Jesse James and the Civil War in Missouri*. Columbia: University of Missouri Press, 1994.

Evans, Clement A., ed. *Confederate Military History*. 13 volumes. Atlanta: Confederate Publishing Company, 1899. Each volume of this series primarily provides the histories of one or two states. Each state military account was written by a different participant in the war, and they vary greatly in quality. All accounts, however, include biographies of the generals from their state. The lack of a comprehensive index is the major drawback of this work.

Franks, Kenny Arthur. *Stand Watie and the Agony of the Cherokee Nation*. Memphis: Memphis State University Press, c. 1979.

Freeman, Douglas Southall. *Lee's Lieutenants: A Study in Command*. 3 volumes. New York: Charles Scribner's Sons, 1941–1946. The premier narrative study of the organizational and command structure of the Army of Northern Virginia.

———. *R.E. Lee: A Biography*. 4 volumes. New York: Charles Scribner's Sons, 1934–1935. Also provides organizational information on the Army of Northern Virginia.

Fulmen, Michael. *Inside War: The Guerrilla Conflict in Missouri During the American Civil War*. New York: Oxford University Press, 1989.

Gained, W. Crag. *The Confederate Cherokees: John Drew's Regiment of Mounted Rifles*. Baton Rouge: Louisiana State University Press, 1989.

Gauge, Isaac. *Four Years with Five Armies: Army of the Frontier, Army of the Potomac, Army of the Missouri, Army of the Ohio, Army of the Shenandoah*. New York and Washington: The Kneel Publishing Company, 1908.

Goldborough, William Worthington. *The Maryland Line in the Confederate Army, 1961–1865*. Middle Atlantic States Historical Publications Series, no. 19. With an Introduction by Jean Baker and Index Prepared by Louise Q. Lewis. 2d ed. Port Washington, N.Y.: Connect Press, 1972.

Gottschalk, Phil. *In Deadly Earnest: The History of the First Missouri Brigade, CA. Columbia, Mo.: Missouri River Press, 1991*.

Grayson, George Washington. *A Creek Warrior for the Confederacy: The Autobiography of Chief G.W. Grayson*. Edited and with an Introduction by W. David Bairn. Norman: University of Oklahoma Press, 1988.

Harrison, Lisle Hayes. *The Civil War in Kentucky*. Lexington, Ky.: University Press of Kentucky, 1975.

Hartwig, D. Scott. *The Battle of Endosteum and the Maryland Campaign of 1862: A Bibliography*. Meckler's Bibliographies of Battles and Leaders, no. 1. Westport, Conn.: Meckler, 1990.

Hartzler, Daniel D. *Marylanders in the Confederacy*. Silver Spring, Md.: Family Line Publications, 1986.

Hauptman, Lawrence M. *The Iroquois in the Civil War: From Battlefield to Reservation*. Syracuse, N.Y.: Syracuse University Press, 1993.

Johnson, Robert Underwood, and Buel, Clarence Clough, eds. *Battle and Leaders of the Civil War*. 4 volumes. New York: The Century Company, 1887. Reprinted 1956. Exceptionally valuable for its tables of organization for major engagements.

Krick, Robert K. *Lee's Colonels: A Biographical Register of the Field Officers of the Army of Northern Virginia*. 2nd edition. Dayton, Ohio: Press of Morningside Bookstore, 1984. Brief but very informative sketches of the 1,965 field-grade officers who at one time or another served with the Army of Northern Virginia but never achieved the the rank of brigadier general. The second edition also includes a listing by name and unit of those field-grade officers who never served with Lee.

Long, E.B. and Barbara. *The Civil War Day By Day: An Almanac 1861–1865*. Garden City, New York: Doubleday, 1971. An excellent chronology of the conflict, with much information on the organizational changes command assignments.

Lonn, Ella. *Foreigners in the Confederacy*. Chapel Hill: University of North Carolina, 1940. Accounts of the foreign-born contribution to the Confederacy.

Manatee, Harold Rental. *Maryland in the Civil War*. Baltimore: Historical Society, 1961.

McDonough, James L. *War in Kentucky: From Shiloh to Perryville*. Knoxville, Tennessee: University of Tennessee Press, 1994.

McKim, Randolph Harrison. *The Numerical Strength of the Confederate Army: An Examination of the Argument of the Hon. Charles Francis Adams and Others*. New York: The Kneel Publishing Company, 1912.

Moire, Albert Burton. *Conscription and Conflict in the Confederacy*. New York: The Macmillan Company, 1924.

National Archives, Record Group 109. Microfilm compilation of the service records of every known Confederate soldier, organized by unit. The caption cards and record-of- events cards at the beginning of each unit provide much valuable information on the units' organizational history.

Priest, John M. *Endosteum: The Soldiers' Battle*. Shippensburg, Pa.: White Mane Pub. Co., 1989.

Rampage, James A. *Rebel Raider: The Life of General John Hunt Morgan.* Lexington, Ky.: University Press of Kentucky, 1986.

Scharf, J. Thomas. *History of the Confederate States Navy: From Its Organization to the Surrender of Its Last Vessels.* Albany: Joseph McDonough, 1887. A rather disjointed narrative that provides some insight into operations along the Southern coast and on the inland waterways. Unfortunately, it lacks an adequate index.

Sifakis, Stewart. *Who Was Who in the Civil War*. New York: Facts On File, 1988.

———. *Who Was Who in the Confederacy*. New York: Facts On File, 1989. Together both works include biographies of over 1,000 participants who served the South during the Civil War. The military entries include much information on regiments and higher commands.

Speed, Thomas. *The Union Cause in Kentucky, 1860–1865, by Captain Thomas Speed, Adjutant 12th Kentucky Infantry and Veteran Infantry Vols. 1861–1865.* New York: G.P. Putnam's Sons, 1907.

Tancig, W.J. *Confederate Military Land Units, 1861–1865*. South Brunswick, N.C.: T. Yoseloff, 1967.

Townsend, William Henry. *Lincoln and the Bluegrass*. Lexington, Ky.: University of Kentucky Press, 1955.

U.S. Navy Department. *Official Records of the Union and Confederate Navies in the War of the Rebellion*. 31 volumes. Washington: Government Printing Office, 1894–1927. Provides much valuable information on the coastal and riverine operations of the Civil War.

U.S. War Department. *The War of the Rebellion: A Compilation of the Official Records of the Union and Confederate Armies*. 70 volumes in 128 books divided into four series, plus atlas. Washington: Government Printing Office, 1881–1901. While difficult to use, this set provides a gold mine of information. Organized by campaigns in specified geographic regions, the volumes are divided into postaction reports and correspondence. The information contained in the hundreds of organizational tables proved invaluable for my purposes.

Wakelyn, Jon L. *Biographical Dictionary of the Confederacy*. Westport, Conn.: Greenwood Press, 1977. Short biographies of 651 leaders of the Confederacy. However, the selection criteria among the military leaders is somewhat haphazard.

Warner Ezra J. *Generals in Gray: Lives of the Confederate Commanders*. Baton Rouge: Louisiana State University Press, 1959. Sketches of the 425 Southern generals. Good coverage of pre- and postwar careers. The wartime portion of the entries leaves something to be desired.

Weeks, Philip. *Farewell, My Nation: The American Indian and the United States, 1820–1890*. Arlington Heights, Ill.: H. Davidson, c. 1990.

Wise, Jennings Cropper. *The Long Arm of Lee: The History of the Artillery of the Army of Northern Virginia.* Lynchburg, Virginia: J.P. Bell Co., 1915. Reprinted 1959. An excellent study of Lee's artillery, providing valuable information on batteries and their commanders and organizational assignments.

Wright, Marcus J. *General Officers of the Confederate Army*. New York: Neale Publishing Co., 1911. Long the definitive work on the Confederate command structure, it was superseded by Ezra J. Warner's work.

PERIODICALS

Civil War Times Illustrated, its predecessor *Civil War Times*, *American History Illustrated* and *Civil War History*. In addition, the *Southern Historical Society Papers* (47 vols., 1876–1930) are a gold mine of information on Confederate units and leaders.

KENTUCKY BATTLE INDEX

References are to record numbers, not page numbers.

KENTUCKY NAME INDEX

References are to record numbers, not page numbers.

MARYLAND BATTLE INDEX

References are to record numbers, not page numbers.

MARYLAND NAME INDEX

References are to record numbers, not page numbers.

MISSOURI BATTLE INDEX

References are to record numbers, not page numbers.

MISSOURI NAME INDEX

References are to record numbers, not page numbers.

CONFEDERATE BATTLE INDEX

References are to record numbers, not page numbers.

CONFEDERATE NAME INDEX

References are to record numbers, not page numbers.

INDIAN BATTLE INDEX

References are to record numbers, not page numbers.

INDIAN NAME INDEX

References are to record numbers, not page numbers.